Advance praise for

Fighting Academic Repression and Neoliberal Education

"In an era of corporatization—which breeds greed, fear, and compliance—the topics discussed in *Fighting Academic Repression and Neoliberal Education* are both necessary and refreshing. There are pockets of resistance throughout the ranks of higher education, and Anthony J. Nocella II and Erik Juergensmeyer are helping to connect those pockets into a coherent force for progressive social change. This book is a must-read for all those who are involved with—and who care about changing—the current state of higher learning."

—*Jason Del Gandio, Author of* Rhetoric for Radicals:
A Handbook for 21st Century Activists

"In a time where academic repression seems to be increasing in educational systems across the world, it is refreshing to encounter a book that so brilliantly provides avenues for resistance of critical pedagogy. *Fighting Academic Repression and Neoliberal Education* brings together an amazing collection of scholars and activists to show how students and teachers alike can come together to challenge various forms of oppression within academic settings in order to provide a true liberatory framework for the future. A must-read for anyone interested in making the classroom a safe space for resistance and change."

—*JL Schatz, Director of Speech & Debate, Binghamton University*

"Anthony J. Nocella II and Erik Juergensmeyer's collection of essays in *Fighting Academic Repression and Neoliberal Education* stress the importance of collaboration, generating conversation, and practicing care. A reader learns not only about academic repression but about various educational spaces and the struggles to change them. For those who believe that agency is central to freeing academia, the knowledge arising from this text is irreducible and essential."

—*Amber E. George, Cornell University*

"The compilation of essays within *Fighting Academic Repression and Neoliberal Education* reflects a robust lineage of subversive and counterhegemonic educational discourse that is desperately needed in the contemporary moment. A symbiotic combination of educational and social theory and activist practices, *Fighting Academic Repression and Neoliberal Education* offers academicians a comprehensive radical framework for critiquing the neoliberal sensibilities that endanger higher education as well as poignant and insightful narratives about how the ideals of social justice can inform research, teaching, and community service."

—*Ahmad R. Washington, Assistant Professor,*
Department of Counseling and Human Development,
University of Louisville

More advance praise for

Fighting Academic Repression and Neoliberal Education

"If the role of the scholar-activist is to provide an in-depth, poetic, practical, and critical analysis of the society in which we all live, these essays accomplish that. If our mission is to imagine, study, and birth other worlds in this global transformational project, it will do us well to pay attention to the voices within *Fighting Academic Repression and Neoliberal Education*."

—*Keno Evol, Poet, Independent Scholar, and Collective Member of Poetry Behind the Walls*

"Once upon a time, higher education provided opportunities for students to explore controversial, oppositional, and marginalized perspectives in efforts to develop solutions and conclusions that were oriented toward the greater good. *Fighting Academic Repression and Neoliberal Education* reminds us that this bygone era, prior to the advancement of academic fascism, is worth fighting for."

—*Leslie James Pickering, Author of* Mad Bomber Melville

"Academia must remain a crucible for social justice, even as freedom of thought and action are threatened and coerced by powerful corporate interests. In *Fighting Academic Repression and Neoliberal Education*, Anthony J. Nocella II and Erik Juergensmeyer give voice to the scholar-activists who will transform education in our own time; and they give us all the tools of transformation: meaningful dialogues, productive alliances, and deeper knowledge of how to recognize and resist the many forms of corporatization that reify and reinforce injustices, great and small."

—*Judy K. C. Bentley, Associate Professor, State University of New York at Cortland*

"In the past several decades since *A Nation At Risk* manufactured the current educational crisis, the government has dictated and standardized education starting with K–12. Teachers were handed scripts and told that they must teach a standardized curriculum with fidelity. Teacher evaluations became based on standardized test scores, ensuring compliance with the threat of job loss. Schools with the least amount of assimilation, i.e., low standardized test scores, were targeted for closure. Yet, the elite enjoy private school education that promotes free thinking over this standardization. After thirty-plus years of this academic repression, the rebellion is starting. *Fighting Academic Repression and Neoliberal Education* outlines how others have fought this repression and helps to inspire and engage others in this fight."

—*Eve Shippens, Teacher and Parent, Buffalo Public Schools*

Fighting Academic Repression and Neoliberal Education

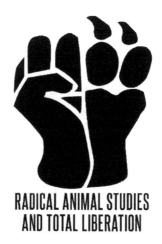

RADICAL ANIMAL STUDIES
AND TOTAL LIBERATION

Anthony J. Nocella II
Series Editor

Vol. 3

The Radical Animal Studies and Total Liberation series
is part of the Peter Lang Education list.
Every volume is peer reviewed and meets
the highest quality standards for content and production.

PETER LANG
New York • Bern • Frankfurt • Berlin
Brussels • Vienna • Oxford • Warsaw

Fighting Academic Repression and Neoliberal Education

Resistance, Reclaiming, Organizing, and Black Lives Matter in Education

Edited by Anthony J. Nocella II
and Erik Juergensmeyer

PETER LANG
New York • Bern • Frankfurt • Berlin
Brussels • Vienna • Oxford • Warsaw

Library of Congress Cataloging-in-Publication Data

Names: Nocella II, Anthony J.
Fighting academic repression and neoliberal education:
resistance, reclaiming, organizing, and black lives matter in education /
edited by Anthony J. Nocella II, Erik Juergensmeyer.
Description: New York: Peter Lang, 2017.
Series: Radical animal studies and total liberation; vol. 3
ISSN 2469-3065 (print) | ISSN 2469-3081 (online)
Includes bibliographical references and index.
Identifiers: LCCN 2016039512 | ISBN 978-1-4331-3314-5 (hardcover: alk. paper)
ISBN 978-1-4331-3313-8 (paperback: alk. paper) | 978-1-4331-3894-2 (ebook pdf)
ISBN 978-1-4331-3895-9 (epub) | ISBN 978-1-4331-3896-6 (mobi)
Subjects: LCSH: Education, Higher—Sociological aspects.
Education, Higher—Political aspects. | Education and state. | Neoliberalism.
Academic freedom. | Teaching, Freedom of.
Classification: LCC LC191.9 .F54 2017 | DDC 379—dc23
LC record available at https://lccn.loc.gov/2016039512
DOI: 10.3726/978-1-4331-3894-2

Bibliographic information published by **Die Deutsche Nationalbibliothek**.
Die Deutsche Nationalbibliothek lists this publication in the "Deutsche
Nationalbibliografie"; detailed bibliographic data are available
on the Internet at http://dnb.d-nb.de/.

The paper in this book meets the guidelines for permanence and durability
of the Committee on Production Guidelines for Book Longevity
of the Council of Library Resources.

Printed in the United States of America

This book is dedicated to those who have been pushed out of school and are products of the school-to-prison pipeline along with those who are targeted because of their politics, identity, or pedagogy that do not fit within orthodox, noncritical, classic, normative schooling.

Table of Contents

Foreword

Remembering the Future?

WARD CHURCHILL

In 1963, acclaimed liberal administrator Clark Kerr, then-president of the University of California (U/Cal) system, published a revealing little book titled *The Uses of the University*. Therein, he likened such institutions to "knowledge factories" designed to function in a manner serving specific social and political purposes. In essence, Kerr explained, they were facilities owned by the State together with its corporate partners, run by executive hirelings like himself who, with the assistance of a managerial staff, coordinated a nonunionized workforce consisting of a faculty guild and supporting personnel whose collective task was, at defined intervals, to have completed the processing of raw material into particular types, numbers, and qualities of products desired by the owners. The latter were adjusted from time to time in correspondence to the owners' perception of their needs, and workforce composition altered accordingly, but, while subject to quantitative variables, the nature of the raw material remained constant.

The "raw material" in Kerr's remarkably candid rendering was of course students, figuratively arriving at the factory in the form of the crude ores from which over a four-year period, allowing for a certain amount of "wastage" along the way, the workforce would smelt, mold, and otherwise shape into the quota of graduates certifiably imbued with "threshold" levels of proficiency in the fields State/corporate planners deemed necessary to meet the demand for a "qualified" base of entry-level employees in their various development scenarios. Much the same applied to the much smaller numbers selected from each production run to undergo further processing in professional and grad schools, both to meet the owners' need for personnel with somewhat more rarified competencies and to replenish the factories' own workforce.

Plainly, what Kerr described was an institutional reality sharing nothing in common with that in which the "life of the mind" would be cultivated along with "pursuit of knowledge for its own sake" and all the other lofty ideals supposedly defining the mission of universities in the United States since the first raft of them were being established during the last third of the 19th century, purportedly following the example of the esteemed "German model." That, of course, was *never* true, not least because, as Thorstein Veblen pointed out rather emphatically in his 1904 book, *The Higher Learning in America*, universities in Germany were by definition entirely distinct from such "vo-tech" enterprises as business and engineering schools. Nor could German universities be owned—they occupied a unique legal status precluding even the State from asserting proprietary interest—and faculty were institutional freeholders, not employees.

Most tellingly, perhaps, while philosophical endeavors formed the very core of the German university, philosophy was never so much as mentioned in *The Uses of the University*. This is not to say that in the Kerrian formulation student processing didn't require a substantial dose of ideological indoctrination. It did, mainly for purposes of inculcating an unquestioning sociopolitical homogeneity in those slated to fill the lower echelons of the burgeoning U.S. technocracy, the more so in those selected for advanced processing in doctoral programs devoted to the manufacture of the products destined to become designated members of the country's intelligentsia and policymaking élites. To observe that such conditioning had nothing in common with the modes of critical engagement defining the Germanic or any other philosophical tradition would be to radically understate the case.

If all of this is sounding more like a report on the current state of American universities than a distillation of what was said in a little-read and less remembered book released more than a half-century ago, it should.* Other than that they've become ever more refined, sophisticated, and entrenched over the past fifty years, Kerr's horrifyingly lucid description of the mechanics and objectives of what he preferred to characterize as "multiversities" at the dawn of the 1960s is no less illuminating of the institutional/systemic realities of American "higher education" in 2016. That being so, it seems worthwhile to cast a backward glance at the response to his exposition, couched as it was in a tone offering no hint of criticism, but rather a degree of self-congratulatory enthusiasm that seems entirely consonant with sentiments routinely expressed by owners and their administrative minions, together with a rather craven stratum of faculty sycophants, in the present moment.

---

* Those interested in pursuing what is said herein are cautioned to consult the first edition of *The Uses of the University*. Kerr published new editions in 1972, 1982, 1995, and 2001, essentially rewriting the book each time, and never repeating what he'd originally said.

As it happened, Kerr's eagerness to please his bosses led him to overplay his hand by seeking to impose their desired ideological boundaries not only in the classroom but more broadly. In mid-September 1964, he ordered a campuswide ban at U/Cal Berkeley on student activities "advocating political causes" other than those espoused by the administratively sanctioned Democratic and Republican clubs. This resulted in a major confrontation on October 1 when a former student was arrested for distributing civil rights literature *outside* the university's main gate. A week later, veteran Berkeley radical Hal Draper released *The Mind of Clark Kerr*, a widely circulated pamphlet summarizing the views expressed in *The Uses of the University*.

Student reaction was swift, delivered in a spiraling series of protests, and expressed most eloquently by an undergrad named Mario Savio in an impassioned speech delivered during a mass demonstration outside the campus administration building on December 2:

> We're human beings [...] [not a] bunch of raw materials [and we] don't mean to be made into any product [or] bought by some clients of the university, be they the government, be they industry, be they anyone! There's a time when the operation of the machine becomes so odious, makes you so sick at heart, that you can't take part! You can't even passively take part! And you've got to put your body upon the gears [...] upon the wheels [...] upon the levers, upon all the apparatus, and you've got to make it stop! And you've got to indicate to the people who run it, to the people own it, that unless you're free, the machine will be prevented from working at all!

The Berkeley students never managed to bring the machine to a halt, but they were sufficiently disruptive force rescission of Kerr's ham-handed ban in January 1965. By then, Chancellor Edward Strong had been compelled to resign, and Kerr himself was fired in early 1967, never to hold another academic position. Having meanwhile gained increasing moment, the "student power" movement as it came to be called—not just at Berkeley, but nationally—had expanded its horizons, shifting from simply demanding free speech on campus to pushing over the next decade for structural changes with a force that left the universities little alternative to making noticeable concessions, for the first time admitting Students of Color in significant numbers, hiring Faculty of Color, and allowing establishment of programs—in some places whole departments—focusing on non(Eurocentric)/antipatriarchal subject matters and critical theory.

To be sure, the effort ended far too soon, its goals were too limited, and other errors abounded. The institutional strategy, after all, was one combining near-term containment with cooptation over the longer run. That the approach taken by *Those In Charge* had been successful might have been apparent to anyone who cared to look by the early 1990s and is glaringly obvious in the institutional realities we confront today: students neutralized by the ruinous debt incurred for the "privilege" of attending "public" schools; the programs and departments launched with such promise largely neutered, many now serving as mere rubber stamps to orthodoxy; "radical" faculty members largely absorbed in the self-serving stupidities of "professionalism" while a mushrooming segment of the "professoriate" has been reduced to little more than day labor.

That the situation is intolerable should be self-evident. So, too, the facts that there is inspiration to be drawn from the events at Berkeley during the mid-1960s and profound lessons to be gleaned from the movement that followed. Should both be heeded, the old adage of the past serving as prologue may yet be vindicated. Vindication, however, will be contingent upon the twin realizations that this time there can be no resort to the half-measures of shallow compromise in the institutional setting and that success therein is entirely dependent upon an equally uncompromising transformation of the broader sociopolitical/economic status quo. The "owners," in effect, must be dispossessed. Can it happen? Of course. Will it happen? We'll see.

Preface

EMMA PÉREZ

We are in a crisis. This explicit crisis has always been at the root of US history molded by settler colonialism, slavery, worker exploitation, gender inequities, ableism, and LGBTQI negation—all to privilege white, colonialist, Christian, heteronormative values in the twenty-first century. The crisis disrupts every aspect of our lives—health care, economic parity, the environment, and education while advancing the prison industrial complex and anti-immigrant detention centers. In the aftermath of cultural uprisings of the 1960s and 1970s, we have seen the pendulum swing so far to the right that the middle is now what the right used to be. Extremists, who despise all that is different from their purported mainstream of whiteness, have set a neoliberal, capitalist agenda while cheering "make America great again," longing for their own brand of the 1950s unquestioned authority. But here's the thing: history has revealed that strike activity of the 1920s, union organizing of the 1930s and 1940s, civil rights protests of the 1950s, and the student, gay, Black, Chicana/o, Native, and women's movements of the 1960s have pushed against privileged authoritarians who enforce profiteering at the core of all they value. In fact, if we follow the money, we see quite clearly a history of white colonialist choreography that justifies racism, misogyny, and economic injustice.

When I landed in the Ethnic Studies Department at University of Colorado (CU), Boulder in 2003, I was fully aware of historical legacies that revered frontier pioneers who massacred Native Americans at Sand Creek in the nineteenth century and posted sun down signs, "No Mexicans After Night," in the early twentieth century. It is a state built upon the blood of indigenous tribes and Mexican laborers. I was, however, unaware that in 2001, the Colorado Commission on Higher Education paid the neoconservative National Association of Scholars (NAS) to prepare a report that argued against racial diversity at CU Boulder while reasoning that Western European classics had to remain the core curriculum. The report became so entrenched that the more liberal administrators and professors at CU continue to endorse a Eurocentric curriculum either through reticence or sheer unquestioned elitism. By 2005, the NAS and the American Council of Trustees and Alumni (ACTA, founded in 1995 by Lynne Cheney, spouse of George W. Bush's Vice-President Cheney) gained so much support that Colorado became a test case for abolishing tenure. *The New York Times* has defined ACTA as "a conservative nonprofit group devoted to curbing liberal tendencies in academia" in the name of academic freedom. When University President Elizabeth Hoffman (2000–2005) refused to fire tenured, full professor and Native American scholar, Ward Churchill while tackling the Colorado legislature for their McCarthyism, she was promptly asked to resign by the state Governor Bill Owens (born and educated in Texas, early supporter of George W. Bush and alleged member of ACTA). In her place ACTA member Hank Brown (2005–2008) was appointed President of CU to oversee Churchill's unmerited firing.

But let's back up historically. According to Colorado journalist Ed Quillen the Ku Klux Klan (KKK) made inroads in Colorado's government at the beginning of the 20th century. In 1924, Governor Clarence Morley was a Klansman who took direction from Dr. John Galen Locke, the Grand Dragon of the Colorado Realm. At that same time, Mayor Benjamin Stapleton of Denver consulted the Klan when making appointments and a Klan majority thrived in Colorado's House of Representatives (*Colorado Springs Independent*, May 22, 2003). In a state and country with KKK antecedents, I would venture to point out that NAS and ACTA promote white colonialist Western European standards inherent in KKK white supremacy.

The Common Core for K-12 is just another method for spreading Western European colonialist knowledge in the name of standards. Senate Bill 08–212, passed in 2008, adopted the new Colorado Academic Standards, which incorporate the Common Core State Standards in mathematics, reading and writing. Common Core is a neoliberal, profiteering, capitalist enterprise that has done considerable damage to children's education forcing them to memorize facts and figures while holding them hostage to hours of test preparation to take tests that gauge memorization, while devaluing critical thinking. When these same students enter college, they have not been trained to think critically and are perplexed because professors do not coach them with the answers to tests. Even my nine-year-old daughter, who is in the fourth grade, understands that she is not being prepared for college through Common Core curriculum but instead being told what to memorize. Once again, we must follow the money and ask, who benefits from Pearson, the testing conglomerate that earns $9 billion annually administering faulty tests with so many glitches that results remain questionable. Fortunately, a grassroots movement by parents has begun to question the purpose of testing that began to be enforced with Bush's No Child Left Behind, yet another neoliberal program designed to make private business's money at the expense of children's creativity. Moreover, the neoliberal trend is that of reallocating money from public schools that need it to charter schools (pseudoprivate) with few unionized employees, less oversight, and a higher teacher turnover rate compared to public schools.

I point out K-12, not only because I observe my daughter's experience in public school, but also because I have experienced firsthand how incoming college students are not primed to think critically as they navigate college. Many, however, are rising to the challenge and rebelling against corporate America, modern day colonial boarding schools, police brutality against Blacks in America, and fascist immigration policies against Latinas/os.

The prescient editors of this timely volume gathered essays that address our current crisis and offer solutions to the ways in which student, staff, and faculty activism on college campuses combat the growing neoliberal, corporate university. The scholar-activists writing here pick up vital questions about how we must take back our universities from anti-intellectual profiteers such as Pearson profiting off standardized and teacher licensure tests. Those who are not trained educators have infiltrated every level of public education for profit such as those emerging out of Teach for America. The authors here are aware of the crisis and provide examples of grassroots movements, strikes, and protests resisting neoliberals eager to wipe out differences that are already here, that have been here for centuries. These scholars venerate those already in the midst of crucial activism and propose a welcome blueprint of hope.

Acknowledgments

Acknowledgments are so critical and a radical humbling of oneself because it publicly notes that no one is an island and that everyone is interdependent and needing support because we are living creatures and part of an ecosystem, where everything is interwoven and interdependent on one another. We would like to thank first our publisher, Peter Lang Publishing, and Chris Myers, Stephen Mazur, Farideh Koohi-Kamali, Sophie Appel, and Alisa Pulver. We would also like to thank everyone who wrote a prereview of the book: Eve Shippens, Judy K.C. Bentley, Leslie James Pickering, Keno Evol, Edward Avery-Natale, David Nibert, Meneka Thirukkumaran, Don C. Sawyer III, David Gabbard, Ahmad R. Washington, Peter Mclaren, Amber E. George, JL Schatz, Jason Del Gandio, and Bill Ayers. Anthony and Erik would of course like to thank the contributors who made this book possible: Ward Churchill, Emma Pérez, Nick Clare, Gregory White, Richard White, Mary Heath, Peter Burdon, Mark Seis, Sue Doe, Laura L. Finley, Ryan Thomson, John Lupinacci, Diana Vallera, Sean Donaghue-Johnston, Tanya Loughead, Shannon Gibney, Emil Marmol, Mary Jean Hande, Raluca Bejan, Kelly Limes-Taylor Henderson, Z. B. Hurst, Becky Clausen, Keri Brandt, Janine Fitzgerald, and Carey Vicenti. We would also like to thank John Baranski and the Association for Humanist Sociology for the vibrant discussion about this book's potential impact. We would like to also thank our family, friends, and the Earth for providing love, support, and joy.

Introduction—A Tactical Toolbox for Smashing Academic Repression

ANTHONY J. NOCELLA II AND ERIK JUERGENSMEYER

This book makes the fourth book on the specific subject of academic repression, following *Academic Repression: Reflections from the Academic Industrial Complex* (Nocella II, Best, & McLaren, 2010), *Policing the Campus: Academic Repression, Surveillance, and the Occupy Movement* (Nocella II & Gabbard, 2013), and *The Imperial University: Academic Repression and Scholarly Dissent* (Chatterjee & Maira, 2014). Prior to and during the rise of the above texts, there was and is ongoing discussion on defending academic freedom. The books that anyone interested in academic freedom should read include *The University in Ruins* (Readings, 1997), *Uncivil Rites: Palestine and the Limits of Academic Freedom* (Salaita, 2015), *Academic Freedom After September 11* (Doumani, 2006), *No University is an Island: Saving Academic Freedom* (Nelson, 2011), Academic Freedom in the Post-9/11 Era (Carvalho & Downing, 2011), *The Humanities, Higher Education and Academic Freedom: Three Necessary Arguments* (Berube & Ruth, 2015), *University Inc.: The Corporate Corruption of Higher Education* (Washburn, 2006), *Neoliberalism's War on Higher Education* (Giroux, 2014), *Universities in the Business of Repression: The Academic Military Industrial Complex in Central America* (Feldman, 1999), and *The University in Chains: Confronting the Military-Industrial-Academic Complex* (Giroux, 2007).

Anyone interested in the future of education must be knowledgeable about how academic repression works as it affects us all—students, politicians, teachers, professors, staff, administrators, and community members. Only an unwise individual enters a space not knowing the possible dangers ahead. Academic repression is the strategy to target, control, and eliminate a person or group of people for their ideas, actions, or identity by those in authority within the school/academic system. The two largest dangers within academia that foster the rise of academic repression and use of academic repression from kindergarten to higher education are: (1) the corporatization of education and (2) the industrialization of education.

Corporatization of education is the takeover of education for the purpose of profiting the private sector. There are four ways this is carried out: (1) corporations hijack programs and departments for the purpose of the professors teaching and training possible future employees; (2) corporations use school facilities and resources for free or reduced rates for meetings, courses, seminars, and forums; (3) corporations request administrators to control and eliminate any negative scholarship, teaching, or research from students and professors; and (4) corporations are accepted and welcomed on campus because they appear charitable and caring about the public good. The industrialization of education is the process of making education for the purpose of achieving the utmost efficiency in developing a product (i.e., diploma) for the consumer (i.e., student).

Industrialization through the philosophy of Taylorism and Weberism is carried out in four ways: (1) developing a strong and overreaching administrative body that can micromanage, which limits inconsistency and independence (i.e., creativity); (2) eliminating any control or authority of the subordinate; (3) creating one path for all consumers to take and give as much structure to that path including timeline; and (4) categorizing and siloing everything from resources, buildings, departments, degrees, curriculum, courses, pedagogy, teaching practices, syllabi, professors, staff, and students.

The question is how and why did education become motivated by these two initiatives? The answer is simple, education is only useful for the purpose of receiving a job, and we live in a competitive economic system, that is, capitalism; and for every job offer the company is looking for the best and the brightest; therefore, students want to know and show that they have received a high-quality education. This cannot be proven if we do not have a standard method of evaluating education. Therefore, schools, colleges, and universities have to be accredited. If they are not accredited, they are not allowed to be ranked and are not valued in our society and by our popular corporate poles, such as *U.S. News and World Reports*. Education is not about learning or making the world a better place; it is today about making money—this is the fundamental battle that must be waged.

EDUCATION FOR DEMOCRACY

The foundational purpose of school is simply to create and sustain a healthy and engaged community through an educated and critical citizenry. The mission of schools is to create public intellectuals. A public intellectual is one who educates the public, specifically students on the relationship between disciplinary knowledge and the good of the community to encourage community leadership. In analyzing different levels of leadership important for peacebuilding, Lederach (1997) identified the level of middle-range leadership/hybrid (the grouping in between top and grassroots) as important and unique to peacebuilding (p. 39). This positioning allows "academics and intellectuals" to mediate between actors that commonly are in opposition with each other (p. 41).

bell hooks (2003) opposed the concept of the "public intellectual" because it is passive and has been coopted by neoliberalism. Instead, hooks argued for what Chomsky described as "dissident intellectuals," active and resistant scholars who fight oppression, are "critical of the status quo," and "dare to make their voices heard on behalf of justice" (p. 187). In the last few decades, the scholar-activist has become a common term adopted by those who are bridging that gap between schools and the community. Notably, Angela Davis, Howard Zinn, Gloria Anzaldúa, Marc Lamont Hill, and Dana Cloud demonstrate the importance of the scholar-activist. To be a scholar-activist, one should participate in social media, publish on blogs and other public media outlets, organize public forums and protests, conduct participatory action/activist research for the community, and publish in activist and scholarly presses. An excellent example of how scholar-activism can benefit democracy can be seen in the recent Black Lives Matter movement. Shamell Bell's work on Hip Hop dance, Peniel E. Joseph's work on Black liberation, Bettina Love's work on Black women and girls, Barbara Ransby's work on social justice, and Blair Kelley's work on racial injustice exemplify the important role of the scholar-activist.

As scholar-activists, all of the authors, including the editors, in this book are writing as citizens of a democracy, not as representatives of their individual institutions—they are in no way speaking for their institutions. Higher education is a microcosm of society that contains a wide diversity of opinions, identities, and actions that are often in conflict. We hope this book creates an opportunity for opposing views and people to reclaim the democratic need for education, away from the clamps of the corporate industrial machine. This being said, this book is deliberately providing space and place for marginalized voices within academia that are often silenced and not heard—an important component of citizenry and democracy that is upheld by the American Association of University Professors' "1940 Statement on Principles on Academic Freedom and Tenure."

TACTICS OF FIGHTING ACADEMIC REPRESSION

There are many tactics in creating change, but not all tactics are applicable or relevant to the politics within higher education, for this reason this book is essential.

There are many tactics to use, but some essential ones to gain attention and control the narrative include:

(1) using social media including Facebook, Twitter, Instagram, Linkedin, Tumblr, Snapchat, Academia.edu, Myspace, Flickr, Pinterest, Google+, Vine, YouTube, Yik Yak, and Reddit to name a few to spread information about an event or injustice;

(2) having a large network to tell about an event or injustice through list-serves, phone banks, and mass mail and e-mail;

(3) having resources such as printer, chalk, posters, banner, paint, markers, bullhorn, sound system, flyers, stickers, websites, business cards, buttons, shirts, postcards, e-mail, phone numbers, and office equipment to assist in organizing events; and

(4) developing an organization with bylaws, mission, purpose, goals, strategies, tactics, subcommittees, and regular meetings to create events and to gather information.

The four most effective tactics to resist academic repression beyond just controlling the narrative include:

(1) occupying places short term such as chalking sidewalks and buildings, protest in classrooms, halls, dorms, sidewalks, streets, and quads and long term such as creating blockades in the front of entrances of buildings, roadways, walkways, and takeover buildings, rooms, and offices;

(2) promoting a boycott by doing mass walkouts or strikes as well as transfer to another school;

(3) mapping out administration and school leadership's vulnerabilities and protest locations where they and their friends and families frequent, such as their churches, homes, country clubs, work, restaurants, cafes, doctors, movie theatres, and grocery stores; and

(4) developing a smear campaign by creating flyers, posters, memes, stickers, buttons, shirts, and graffiti to bring light to the specific injustices and private unethical acts that the people who are responsible for the academic repression.

MARTIN L. KING JR.'S SIX STEPS OF NONVIOLENT SOCIAL CHANGE

The following was written by Martin L. King, Jr. (2014) on how to create social change by organizations, activists, community organizers, collectives, and individuals.

1. Information gathering: To understand and articulate an issue, problem or injustice facing a person, community, or institution you must do research. You must investigate and gather all vital information from all sides of the argument or issue so as to increase your understanding of the problem. You must become an expert on your opponent's position.

2. Education: It is essential to inform others, including your opposition, about your issue. This minimizes misunderstandings and gains you support and sympathy.

3. Personal commitment: Daily check and affirm your faith in the philosophy and methods of nonviolence. Eliminate hidden motives and prepare yourself to accept suffering, if necessary, in your work for justice.

4. Discussion/negotiation: Using grace, humor, and intelligence, confront the other party with a list of injustices and a plan for addressing and resolving these injustices. Look for what is positive in every action and statement the opposition makes. Do not seek to humiliate the opponent but to call forth the good in the opponent.

5. Direct action: These are actions taken when the opponent is unwilling to enter into, or remain in, discussion/negotiation. These actions impose a "creative tension" into the conflict, supplying moral pressure on your opponent to work with you in resolving the injustice.

6. Reconciliation: Nonviolence seeks friendship and understanding with the opponent. Nonviolence does not seek to defeat the opponent. Nonviolence is directed against evil systems, forces, oppressive policies, unjust acts, but not against persons. Through reasoned compromise, both sides resolve the injustice with a plan of action. Each act of reconciliation is one step close to the "Beloved Community."

GANDHI'S FOUR STEPS FOR SOCIAL CHANGE

The following are four steps that come from Gandhi's quote: "First they ignore you, then they ridicule you, then they fight you, and then you win," which we have defined in each step as follows.

1. Ignore you: The stage which the group or individual is not looked at as having power, legitimate argument, and the ability to create change; therefore, those in power do not give space or place to the group wanting change.

2. Stigmatize you: Those in power identify those who are different to discredit them so they are not given space and place to create change.

3. Repress you: Those in power after a particular time period and growth of this group that wants change are recognized as a threat in creating change and are specifically targeted and repressed by arresting, incarceration, assassination, framing, fabricated criminal charges, and infiltration and division of social movements.
4. Accept you: If the group or movement is not destroyed by repression and the fight for change by the group or movement continues to grow with members and garner mass public creditability be accepted by those in power.

GROUND RULES

Here are a set of common and useful ground rules to use in meetings of the group.

1. Volunteer yourself only.
2. No put downs of yourself or others, even in a joking way.
3. One mic (one person speaks at a time).
4. Vegas (whatever said in a space, does not go beyond those that heard it).
5. Participate.
6. Step up, step down (those that have more priviledge speak less in a space).
7. Three then me (do not speak until at least three people spoke).
8. KISS (keep it short and sweet).
9. Keep an open mind.
10. Assume the best.
11. Don't yuck on my yum (do not put down what someone else likes).
12. Don't take anything personal.
13. Attack the idea not the person.

TWENTY-STEP PROCESS FOR ORGANIZING A PUBLIC EDUCATION FORUM

The following is a good list of how to organize a successful event, which will help spread information and educate the public about the issue that the group is concerned about.

1. Pick an event theme with a title and a description.
2. Establish an event committee of two to three people and sponsors.
3. Establish a length of time such as one hour, three hours, day long, weekend long, or week long and format of the event such as, workshop,

roundtable, teach-in, Skype, film screening, lecture, debate, open mic, or conference.

4. Invite and confirm speakers on the topic from the community, universities, schools, and other institutions/organizations.
5. Receive biographies, professional titles, and full name of the speakers.
6. Lock in a location and time that is accessible and in a location that the public can easily find. Think about the bus schedule and parking situation.
7. Develop a flyer and send it out to the event committee, speakers, and sponsors for approval.
8. Promote and advertise through e-mail, media (such as radio and newspapers), Facebook, Twitter, blogs, phone calls, speaking in classrooms and organizations, and texting.
9. On the day and week of the event, repromote.
10. On the day and week of the event, reconfirm speakers.
11. An hour before the event, make sure all the event committee members are at the event location on time.
12. An hour before the event, organize chairs, food, video camera, banners, and a welcoming/information table.
13. An hour before the event, the cofacilitators should practice explaining the purpose, goal, schedule, and presenters' bios.
14. An hour before the event, the cofacilitators should decide how the discussion will be facilitated after the presenters are finished. If possible, call on people with marginalized identities, try not to call on the same person more than once, and do not allow anyone to speak for an excessively long period of time.
15. Make sure the event starts and ends on time.
16. Make sure to thank everyone for presenting, organizing, attending, etc.
17. Make sure to tell everyone about the next event or to tell them where to find out about future events.
18. Make sure to tell people how to get involved with this issue.
19. Make sure to send out, via social media and e-mails, thank yous to those who attended.
20. Make sure to quickly post pictures and videos of the event on social media.

BASIC SECURITY CULTURE

Security culture is the actions an organizer and activist should adopt to be safe against infiltration, sabotage, division, and other forms of repression by the government, school, and corporations.

1. Keep your computer, home, office, locker, phone, tablet, vehicles, etc., always locked, organized, and clean so if someone was to enter your home you would likely know.
2. Don't brag about your or others' activism, especially illegal activity, to family, friends, partners, or other people that have done time.
3. Only do civil disobedience and other illegal activism with people you know very well including where they grew up, work, went to school, and currently live and who their friends and family are.
4. Don't joke or speak about illegal activities. This will aid in spot lighting more attention onto you from law enforcement.
5. Use encrypted software and shorthand communication beyond just writing to protect what you or others are planning.
6. Develop methods in nominations of people into a collective, group, or project to establish one's level of safety and security.
7. Strive to build trust based on honesty and building an open relationship.
8. Don't ask others about their involvement with illegal action.
9. Don't date people or do actions with people you are dating. This will possibly increase the complexity of risk that is taking place.
10. Strive to never have a paper trail of your activism that is "illegal" such as not typing on a computer, e-mail, or piece of paper.
11. Have your meetings in a secure and nonsurveilled location.
12. Do not promote or support rumors about anything about anyone. Strive to end rumors or address them quickly and efficiently.
13. Minimize internalized social movement politics, which aids in information gathering of law enforcement, which could be used against activists.
14. Avoid working with people you don't like rather than publicizing your dislike of them.
15. Know your legal/illegal limits based on job, friends, children, family, organization(s), and movement.
16. Respect and learn each individual's security expectations and abide by them.
17. Leave no trace, meaning leave nothing in your home, car, on your phone, computer, or drop anything at events or locations that might aid in incarceration or information gathering of you or others.
18. All messages with the organization including listserves, board members, volunteers, and coordinators, directors, and social media messages should have the following note at the bottom of all messages discussing events, programs, projects, and general information about the group. All messages about the group should be private and should not be forwarded or discussed with others: CONFIDENTIALITY NOTICE: This communication (including any attachments) is intended only for the use of the

intended recipient and may contain information that is privileged and confidential. This communication along with all verbal, social media, and digital communication about all _____ (the name of the organization here) business and _____ (the name of the organization here) volunteers is private and not to be shared or discussed visually, forwarded, verbally or digitally with others such as friends, family, or members of _____ (the name of the organization here). If you are not the intended recipient, you are notified that any use, dissemination, forwarding, distribution, or copying of the communication is strictly prohibited. Please notify the sender immediately by e-mail if you have received this communication in error and delete this e-mail and all copies of this email from your system. Thank you.

OVERVIEW OF THE BOOK

In the Foreword, internationally respected long-time radical scholar-activist Ward Churchill writes about the 1960s university administrator Clark Kerr, who published *The Uses of the University*, which compares the university to a "knowledge factory" and the students are raw material to be molded and shaped into a product useful and worthy of society's needs. He ends by saying students in the 1960s resisted and protested this framework against Kerr, but today Kerr's idea is a reality. Will it be dismantled and overthrown or continue on its track?

In the Preface, Chicana scholar and feminist Emma Pérez puts names to paper about how kindergarten to higher education is being taken over by for-profit and nonprofit corporations, such as Pearson and Teach for America. Pérez speaks about the effects of this corporate takeover and how youth of color are the largest targets for pushout.

In Chapter 1, observing the ineffectiveness of contemporary forms of protest due to neoliberal reform, Nick Clare, Gregory White, and Richard J. White suggest alternative approaches to collective resistance that both unite all affected parties and effect change.

In Chapter 2, Mary Heath and Peter Burdon trace the origins of unwanted neoliberal reform and argue academics are failing to organize and resist such reform. They provide examples of effective reform through a case study in their native Australia, where faculty from a variety of disciplines united to challenge reform and acknowledge significant material and emotional challenges.

In Chapter 3, Mark Seis details factors leading to and effects of neoliberalization and provides a case study of how neoliberal reformers infiltrated a college campus and divided different constituencies, all under the aegis of "exceptional circumstances" that masqueraded as consistent with principles from the American Association of University Professors.

In Chapter 4, Camila Bassi utilizes privilege theory to argue that intersectionality limits our capability to work together, further enabling academic repression. She demonstrates this division by showing how conflict between radical feminists and transactivists results in *ressentiment*. To this end, she provides strategies for challenging the academic repression of identity politics.

In Chapter 5, Conor Cash and Geoff Boyce argue that neoliberalism does not simply exist in recent occurrences of academic repression but in the overall infrastructure of schooling. Understanding the university as a site of production, they argue, enables critics of neoliberalism to see institutionalized schooling differently, empowering them to enact a new strategy for change—teaching toward entropy.

In Chapter 6, Erik Juergensmeyer and Sue Doe demonstrate how a variety of initiatives initiated by neoliberal think tanks and foundations have whittled away their curricular authority at the expense of student learning. They detail how reform directly targets those who are most vulnerable and offer strategies for combating reform.

In Chapter 7, Laura L. Finley demonstrates how academic institutions are creating repressive systems that limit faculty, staff, and students engaging in activism. By becoming familiar with ways activism is stifled, readers become more engaged at their institutions and develop strategies for demanding more transparency.

In Chapter 8, by comparing student resistance tactics for combating political exclusion and repression, Ryan Thomson's cross-national case study positions educational spaces within contemporary protest, and highlights both positive and negative trends.

In Chapter 9, John Lupinacci articulates a vision for collaborative, intergenerational curricula that challenge existing hierarchical structures. He demonstrates how resistance pedagogy as enacted through a guerilla art project empowers a variety of stakeholders.

In Chapter 10, detailing the intimidation and personal stress incurred by her institution's administration, Diana Vallera documents the steps behind a very successful negotiation process between administration and the part-time faculty union. She then suggests key changes that need to happen in order to successfully combat further efforts at neoliberal reform.

In Chapter 11, differentiating between negative and positive freedoms, Sean Donaghue-Johnston and Tanya Loughead demonstrate how academic repression occurs through trends in staffing that lead to safe teaching practices and limit students' learning opportunities.

In Chapter 12, Emil Marmol, Mary Jean Hande, and Raluca Bejan not only detail the tactics used during a month-long strike that sought to create improved

working conditions, but they also provide research on the conditions leading up to poor working conditions and the administration's reactions to the strike.

In Chapter 13, Shannon Gibney's experiences of accusation, intimidation, and racial harassment illustrate the somber, repressed state of higher education, but her story also provides hope as she details how she involved the community and controlled the narrative to successfully overcome gender and race-motivated repression.

In Chapter 14, to counter dominant narratives that perpetuate oppressive hierarchical structures, Kelly Limes-Taylor Henderson offers different approaches to own discourse. She demonstrates how research methodology and authorship can counter existing paradigms and empower activists.

In Chapter 15, Z. B. Hurst utilizes personal narrative to locate a positionality within an academic system that seeks to homogenize individuals and threatens difference. Interspersing current events with on-campus experiences, Hurst details what it's like to be an outsider in both community and university and offers ways to create more inclusive educational institutions.

In the Afterword, the Southwest Colorado Sociology Collective—Keri Brandt, Becky Clausen, Janine Fitzgerald, Mark Seis, and Carey Vicenti—discuss how to build a unified supportive community of friends rather than a collegial and well-balanced department. They go on to discuss why that is important because of the rise of the factory/industrial/bureaucratic designing of schooling and the corporatization and profiting of schooling. They further claim higher education has become a 21st century boarding school where instead of just Native Americans being conditioned and molded, everyone is.

REFERENCES

AAUP (1940). *1940 statement of principles on academic freedom and tenure.* Retrieved from https://www.aaup.org/report/1940-statement-principles-academic-freedom-and-tenure

hooks, b. (2003). *Teaching community: A pedagogy of hope.* New York: Routledge.

King Jr., M.L. (2014). *Six steps of social change.* Retrieved from http://www.thekingcenter.org/king-philosophy#sub3

Lederach, J. P. (1997). *Building peace: Sustainable reconciliation in divided societies.* Washington, DC: Unites States Institute of Peace Press.

working conditions, but they also provide research on the conditions leading up to poor working conditions and the administration's reactions to the strike.

In Chapter 13, Shannon Gibney's experiences of accusation, intimidation, and racial harassment illustrate the somber, repressed state of higher education, but her story also provides hope as she details how she involved the community and controlled the narrative to successfully overcome gender and race-motivated repression.

In Chapter 14, to counter dominant narratives that perpetuate oppressive hierarchical structures, Kelly Limes-Taylor Henderson offers different approaches to own discourse. She demonstrates how research methodology and authorship can counter existing paradigms and empower activists.

In Chapter 15, Z. B. Hurst utilizes personal narrative to locate a positionality within an academic system that seeks to homogenize individuals and threatens difference. Interspersing current events with on-campus experiences, Hurst details what it's like to be an outsider in both community and university and offers ways to create more inclusive educational institutions.

In the Afterword, the Southwest Colorado Sociology Collective—Keri Brandt, Becky Clausen, Janine Fitzgerald, Mark Seis, and Carey Vicenti—discuss how to build a unified supportive community of friends rather than a collegial and well-balanced department. They go on to discuss why that is important because of the rise of the factory/industrial/bureaucratic designing of schooling and the corporatization and profiting of schooling. They further claim higher education has become a 21st century boarding school where instead of just Native Americans being conditioned and molded, everyone is.

REFERENCES

AAUP (1940). *1940 statement of principles on academic freedom and tenure.* Retrieved from https://www.aaup.org/report/1940-statement-principles-academic-freedom-and-tenure
hooks, b. (2003). *Teaching community: A pedagogy of hope.* New York: Routledge.
King Jr., M.L. (2014). *Six steps of social change.* Retrieved from http://www.thekingcenter.org/king-philosophy#sub3
Lederach, J. P. (1997). *Building peace: Sustainable reconciliation in divided societies.* Washington, DC: Unites States Institute of Peace Press.

Part I.
Neoliberal Education

"Neoliberal democracy. Instead of citizens, it produces consumers. Instead of communities, it produces shopping malls. The net result is an atomized society of disengaged individuals who feel demoralized and socially powerless."

NOAM CHOMSKY

"NGOs have a complicated space in neoliberal politics. They are supposed to mop up the anger. Even when they are doing good work, they are supposed to maintain the status quo. They are the missionaries of the corporate world."

ARUNDHATI ROY

Striking Out! Challenging Academic Repression in the Neoliberal University through Alternative Forms of Resistance: Some Lessons from the United Kingdom

NICK CLARE, GREGORY WHITE, AND RICHARD J. WHITE

INTRODUCTION: THE RESISTIBLE RISE OF THE NEOLIBERAL UNIVERSITY

> "Neoliberalism is not an enduring, inescapable hegemony but instead a reversible set of political-economic practices. It can thus be continually contested... " (Chun, 2009, p.112).

This chapter argues that embracing diverse, alternative, and experimental types of activism is vital in order to more successfully resist and fight the multiple forms of (academic) repression evident within the neoliberal university. In this context, neoliberalization can be recognized by drawing attention toward "the infusion of market and competitive logics throughout universities, the rise of audit process and cultures or accountability, and the replacement of public with private (student and private business) funding" (Dowling, 2008, p. 2). Moreover, the great reluctance by many university staff to passively accept these neoliberal processes has resulted in universities being subjected to "a particular combination of Stalinist hierarchical control and the so-called free market, in which the values, structures and processes of private sector management are imposed" (Radice, 2013, p. 408). In the face of this, the success of top-down forms of collective resistance—exemplified in calls for industrial action in the form of a strike—have been worryingly limited, ineffective, and, in places, highly counterproductive. Thus there is an urgent need to embrace other, potentially more effective, creative, and decentralized forms of activism that do not suffer from the same failings or weaknesses. Significantly, these forms of activism exist in the here and now, and we draw on several examples to illustrate what effective campus-based activism may look like and how these can be employed either as alternatives to strike action or as complementary to them.

The need to foreground new ways of organizing and protesting recognizes both the weaknesses of strike action, and also the new dynamic social-economic realities of twenty-first century universities. Certainly, the changing class composition found within increasingly neoliberalized universities (Paschal, 2013) has created new opportunities for resistance and expressions of solidarity. Indeed, a brief glance to see how protesters are organizing themselves reveals a shift away from mass-centralized and coordinated forms of action in favor of (student-led) direct action that is creative, unpredictable, spontaneous, ephemeral, and strategic. Occupations, teach-ins and sit-ins, and other experiments in critical pedagogy, such as "autonomous universities," continue to (re)invigorate and reanimate the struggle against "University Inc." (Parker, 2013) in new and important ways. Drawing on the diversity of mainstream/predictable and alternative/nonpredicable strategies of resistance offers the best opportunity to challenge, transcend, and transgress the dominant and repressively hierarchical power structures within academia. As a testament to the success of the "alternative" forms of activism, they have increasingly been met with a range of draconian responses that seek to silence, repress, and punish those involved (Nocella II et al., 2010). Where these have been successful, it is important that lessons are learned, and the limits of these alternative forms of protest are recognized and addressed. On this note, yes there are great strengths to be found in diversity, absolutely, but there are also equal strengths harnessed through expressions of solidarity, which we must not overlook. Moving forward, we need to find new forms of activism and protests that unite staff, students, and other exploited groups within and beyond the university.

APPROACH

Within this context, drawing on first-hand experience in two cities within the United Kingdom—London and Sheffield—this chapter explores the relative successes and failures of a series of struggles "in-against-and-beyond" the neoliberal university (Pusey & Sealey-Huggins, 2013). Drawing insight and inspiration from both anarchist and autonomist-Marxist theory, we argue that not only are alternative forms of resistance desirable, and enactable, but in fact essential, if the neoliberal university—and the multiple forms of academic repression it sustains within it—are to be successfully challenged.

THE UNITED KINGDOM AND THE NEOLIBERAL UNIVERSITY

The contested subject of the "neoliberal university" has been keenly and critically debated across a number of disciplines by academics concerned with the "marketization" of higher education (Brown & Carasso, 2013; Molesworth et al., 2011; Parker, 2013; Slaughter & Rhoades, 2000; The Autonomous Geographies Collective, 2010; The SIGJ2 Writing Collective, 2012; Radice, 2013). Before continuing, it is important that temptations to reinforce a monolithic reading of both "neoliberal" and "university" are resisted. Regarding neoliberalism, for example, Springer (2010) argued:

> As a series of protean processes, individual neoliberalizations are considered to "materialize" quite differently as mutated and hybrid forms of neoliberalism, depending on and influenced by geographical landscapes, historical contexts, institutional legacies, and embodied subjectivities (p. 1029).

Recognizing difference and diversity is particularly important as it should suggest that such multiplicity demands appropriately decentered, bottom-up, and variegated strategies of resistance. Such a conclusion is reinforced by Halvorsen's (2015a) observation:

> The university is not a monolithic institution, but is constantly being reworked by individuals within it, pushing it toward different ends. The university not only provides a resource base for doing militant research but, at best, is ripe for the creation of "cracks" [in capitalism] (p. 2).

Beyond doubt, however, is that a marketization of higher education—while uneven and contingent—is becoming increasingly pervasive, challenging, and eroding the not-for-profit grounds upon which public universities still, theoretically at least, stand upon (Martell, 2015). Focusing on the United Kingdom, the last two decades have witnessed a rapid shift in the nature of funding within the higher education system: from a model based on public funding to one reliant on private capital-increasing tuition fees, for example, have been central to the policies of subsequent governments that have sought to shift the burden of responsibility from the state to the individual.

Unsurprisingly, the "neoliberal assault" (Barkawi, 2013) on academia has many serious and far-reaching implications. These include, but are far from limited to:

(1) the steady increase in the cost of education (particularly fees) and retracting state support for the sector (either through grants or loans);

(2) the increase in casualization and flexibility of contracts within the sector, which has led to a depression of wages for lower paid staff;

(3) the outsourcing of contracts, assets, and resources to private companies—under the direction of the university management—which has decentralized control and contributed to wage deflation;

(4) an increase in competition within the academic community as focussed through the Research Excellent Framework (REF), leading to a competition-based market over funding for projects and for staff tenure; and

(5) the exorbitant remuneration of management, particularly at universities within self-selected associations and professional bodies. Indeed the management of the university as an institution, then, has shifted away from advancing perceived "social goods" to arrangements that favour the varieties of competitiveness and market-led approaches which have typified neoliberalism.

Focusing in more detail on the neoliberal scripting of university students as "market consumers" (rather than unique individual learners) has signified a dramatic paradigm shift across the sector, where the privileging of the overall "student experience" over the quality and delivery of pedagogy and critical thinking in particular has had numerous consequences. The cumulative result of these factors is that students are increasingly reconsidering/renegotiating their relationship with the university as an institution—from active learners to passive consumers. If we examine the genesis of these ideas, a body of literature identifies the public school system as the perpetuating force in recycling education—and the process of being educated—as a commodity. As Scott (2012) argued:

> The great tragedy of the public school system [...] is that it is, by and large, a one-product factory. The tendency has only been exacerbated by the push in recent decades for standardization, measurement, testing, and accountability. The resulting incentives for students, teachers, principals, and whole school districts have had the effect of bending all efforts toward fashioning a standard product that satisfies the criteria the auditors have established (p. 71).

In establishing standards that fulfill a certain goal (or end product), there are pre-determined, precisely defined limits that dictate how far students can critically engage with the process of being educated. The result is that students become the subject of their studies as opposed to being iteratively involved in their training (ideally as co-learners). Here, and elsewhere, the embedded nature of such structures in educational institutions is exemplary of the processes which actively (re)produce the conditions for the proliferation of financial capital.

Surveyed as a whole, the impacts of this/ these neoliberal restructuring(s) have been dramatic and keenly felt across the entire sector, at all levels: from academic and administrative staff to casual/temporary workers and students. This is to be expected, as the pursuit of economic profits above human values and needs becomes the new bottom line. The cumulative experiences of neoliberal universities in North America, as Asimakopoulos (2014) emphasized, are increasingly apparent in the United Kingdom:

> Neoliberalism has now transformed universities (at least those for middle and working classes) into publicly funded vocational schools for corporate needs, basically job training centres. The goal is to produce skilled workers, which defines what professionals are. The means are mostly through applied programs where critical thinking is understood as work-related problem solving. Such programs are nonthreatening to the system unlike the social sciences and humanities, which happen to be the first on the policy chopping block when financial crises occur. The colonization of the educational system by capitalist relations is designed to reproduce obedient nationalistic consumers as capitalism's transformation has engulfed the political process equating it with market consumption. Accordingly, everything should be provided by markets, where freedom is expressed by purchasing goods and services, students are customers, teachers are workers, and schools are businesses (literally as in the case for for-profit educational corporations in the United States) (p. 151).

Once these neoliberal goals are allowed to become embedded as new university "norms," the consequences are far-reaching. As Martell (2015) observed:

> Unequal opportunities for applicants and students, and between universities, and managers and their employees, are widen[ed]. Managers impose, push out staff and student unions, and side-line consultation. Community is broken up by inequalities, the exclusion of university members from citizenship, and the fragmentation of the workforce with outsourcing (para. 12).

The neoliberal university has fostered large disquiet and discontent amongst students and staff alike over the quality of education delivered, and the conditions of work that should facilitate a high level of learning and training. Rather than promoting new forms of identity and solidarity, the sense of vulnerability, isolation, and anomie has become pervasive. The next section focuses on the limits of traditional, mainstream forms of protest, and dissent in channelling this discontent effectively and foregrounds the readers' attention to the relative strengths of alternative forms of resistance within and against the neoliberal university.

ALTERNATIVE FORMS OF RESISTANCE: SOME LESSONS FROM THE UNITED KINGDOM

The opening part of this section argues that the traditional model of unionism, as a means of resisting and fighting the neoliberalization processes within higher education, has had rather limited success. Coordinated strike action, as illustrated by those coordinated by the University and College Union (UCU), for example, failed to challenge the increasingly entrenched positions taken by university management on issues such as pay and conditions, and thus left university staff with even fewer options in terms of (re)negotiating terms of pay and working conditions. These outcomes, coming at a time of increasing hostility toward trade union action, strongly suggests that activists should look to develop more effective strategies that embrace a diversity of nonviolent tactics such as, but not limited to, boycotts, sit-ins, walkouts, blockades, hunger strikes, fasts, banner drops, tabling, teach-ins, workshops, flyering, and chalking. Before continuing, it is important to emphasize that this chapter is not a rejection of UCU or trade unions per se. For example, all authors are members of UCU, and have balloted for, supported, and been directly involved with industrial action in the past. Instead, the key arguments made here draw on critical reflections embedded in the difficulties we have personally encountered when engaging in activism designed to contest and counter neoliberalization and have seen other activists endure. More positively, we have also witnessed, and participated in, other meaningful forms of resistance (both complementary, and alternative, to industrial strike action) that offer further possibilities and relevant to inform new approaches to activism and protest within and beyond the university. It is these constructive interventions that we wish to explore more fully later in the chapter. In June 2006, the UCU was successful in negotiating a 10.37 percent pay rise to take place across the next 22 months, as well as a further 2.5 percent rise in the following year. Although it is important to note that this result stemmed from an extended marking boycott of exams and other forms of assessment—a tactic discussed in more detail further—perhaps the most telling issue here has been the fallout from the industrial action: while securing the pay raise was an undoubted success, in many ways it was a pyrrhic victory. Although UCU membership remains relatively high, levels of militancy and active participation have reduced, and in the case of the 2013 industrial action the pay rise achieved in 2006 was cited by some staff as a reason for this downturn. For instance, in one author's experience, conversations with lecturers about the importance of carrying out strike action to combat what was, in real terms, a 13 percent pay cut since 2008 were frequently met with claims that they felt uncomfortable going on strike given that they were well paid in comparison to many other university staff—this point was even made by one department's union representative. On the other hand, among some staff (again, all members of UCU) there was a level of resentment that the pay scales agreed through union-led struggle were such that new staff apparently earned almost as much as more senior lecturers. Either way, for many, a reticence to strike was, counterintuitively, grounded in the 2006 experience, and exacerbating these problems, other staffs were resigned to the fact that going on strike would apparently achieve very little, while others could not afford to be docked wages that close to Christmas.

These were, of course, not universal responses, as there were a significant number of extremely committed and active members of staff. However, the apathy we confronted on the day was, at points, shocking—in one author's experience: the only people present on the picket line for two departments were a handful of Ph.D. students, with no members of staff at all. Although we witnessed relatively few members of staff crossing the picket line, many colleagues chose to work from home instead, using the time to catch up with their own research and administrative tasks. Another common situation for those with teaching responsibilities on the day of the strike was to reschedule the class for a different day. Again, while this avoided the crossing of the picket line, it contributed to the undermining of the strike. Staff who did rearrange teaching typically pointed out that they felt students were paying so much (the social science departments where we work have little contact/teaching time) they felt uncomfortable denying them the services they had paid for. The ubiquity of such comments reinforces the ways in which, as argued above, higher education in the United Kingdom has become increasingly commodified. Perhaps more insidiously, the number of staff who felt they needed to use the day of the strike to catch up with their own research shows not only the pressures facing academics in the United Kingdom, but also the ephemeral and immaterial nature of academic labour, something which makes the withdrawal of such labour a challenge. Accordingly, the next sections will explore the potential for more effective forms of resistance, emphasising the need for solidarity between staff and students (SIGJ2 Writing Collective, 2012).

Perhaps one of the most alarming things about the 2013 strike was the lack of student engagement and understanding. Despite UCU's attempts at outreach to the student body—including a number of discussions, Q&A sessions, and even social events organized by various branches—many students did not know about, let alone understand and support, the strike. The vast majority of students, once they had spoken to people on the picket line, offered their support and chose not to cross into buildings, but admitted this was the first they had heard of the strike. A surprising number of students even admitted that they did not know what a strike or a picket line was at all—all the more depressing for those of us in social science who have taught the self-same students about (class) struggles and resistance. A popular misconception among students was that their threefold rise in fees had helped fund a pay rise of the same magnitude for academic staff. Once this myth was dispelled, and the nature of the real terms of the pay cut explained, support increased. These conversations were, however, comparatively isolated, as only engaging with students who approached picket lines inevitably failed to speak to a huge proportion of the student body. Similarly, the events arranged before the strike by UCU were typically only attended by politicized students who already supported the strike. The challenge, therefore, is to engage productively with much more of the student body. Without these links and successful explanation of the reasons for industrial action, students can often become pitted against staff, with some students deeming staff selfish as their actions were preventing students from accessing the "product" they had paid for. This consumer rights discourse was not only a depressing culmination of higher education's commodification, but it also touched on the problematic alliances being drawn between university management and students.

Without wishing to separate or simplify the university into three homogeneous groups, without significant engagement with the student body, strike action can place academics in an isolated position. In our experiences, university management was adept at positioning itself as "on the students' side," something which contributed to animosity toward academic staff. The position of academic staff (i.e., lecturers, researchers, and postgraduate teaching assistants) becomes less tenable in the face of hostility from both university management and from students. The experiences of the authors suggest that, during the period of strike action, university management was able to occupy an advantageous position, being both critical of strike action whilst simultaneously supporting students, that, in the main, viewed such industrial action negatively. The resulting effect is that the university, despite the disquiet of academic staff, is still able to gain from a contentious situation as the withdrawal of labour on isolated days fails to compromise those things most important to universities: teaching and learning indicators, student satisfaction and academic work that ultimately contributes to overall "research power" (i.e., in the Research Excellence Framework). In terms of where this situation leaves the position of the academic, it is clear that the nature of work within the neoliberal university has become increasingly precarious. Not only are we faced with a situation where academics and researchers find themselves pitted against the student body, the types of work, and immaterial labour that academics engage in have increasingly been commodified (Barkari, 2013). This has had a direct impact on the ability to bargain—especially since publishing in academia is viewed as an essential component of one's training and/or career progression. Viewed as actions in isolation, we suggest that the efficacy of the one-day strike and the tactics employed in contemporary industrial action do not pose effective challenges since university management structures—and broader academic practices—have fostered conditions such that researchers are placed in increasingly stressful and precarious positions. Actions, in our view, must be coordinated.

ALTERNATIVE FORMS OF RESISTANCE AND THE NEED
TO COORDINATE ACTION

Vibrant, decentred dynamic forms of student-led activism have emerged in recent years—particularly since the passing of a government bill to raise tuition fees to £9,000 per year in 2010—specifically targeting the "marketization" of higher education. There have been many positive impacts and new transformative spaces that have directly emerged through such inventions, and we begin by discussing, in some detail, two of these. Following this, we conclude with a series of points that reflect on these two experiences and provide a series of practical examples we believe can help in the fight against (and from within) the neoliberal university.

WITHIN AND AGAINST THE "NEOLIBERAL UNIVERSITY":
THE ROLE OF STUDENT OCCUPATIONS

The recent wave of occupations in universities across the United Kingdom provides important examples of how coordinated, democratic actions can have a measurable impact. The University College London (UCL), Sheffield, Warwick, Sussex, Edinburgh, and School of Oriental and African Studies (SOAS) provide some recent examples of institutions that have seen coordinated action from students opposing rising tuition fees and the increasing privatization of university services. In many ways, these have been successful, and have joined groups together, increasing levels of student activism. The recent visibility of some of these occupations—particularly in 2010, during and after the vote on increasing tuition fees to £9,000—have helped to draw some staff in that have sympathies with the student movement but have in previous years felt unable to demonstrate solidarity. Whilst it should be recognized that there are gains to be made from the wave of occupations, the authors note that there can be significant limitations to them.

One particular issue with the occupation of university premises is that they become difficult to maintain, with interest and levels of morale typically waning after a few weeks. Further, occupations can become insular, and there are attendant issues with radical posturing, which only serve to alienate some members of the student body. The theatrics of an occupation also pose interesting questions around the fetishization of the spectacular over the everyday experience of maintaining acts of resistance, examples of which are discussed later in the chapter.

When done strategically, however, occupations can be extremely productive and also complement forms of action taken by staff. One excellent example to mention is the occupation by students from the University of Sheffield of a major administration building the night before a strike began. The action taken in the

Arts Tower at the University of Sheffield, while extremely disruptive for university management, was able to minimize the direct disruption of students' classes, avoiding some of the problematic consequences (of strike action) that have already been discussed. In deploying this particular tactic in an administrative center, the occupation of the Arts Tower—joined both by students and staff—demonstrated a level of unity that might otherwise have been difficult organizing via the traditional routes of industrial action, and helped redraw the lines of solidarity that created a more united front of students and staff against management, which inevitably increased the impact of strike action.

Nevertheless, as has been discussed, levels of repression have also become high, and this can have consequences for both students and staff involved with occupations. For instance, in the wake of various occupations, the University of Sheffield not only implemented a series of injunctions against all forms of protest on university property, but there have also been targeted actions against students and staff. In conjunction with as well as the attendant increases in persecution and surveillance, this presents significant questions around the viability for students to take action if the university decides to take punitive measures. Further, in one author's experience, threats have previously been made to cut his funding (emphasizing the precarity of research students), and security has been particularly repressive, resulting in additional surveillance (Lewis, 2013). Elsewhere, there have been problematic issues with other staff facing disciplinary action for offering teach-ins at previous occupations. Thus, not only do students and staff alike need to consider ways to carry out such experiments in occupations and demonstrations, but also in ways that are sustainable and can withstand overt pressure by university management. In spite of these concerns over the instances of occupations as a tactic, the re-emergence of student occupations has been an important moment, with tangible and material successes. But in moving forward, a couple of key points should be considered. First, alternative strategies must complement occupations, especially at times where the momentum of the occupation movement is dwindling. And second, it is vital to build links and solidarity between staff and students, as well as those outside of the activist milieu. An example of this is therefore discussed next.

"FREE UNIVERSITY OF SHEFFIELD"

To take one example of recent activism within and against the neoliberal university, we would like to draw attention to the "Free University of Sheffield." As an action, the organization—formed in 2014 as a response to the increasing marketization of higher education—aims to break down barriers and hierarchies between staff and students, forging the links between these two groups. The organization itself promotes alternative methods of educating and disseminating ideas, outside of the parameters of neoliberal pedagogical structures, and sessions/events set up by the Free University of Sheffield (which have taken place in recent years at both Sheffield and Sheffield Hallam University) have ranged from discussions around anarchism, education, street politics, queer liberation to workshops on consent and comedy and art therapy. To discuss such topics, the "Free University" has been successful in occupying and reclaiming university premises and transforming them in to spaces of bottom-up, democratic debate. These challenges have been particularly important in the struggle for maintaining interest since previous occupations—particularly around 2010—lost momentum.

The authors note here, however, that tensions can emerge in the contemporary struggles against the university. There were a number of debates circulating during the recent wave of occupations on whether or not it would be better to occupy and carry out something ostensibly more "radical," or proceed on a more official route. The authors found that there were material gains to be made by acknowledging and confronting the relative privileges afforded to staff and some students—as with taking an official route and booking university spaces officially. Work on the Occupy Movement has considered the fundamental importance of dovetailing the more everyday experiences associated with social reproduction with the more combative taking of space, if the transformative potential of such actions are to ever be realized (Halvorsen, 2015b). This dialectical relationship between the quotidian and the spectacular should, therefore, underpin action within and against the neoliberal university. Our experiences suggest that there was more scope for productive engagement in taking an official route, as unfortunately a more aggressively occupied space failed to reach out as much, ending up in notions of the spectacular and isolating, as opposed to the sustained and inclusive. In thinking prefiguratively, the notion of building a new university in the shell of the old, and doing this in a sustainable way is, as the authors are keen to suggest, a method that could be useful in the future when considering tactics and actions. However, there is also a need to find ways to encourage these types of interventions to gain momentum, and animate new, multiple and more visible types of praxis into being.

For many reasons this remains the primary challenge, and something that students have been taking up; the "Free University" has become an organization in its own right, undertaking a number of activities. A key part of this is the idea of (re)appropriating spaces, for example, the "Free University of Sheffield" recently occupied premises within the student's union. The strategic occupation of the "Inox" dining area in 2015 and the subversive elements that came with it presented a new challenge to university management and security. The dining area itself, a high-end restaurant and flagship part of the University's project to expand corporate engagement, was specifically targeted for occupation since it had seen very little use, and also provided an additional study space for students—who themselves went on to produce a number of satirical posters about the reclamation of university property. Symbolically, the reclaiming of such spaces aimed to put the needs of staff (particularly those in precarious positions) and students above the business interests of the university, but in such a way that was outward facing and immune from university recrimination—the students were, after all, making the most of study space.

Tactically and strategically this needs to be part of broader movement, that is often student-led, but with involvement from staff. While the Free University of Sheffield has made some important strides forward with their work, inevitably issues and difficulties remain. As with our analysis of limitations thus far, there is a need to be reflective, and realize the limits of certain actions. Especially pressing is the problem is that much of the population—both student and staff—is temporary. As contracts for staff become shorter continuity in such projects is a challenge. There is always a need to maintain consistency with such projects, and, combined with short-term staff contracts, the typical three-year undergraduate course in the United Kingdom causes issues. A further issue is that, despite the best attempts of those involved, such university-centric activities typically remain off limits for the wider community. As campuses become more securitized, nonstudents may feel unwelcome/uncomfortable, and may even be prevented from attending such events. Likewise, beyond simply the physical spaces of protest themselves, the atmosphere of political events is crucial in the extent to which they are successful. Accordingly, there needs to be a frank acknowledgment of the regular use of inaccessible language as well as the fetishization of an activist milieu that can become counterproductively and counterintuitively reactionary and insular.

Considering these points, we suggest that such innovative actions are best understood as part of a broader repertoire that can build solidarity and help to decommodify the experience of studying and working within the university institution. Before concluding, therefore, we have provided a list of ideas and tactics that we believe are fundamental to reclaiming the university:

1. *Create new "alternative" critical spaces of pedagogy within the academy.*
   This has been an important positive form of action that both reclaims "privatized" classrooms and student unions, and disseminates critical ideas that challenge the everyday practices within the neoliberal institution, and within wider society.

2. *Cocreate a meaningful commons.*
   It is vital to promote open spaces that can foster important—and inclusive—dialogue and debate between staff and students. This commoning has been successful in Sheffield and has included a teach-in focused on the causes and responses to The Global [Neoliberal] Economic Crisis co-organized by Richard White (Sheffield Hallam) and Jamie Gough (Sheffield

University) which took place in the Sheffield University Students' Union in 2009.

3. *Reach out beyond the academy.*
   While recognizing the need to create "alternative" critical spaces of pedagogy within the academy, it is also so important to reach out to broader activist and public communities. The use of social media: from Tumblr, to Twitter to Facebook (see https://www.facebook.com/thefreeuniversityof-sheffield/) has been extremely important in circulating these ideas and generating broader levels of interest and engagement.

4. *Physically occupy university space.*
   While such solidarity building activities can often take place within formally organized university spaces, there is also benefit in physically occupying university space. This not only can prove disruptive for management and support staff strikes, but it can build momentum among the student movement and raise awareness of key issues and debates.

5. *Student strikes.*
   An interesting recent development to note has been the (re)emergence of the student strike among UK institutions. Historically and globally this tactic has proved extremely successful, and, leaving aside semantic debates about the use of the word "strike," there is UK precedent. In 1971 the National Union of Students (NUS) called and supported a five-week student strike against then education secretary Margaret Thatcher's plans to modify the membership of the union. The strike was successful and ultimately contributed to Thatcher withdrawing her proposal. The presence of the student strike suggests many interesting possibilities for students to reclaim their education and, given the amount they pay in tuition fees and the lack of public-funding universities receive, acknowledge the potentially powerful position they are in. Importantly, in the context of this chapter, there is also great potential for expressions of staff-student solidarity and deeper resistance here through coordinated actions such as student strikes and marking boycotts.

6. *Engage with broader student organizations.*
   Recently the NUS has bucked its typically timid stance and voted to support a student strike. At the same time the more radical, student-led group the National Campaign against Fees and Cuts (NCAFC) is asking students' unions across the United Kingdom to ballot for strike action. If a student strike (or collective boycott of classes, assessments, and exams) is to be successful, it obviously requires large-scale support from the student body, or

else those students who strike could face failing to graduate or more serious repercussions. In this context forging meaningful links (to reflect, share and learn from different experiences and good-practice) with different universities (in the United Kingdom and elsewhere) is vital.

7. *Promote awareness and understanding through dialogue and discussion.*
Analogous with students lacking awareness and knowledge of staff strikes, among academic staff there tends to be very little awareness of student actions/politics. There are multiple reasons for this, but through conversations with students and staff, a number of key factors appear time and again. First, the increasingly atomized nature of academia means that, through a lack of serious engagement with colleagues and especially students, staff are often simply unlikely to have heard about such actions. But even for those who have, issues surrounding workloads and the precarity associated with lack of tenure and short-term contracts means that early career academics may lack the time and job security to engage significantly with more radical student movements. From the students' perspective, low engagement with staff typically came from a combination of lack of knowledge about whom to speak to and fear. Given the levels of repression and intimidation toward student (and staff) activists in universities, students can be reticent in outing themselves as ostensibly radical. The levels of surveillance on university campuses have increased noticeably in recent times. Similarly, increases in the securitization of university premises (Nocella II & Gabbard, 2013), along with the presence of policing, are now common across institutions in the United Kingdom, especially where universities have sought to curb dissent. During this period of increasing repression on university premises, some radical and critical academics have played down elements of their research and personal politics, which can make student activists feel more isolated. The hierarchical nature of universities also adds to these issues, as students can feel uncomfortable approaching staff to ask for support and advice.

8. *Identify and (ab)use hierarchy.*
Consideration needs to be taken over the position of research students, which is simultaneously liminal and precarious. Two of the authors' experiences as research students demonstrate the value that a senior academic can offer when defending someone against charges within the university as an institution and so on. So, we propose what is needed is a form of class composition analysis, and work out what different people within the university can offer. It is clear that what is needed, then, is a confrontation and subversion of privileges. We must recognize the power that comes with a tenured position—as with a head of department, etc. It is proposed that

staff and students alike need to make sure people are engaged and can do what they can, while still maintaining a bottom-up, democratic movement. In this sense, it is possible to do things against and beyond the university, building solidarity between staff and students, linking the struggles against management, and moving forward productively.

CONCLUSIONS

While the complex socio-spatial transformations associated with the neoliberalization of the university have created and perpetuated "the multiple crises of higher education (HE) in the UK" (Radice, 2013, p. 401) they have also provoked new forms of activism into being. What the chapter has sought to emphasize is that these other forms of activism can be alternative, complementary and/ or antagonistic when held against traditional top-down appeals to protest, exemplified by strike action. What is beyond doubt Is that new forms of dialogue—and new expressions of solidarity within the academy—are urgently needed. At the same time, we must recognize our own positionality and privilege within the academy, in order to meaningfully "confront the question of whether we can actually challenge or change our institutional environments or our relationships with one another" (The SIGJ2 Writing Collective, 2012).

Drawing on both personal experiences, and the related experience of others, the chapter has drawn critical attention to several examples of campus-based direct action and expressions of solidarity. Hopefully these will have a broader relevance and interest for other university struggles against neoliberalization and its impacts. Of course, though, we also hope that the content of this chapter should be an invitation to think creatively, not prescriptively: for there is a real need to embrace—and communicate—new and contingent strategies of resilience and resistance at this time. Importantly, embracing praxis which is both experimental and spontaneous, should not be at the automatic expense of those traditional forms of activism that may seem more mundane, but are in fact still important and significant. In that sense, we are hopeful that current student activists will engage in a diverse front of tactics against repression and oppression, and be open to the possibility of pushing these in new and critical directions where possible. In short, the students, faculty, staff, and community members must unite and destroy the current corporate neoliberal administrative-run university and pave the way for a "deneoliberal" era. We must reclaim its not-for-profit roots, thereby creating a non-negotiable space and place for higher education that embraces: (1) free (in every sense) education, (2) community-based leadership, (3) locally supported curriculum, (4) critical dialogue, and (5) inclusive social justice pedagogy. All these we hope will empower every student and professor by impressing upon them the need to develop their academic knowledge, relevance, and understanding of activism, helping them fight oppression and repression in all its forms, and in doing so reject the hollow alternative as a passive citizen of a nation state used to promote complicity, capitalism, and consumption.

REFERENCES

Askimalopoulos, J. (2014). *Social structures of direct democracy: On the political economy of equality.* Boston, MA: Brill.

Bailey, M., & Freedman, D. (2011). *The assault on universities: A manifesto for resistance.* London, UK: Pluto Press.

Barkawi, T. (2013). The neoliberal assault on academia. Retrieved from http://www.aljazeera.com/indepth/opinion/2013/04/20134238284530760.html

Barber, M., Donnelly, K., & Rizvi, S. (2013). *An avalanche is coming: Higher education and the revolution.* London, UK: Institute for Public Policy Research.

Barnett, R. (2005). *Reshaping the university: New relationships between research, scholarship and teaching.* Maidenhead, UK: Open University Press.

Bok, D. (2004). *The commercialization of higher education.* Princeton, NJ: Princeton University Press.

Brown, R., & Carasso, H. (2013). *Everything for sale? The marketisation of UK higher education.* London, UK: Routledge.

Chun, C. W. (2009). Contesting neoliberal discourses in EAP: Critical praxis in an IEP classroom. *Journal of English for Academic Purposes, 8*(2), 111–120.

Collini, S. (2012). *What are universities for?* Harmondsworth, UK: Penguin.

Cooper, D. (2014). *Everyday utopias: The conceptual life of promising spaces.* Durham, NC: Duke University Press.

Davies, W. (2014). *The limits of neoliberalism: Authority, sovereignty and the logic of competition.* London, UK: Sage.

Dowling, R. (2008). Geographies of identity: Labouring in the 'neoliberal' university. *Progress in Human Geography, 32*(6), 812–820. doi: 10.1177/0309132507088032.

Halvorsen, S. (2015a). Militant research against-and-beyond itself: Critical perspectives from the university and Occupy London. *Area, 47*(4), 466–472. doi: 10.1111/area.12221.

Halvorsen, S. (2015b). Taking space: Moments of rupture and everyday life in Occupy London. *Antipode, 47*(2), 401–417.

Levitas, R. (2013). *Utopia as method: The imaginary reconstruction of society.* London, UK: Palgrave MacMillan.

Lewis, J. (2013). The college campus as panopticon: How security and surveillance are undermining free inquiry. In: Nocella II, A. J. & Gabbard D. (Eds.), *Policing the campus: Academic repression, surveillance, and the Occupy Movement.* New York: Peter Lang.

Olssen, M., & Peters, M. A. (2005). Neoliberalism, higher education and the knowledge economy: From the free market to knowledge capitalism, *Journal of Education Policy, 20*(3), 313–345.

Martell, L. (2015). The marketisation of our universities is fragmenting the academic workforce at the students' expense. LSE British Politics and Policy Blog. Retrieved from http://blogs.lse.ac.uk/impactofsocialsciences/2013/12/04/the-marketisation-of-our-universities/

Molesworth, M., Scullion, R., & Nixon, E. (Eds.) (2011). *The marketisation of higher education and the student as consumer*. Oxford, UK: Abingdon.

Nocella II, A. J., & Gabbard, D. (Eds.). (2013). *Policing the campus: Academic repression, surveillance, and the Occupy Movement*. New York: Peter Lang.

Nocella II, A. J., Best, S., & McLaren, P. (Eds.) (2010). *Academic repression: Reflections from the academic industrial complex*. Oakland, CA: AK Press.

Parker, M. (2013). University, Ltd: Changing a business school. *Organization, 21*(2), 281–292. doi: 10.1177/1350508413502646.

Radice, H. (2013). How we got here: UK higher education under neoliberalism. *ACME: An International E-Journal for Critical Geographies, 12*(2), 407–418.

Scott, J. C. (2012). *Two cheers for anarchism: Six easy pieces on autonomy, dignity, and meaningful work and play*. Princeton, NJ: Princeton University Press.

Springer, S. (2010). Neoliberalism and geography: Expansions, variegations, formations. *Geography Compass*, 4(8), 1025–1038.

The SIGJ2 Writing Collective. (2012). What can we do? The challenge of being new academics in neoliberal universities. *Antipode, 44*, 1055–1058. doi: 10.1111/j.1467-8330.2012.01011.x.

CHAPTER TWO

Academic Resistance: Landscape of Hope and Despair

MARY HEATH AND PETER BURDON

Australian higher education, along with higher education in many other parts of the world, has undergone successive waves of neoliberal and managerialist changes in recent decades. One commentator argued that Australian higher education has experienced "the most profound changes anywhere in the developed world" (Coates et al., 2010, p. 382). University education which was free for a short period, from the mid-1970s to the mid-1980s has been increasingly subjected to fees and then to systems which increase the proportion of the cost of education paid by students. Multiple waves of change to university funding arrangements have been made (Ryan, Guthrie, & Neumann, 2008, pp. 172–173) as the higher education sector has been subjected to reforms also imposed upon the wider public sector (Parker & Jary, 1995; Ryan, Guthrie, & Neumann, 2008, pp. 171–187). These changes have been designed to increase accountability and microlevel government control (Ryan, Guthrie, & Neumann, 2008, p. 174). They have been accompanied by major changes in industrial relations (Ryan, Guthrie, & Neumann, 2008, p. 177). In the process, the Australian government has gone from speaking of higher education as a public service with the capacity to increase the fairness of Australian life to speaking of higher education as a competitive globalized market in which Australian institutions should participate as exporters.

Student numbers rose by fifty-one percent between 1996 and 2005 while teaching-only and teaching-research staff slightly decreased (Bradley et al., 2008, p. 74; Ryan, Guthrie, & Neumann, 2008, p. 178). These increased student numbers represent an increase in access to higher education that is to be welcomed.

However, the lack of equivalent rises in staffing levels has led to rises in workload and work-related stress for staff. It has led to escalating levels of casualization, which mean that up to half of all university teaching in Australia is now undertaken by hourly paid, or "sessional" staff whose working conditions are precarious and often underpaid and poorly supported. Junor (2004) estimated forty percent of academic staffs were employed on a sessional basis a decade ago. Coates *et al.* (2010) showed a doubling of contingent staff as a proportion of the academic workforce from staff increased, from 12.6 percent of all teaching staff in 1989 to 22.2 percent in 2007; May, Peetz, and Strachan (2013) surveyed nineteen universities in 2011 and found that forty-nine precent of all academic staff and fifty-three percent of all teaching and research academic staff (excluding research-only/research-intensive staff) were contingently employed (p. 258). Government-funded regulatory body the Tertiary Education Quality and Standards Agency (TEQSA) found that casual staff made up twenty-two percent of the academic staff employed at Australian universities in 2012 (TEQSA, 2014).

This reduction in resources and staffing for each student, together with changes to student support, and assessment driven by underfunding and under-staffing, has impacted the quality of tertiary, or postsecondary, education in Australia (Thornton, 2008, p. 17; Thornton, 2012, p. 27). Moreover, it has created a new class of precarious workers who are responsible for a significant portion of university teaching and raised levels of anxiety and despondency amongst academic and administrative staff.

This context gives rise to a tension that we will unpack and develop in this chapter. On the one hand, universities around the world are undergoing significant and largely undesirable neoliberal reform. On the other hand, academics, despite their sometimes intimate knowledge of these reforms, analytical skills, and relative privilege, report feeling more focused on survival than organized resistance. Part one of this chapter summarizes research into why, in Australian universities, most academics are not overtly resisting. This discussion is followed in part two by a case study of a resistance project initiated by the authors and involving academics from several South Australian universities. In the case study, we describe the activities we engaged in, difficulties we encountered, and some lessons we learned. In describing this case study, we underline the importance of understanding and taking seriously the material and emotional challenges that prevent many academics from engaging in organized resistance. At many institutions the immediate challenge is not to overthrow the encroachment of neoliberalism into higher education—it is to get a group of diverse people into the same room for a sustained period of time to discuss common goals and strategies for realizing them and to overcome a profound sense of disempowerment and despair that seems ironic in the case of tenured academic workers given their relative social power and privilege.

LITERATURE ON ACADEMIC RESISTANCE

As the educational resources offered to students decline, security of staff employment falls away, and the university becomes more like a for-profit corporation and much less like an institution dedicated to the discovery of knowledge and the provision of education as a public and civic good—staff stress and dissatisfaction is demonstrably rising. These processes are discussed in more detail further. As a cohort of relatively privileged workers with more autonomy than most, it might seem that academics, particularly those who have more secure tenure, might be uniquely well equipped to take action against these processes. Gina Anderson (2008), for example, pointed to academics' skills in critical thinking and argued that academics are "unlikely to passively accept changes they regard as detrimental" (p. 252). Yet there is little obvious evidence of *organized* resistance to these changes in Australian universities (Davies & Bansel, 2005; Gill, 2009; Ryan, Guthrie, & Neumann, 2008, p. 3; Thornton, 2004, pp. 482–483, 500; Trowler, 1998, p. 13). Commenting specifically on law schools, Thornton (2012) observed that neoliberal reform has proceeded "with alacrity" (p. 482).

Various commentators have tried to explain the lack of organized resistance. Some explain the lack of resistance as arising from reductions in government funding and strategies for funding which pit universities and academics against one another in relentless competition for government funding, research funding, and tied grant moneys (Ryan, Guthrie, & Neumann, 2008, pp. 171–187). These processes have produced a hostile, overworked, precarious, and competitive environment, which some suggest is not conducive to organized resistance.

Others point to the ways in which reform of the higher education sector has been designed to reduce the industrial power of academic workers. In the 1990s, government funding for universities was tied to the imposition of a host of repressive working conditions and the use of individual work agreements (rather than enterprise agreements negotiated by unions) on academic workers. The two unions most directly targeted by the government in this period were the Maritime Union of Australia (a famously militant union) and the National Tertiary Education Union (NTEU). Since then government funds have repeatedly been tied to the imposition of conditions, which dramatically affect the working conditions of academic workers and the education of tertiary students (Macintyre, 2007, p. 41).

Still other authors argue that changes designed to limit democratic and participatory decision making and reduce academic autonomy have enabled the intensification of academic work as one way of achieving that outcome, rather than increased workload being an incidental side effect (Parker & Jary, 1995, p. 324). Finally, harnessing university "reform" to the neoliberal rhetoric of efficiency and productivity while simultaneously ridiculing academic work and academic workers has been a very effective strategy used by both conservative and labor governments (Macintyre, 2007, p. 43; Parker & Jary, 1995, p. 323).

Whatever the direct cause, a growing body of research supports the conclusion that both academics and universities as focused not on resistance, but on survival. Suzanne Ryan (2012, p. 4), for example, evoked imagery from zombie films while Bronwyn Davies and Eva Bendix Petersen's (2005) qualitative research described "disillusioned and distressed individuals" rather than "collective academic critique and resistance" (p. 80). Other commentators on the failure of academic workers to organize and the failure of more securely employed academics to support their more precariously employed colleagues have been labeled as "gutless" and "hypocritical" (Schmidt, 2013).

This picture is concerning for those who would resist neoliberalism in higher education, both in the sense that they suggest that despair rather than resistance currently prevails and because they call into question any ground from which resistance might emerge. Fear results in self-policing and a discipline which university management could not hope to force academics to embody (Foucault, 1995). Moreover, the fear described by academics (Macintyre, 2007) seems out of proportion to known instances of institutional repression. That is not to suggest that there has not been retaliation, suppression, and "unprecedented surveillance" (Macintyre, 2007, p. 49; Martin, Baker, Manwell, & Pugh, 1986; Nocella II, Best, & McLaren, 2010). Further, controversy over research funds being dispensed and withheld on political grounds has been documented in the past (Macintyre, 2007, p. 50) and continues in the present with the controversy of the Australian government's decision to fund a Lomborg Consensus Centre (Taylor, 2015). However, universities remain a relatively favorable and privileged space for projects of resistance to occur.

In Australian universities, there is limited evidence to support the claim that academics are routinely repressed on political grounds. One study included a list of documented instances of intellectual suppression in Australia which is striking for the small number of documented cases with serious repercussions documented over a lengthy period including much of the cold war (Martin, Baker, Manwell, & Pugh, 1986, pp. 164–169). In some fields (e.g., research into abortion), numerous instances of repression have been documented (Baird, 2013), while in others, there is clear evidence of censorship and defunding on political grounds (Macintyre, 2007, pp. 50–51). A recent collection focusing on dissent during the years of John Howard's term as conservative Prime Minster (1996–2007) demonstrates all too clearly that government policy, funding strategies, and lack of transparency in relation to decision-making processes about grant funding and the role of government interference in them can induce fear and change the behavior of academics more effectively than direct repression ever could, and with more far reaching effects (Hamilton & Maddison, 2007). Hamilton and Maddison discussed a range of examples (some well publicized) in which the outcomes of scholarly peer review processes for awarding grants were overturned on the apparent whim of a government minister, as well as others in which oversight (and power of veto) over such processes was given to bodies peopled with commentators whose views were shared by the government, with no obvious expertise or qualifications for their new roles. As one contributor to the collection noted: "The surrender of academic freedom is far more insidious than the attack upon it" (Macintyre, 2007, p. 48). Of course, studies which focus only documented cases will understate the extent of repression, and the cases we refer to have been rightly condemned.

We question whether instances of individual and direct repression are the main source of academic inaction, particularly in relation to neoliberal policies within universities. The examples of suppression of research we have referred to create a long, cold shadow in which many academics conceive of speaking out as requiring courage they do not possess (Macintyre, 2007, p. 48). We question why they do not, instead, incite academics to a courageous and principled defense of academic freedom, and why the rhetoric of academic freedom is instead being wielded by conservatives. In one vivid recent example, it has been argued that opposition to climate change denial is an impost on academic freedom (rather than evidence of evidence-based academic rigor) (Taylor, 2015).

The forms of repression we identify here are not those identified in sociological studies of academics, which seek to understand low levels of academic involvement in resistance to neoliberalism, which refer instead to fear of disapproval and trivialization (Davies & Bendix-Petersen, 2005). These microaggressive forms of repression could be resisted through building up support networks and other strategies (Flood, Marin, & Dreher, 2013). This, in turn, however, would require academics to take (some of) what we do seriously as activism and many academics have not taken this step. As Maisto (2013) has argued, for many academics, organizing instils a fear of being labeled as "the kind of person" who organizes or joins a union.

Academic repression should not be overstated or misrepresented. Far from describing existing realities, writings that employ military imagery, i.e., "scholars under siege" or the "war against academics" may unintentionally perpetuate a fear that immobilizes academics from taking action. Repression may grow in response to academic activism, but it may not succeed and for the present there is no strong reason for pessimism.

RETHINKING RESISTANCE

The limited literature on academic resistance suggests a dramatic disconnect between much radical writing on the future of higher education and the actual practices of most academics. While some authors are proposing revolutionary projects for higher education, the existing research on what academics do shows that despair, fear, and misery predominate and that most academics are taking no action against the practices that represent incursions of neoliberalism in our workplaces.

The actions that are reported by academics tend to be individual and passive rather than coordinated acts with a durable public presence. Anderson (2008), for example, sought to expand our understanding of resistance to include routine and informal actions—what Scott (1985) has called "everyday forms of resistance" (p. xvi). Examples recorded by Anderson (2008) included "forgetting" or not completing certain tasks (p. 260). More overt forms of resistance include teaching students about changes to higher education. Anderson (2008) argued that these forms of resistance are widespread and effective in enabling academics to "resist many of the microphysics of power associated with managerialism in Australian universities" (p. 254). Most academics are, after all, far less interested in radically changing the larger structures of higher education in their given location than in what Hobsbawm (1973) called "working the system [...] to their minimum disadvantage" (p. 7).

It is our observation as activists that holding out visions of social change that are immense, and constantly arguing that anything falling short of this is insufficiently radical or a form of collaboration is a barrier to recruiting people to participate in any progressive project. We are not rejecting the wider radical project. However, as with other aspects of our activism, we are interested in practices and goals that have some correspondence with the lived experience of those we would call upon to resist. Only by starting from this point, we contend, can we hope to build the skills and preparedness required to take larger actions. Moreover, we are interested in how relationships that might ground wider collective action begin to build up. We are curious about what we and others might do in the interim period between the current state of affairs and large-scale action.

One of us has spent a lot of time working toward a rape-free world—but this project has taken many forms none of which have achieved that wider goal. Nor is it ever likely such a goal that would be achieved in the short term, by one person, one protest, or even one organization. However, the fact that these actions do not reach their ultimate goal does not mean that they are failures. The same point can be made about ending capitalism or halting climate change. Rather, they represent incursions which are part of addressing the problem or reconceptualize it as capable of being addressed. They offer openings in which conversations can be started and cultures can begin to change. They generate opportunities to build alliances and relationships, learn skills, and pass them on. They create places to understand what might be necessary for long-term change and work toward it and to build organizations that might be prepared to participate in reaching larger goals. Sometimes the demise of an organization, a strategy, or an experiment in strategy is necessary for a better alternative to come into view.

Our interest in theorizing and organizing from lived experience grounded our decision to initiate a meeting between academics working at universities in South Australia who were interested in responding to neoliberalism in our workplaces. Participants were from a range of disciplines and combination of union and nonunion members. In the next section, we describe our experiences as well as some of the difficulties we encountered in maintaining an activist project with our coworkers.

CASE STUDY: ACADEMIC ACTIVISTS, ADELAIDE

Between 2013 and 2014 a group of eight to twelve academics came together on a fortnightly basis to discuss challenges in higher education and how we might take action to respond to them. Between us, the group had experience in each of our state's three universities and some further afield, and worked in a range of disciplines including law, criminology, media studies, and social policy.

We sought a model of organizing that could contradict people's felt sense of being time-poor and isolated by organizing meetings over dinner that we hoped would feel well connected and warm, as well as offering an environment in which people could get to know one another better and speak about issues of mutual concern. We organized primarily through word of mouth. In recruiting participants, we put effort into asking people one to one whether they would be interested not just in talking about neoliberalism, but in taking action against it together. We also asked whether they would be able to attend a gathering to speak further about what we might do. Word began to spread through our coworkers and we welcomed everyone who expressed interest. We met at someone's home, with a view to making these gatherings feel less like "work." The location was accessible by public transport and was between the campuses of all three universities. We put effort into finding times that would work for the maximum number of people, including the parents among us. We cultivated warm introductions and relationship building at gatherings. We stayed in touch and organized meeting times through an email group between gatherings and shared readings chosen by members electronically.

The diversity of our group meant that we were able to compare and contrast experiences cross-institutionally and between disciplines. For example, it was obvious that the impacts of neoliberal reform were being felt with much greater intensity in the arts faculty than in law. This provided a prompt for thinking beyond the perspective of one's own school and how solidarity actions might occur between faculties.

However, the breadth of participation also gave rise to unique challenges. It meant that we did not have a common basis of experience or even necessarily a shared language for articulating problems in higher education. Some members had previously participated in reading groups together where we discussed Marx (1992), Kropotkin (1974), Hardt and Negri (2011), and Klein (2015). Those participants were comfortable describing their experience using the language of "neoliberalism." However, for others in the group, such terms were alien and incomprehensible. Moreover, while some participants had lifelong associations with unions or social movements, others had no experience with collective organizing.

To respond to these challenges we decided that between meetings we would read literature on the corporatization of higher education. Readings were suggested by various participants and included Lang (2013), Williams (2013), and Mackenzie (2014). We also read blogs such as Bad Cover Version (http://badcoverversion.wordpress.com/) in which an adjunct professor at two U.S. universities applies feminist insight and a critique of privilege to the predicament of casual staff and Changing Universities (http://changinguniversities.blogspot.com.au) for news on higher education in the United States.

The readings were discussed near the start of each meeting and we also set aside time for people to describe how their experience corresponded or differed from the authors' accounts. While there were a wide variety of reactions to the texts, we were struck by how frequently participants used these discussions as an opportunity to debrief and "get things off their chest." It was clear that for many participants this was the first time they had a public space to talk about reforms in their area and concerns they had for themselves, their students, and administrative staff. This in itself is suggestive of the intensification of academic work, which means that few academics now take meal breaks away from their desks (and many now have classes scheduled when once there would have been an institutionwide free hour in the middle of the day). Opportunities for what would once have been understood as ordinary collegial conversation—let alone opportunities to meet with any confidence that large numbers of staff would be able to attend should they choose—have all but evaporated.

It was also common for participants to preface their comments with the phrase "I really shouldn't complain" or "we are so lucky compared to other workers." These statements of privilege, while undeniably true, appeared to be part of a narrative that academics employ to reconcile themselves to undesirable reform. This was true at a general level but we have also noted it between schools, i.e., "I know our casual teaching budget has been slashed but you should see what they have done to other schools." Under neoliberalism, we are all too conscious that things could be so much worse—because as relatively privileged workers, they are already worse for many people in the workforce, and we all know of places where we think things are worse in other universities now.

Group meetings ended without ceremony in early 2014. The main reasons for this were consistent with the experience of some activist groups in the community. They included the difficulty participants had in carving out time for meetings; lack of consistency between participants making it difficult to have progressive conversations from one meeting to the next; and difficulties in spreading responsibility and leadership roles within the group. These challenges arose in the context of a relatively modest project, which revealed that how lacking many of the fundamentals for more radical organizing are in our universities. If we could not sustain a fortnightly meeting, what hope did we have of stopping neoliberal reform, overthrowing managerialism, or supporting precarious workers?

Rather than deter us from these goals, our experience provided several valuable lessons:

1. Organize in a way that responds to the skills, interests, and experience of the community you are working with. This insight introduces an important contingency into organizing and eschews vanguard notions of handing down a blue print for others to follow. This sentiment is captured eloquently by educators like Paulo Freire (1978) in the context of his adult literacy program in the West African nation of Guinea-Bissau: "Authentic help means that all who are involved help each other mutually growing together in a common effort to understand the reality which they seek to transform" (p. 4). A similar sentiment is expressed by labor-lawyer Lynd (2012, p. 4) in his description of accompaniment. For Lynd, accompaniment is a nonhierarchical method of organizing that challenges individualization and isolation by conceiving of movement participants as experts, exploring a path forward together.

2. When organizing meetings such as ours, avoid imposing a description of the problem or a course of action. Such ideas can be contributed but the analysis must emerge from the group and take a form that matches their own lived experience. Moreover, decisions about action must be owned by those who will participate. That might mean that rather than initiating a mass strike, the group begins with education, skills training, despair and empowerment work, or simply airing grievances. We cannot expect our colleagues to go from zero to a hundred overnight, and if we are serious about building a movement for change, we may need to start with tangible basics like getting five people into a room.

3. Don't expect immediate results. For example, despite a cessation of group meetings our short-lived project resulted in several tangible outcomes. Most obviously, our readings gave participants a theoretical framework through which they could understand their own experiences and place them in a wider context. Concepts and language from our discussions made their way

into conversations and meetings in our workplaces, where some of us began to speak openly about neoliberalism and corporatization or to articulate higher education as a public good and not a source of private profit making, for example. Discussions also provided participants with a space to share their concerns and, despite the various ways we articulated the problem, understand that they were not alone in how they were feeling and open the potential to politicize our experiences for those of us who had not already taken this position. While perhaps modest, projects that combat the fear and isolation, which many academics describe in the face of neoliberalism, are necessary precursors to any other radical project. In our view, empowerment, collective organization, and politicization are radical undertakings in their own right.

As a result of the meetings, some participants joined or became more engaged with the work of the NTEU, a labor union consisting of sessional, contract, and tenured academics and professional/administrative staff. Approximately one third of university staff in Australia are members of the union (over 28,000 members in total). The NTEU is organizing against fee deregulation, corporatization, the casualization of the university sector, and increased fees for students. Under the conservative Howard government (1996–2007), the NTEU was the target of union-breaking legislation and action alongside the far more militant Maritime Union of Australia.

In another instance, several participants organized a series of school meetings to discuss the enterprise bargaining negotiations that were taking place between the union and university management. This resulted in a widely signed statement that put pressure on the university and the position it was taking with respect to postgraduate workers. Participants also volunteered to accompany professional staff members in meetings with university management so that they could give expression to their grievances in a supportive space. Several group members found ways to incorporate discussions of the corporatization of higher education into their teaching, extending a framework and language into parts of the student body with less social power.

Members involved in a results ban were able to strategize about how to get maximum participation in the ban, mutual support among participants, and minimize opposition. They cowrote an explanation of their actions for dissemination to other staff. Some members chose to organize small-scale events in their workplaces and initiate involvement from other staff—for example, by inviting other staff to meet and write letters as part of a wider union campaign about university funding and policy. Members at one institution were part of instigating industrial action, and members of our group from another discipline organized to support them. The authors wrote a paper which inspired staff at two other institutions, we know of, to take action and begin to organize in their workplaces. Some of us spread information about the National Alliance for Public Universities Charter (http://napuaustralia.org/) in an effort to collectively organize to articulate higher education as a public good and oppose the further corporatization of Australian higher education and policies designed to implement a system closer to that of the United States, including charging higher fees, providing less public support for students, the deregulation of university fees, and further reductions in public funding and support for Australian universities.

Through discussion of the situation facing sessional staff (some of us were only recently contingent staff ourselves), some members became more conscious of the situation facing sessional academics and more conscious of the actions they could take to support sessional staff. At least one of us spent time investigating the potential for the union to support sessional teachers at their own institution and supporting sessional staff to take action on their grievances, as well as inquiring about contingent staff entitlements and insisting on their being complied with. Several of us felt more courageous or perhaps more empowered to share information about union membership and campaigns with our colleagues and did so. While ultimately our work had a modest life, it nevertheless achieved influence that extended beyond the meetings we organized and that evidently continues to have an impact on some people who came to meetings in their daily lives and work.

CONCLUSIONS

The success of future resistance projects inside the University will depend on our ability to acknowledge and take seriously feelings of isolation and disempowerment that are reported by university staff and students. These feelings may be exacerbated by a narrative that exaggerates the risks of resistance or which demands goals which are beyond the grasp of participants. As our experience shows, feelings of disempowerment can be mitigated by strategies that bring people together to share experiences, develop common understandings, and work on common projects. Projects of resistance must also take account the challenges that organizing presents and learn from the experience of peers around the world.

Thankfully, this learning is made easier by the global network of academics, students, and staff around the world who are sharing their experiences and resources. As well as the groups already mentioned in this chapter, there is the Undercommoning project which is an Anglophone North American successor to Edu-Factory. The Undercommoning project takes its name from an expression articulated by Harney and Moten (2013, p. 26) and refers to the underground multitude within the university which refuses to passively accept the further corporatization of higher education. The project also seeks to create a space for critical discussions called "encounters" and offers a "Toykit" with resources and ideas for future projects. Networks and resources like these help to reduce feelings of isolation and the immobilization that can occur from thinking that resources need to be invented from scratch.

The challenges we face inside the university can be difficult to think about and we need resources that show us how to strengthen our capacity to face these challenges so that we can respond with resilience and creativity. Williams (1989) puts it well: "To be truly radical is to make hope possible rather than despair convincing" (p. 118). That is a political challenge of the highest order and one that confronts us today.

REFERENCES

Anderson, G. (2008). Mapping academic resistance in the managerial university. *Organization, 15,* 251–270.

Baird, B. (2013). Abortion politics during the Howard years: Beyond liberalisation. *Australian History Studies, 44*(2), 245–261.

Bradley, D., Noonan, P., Nugent, H., & Scales, B. (2008). Review of Australian higher education: Final report. Canberra, AU: Department of Education, Employment and Workplace Relations.

Coates, H., Dobson, I., Goedegebuure, L., & Meek, L. (2010). Across the great divide: What do Australian academics think of university leadership? Advice from the CAP Survey. *Journal of Higher Education Policy and Management, 32*(4), 379–387.

Davies, B., & Bansel, P. (2005). The time of their lives? Academic workers in neoliberal times. *Health Sociology Review, 14,* 47–58.

Davies, B., & Petersen, E. B. (2005). Neo-liberal discourse in the academy: The forestalling of (collective) resistance. *LATISS-Learning and Teaching in the Social Sciences, 2*(2), 77–98.

Foucault, M. (1995). *Discipline & punish: The birth of the prison.* New York: Vintage Books.

Flood, M., Martin, B., & Dreher, T. (2013). Combining academia and activism: Common obstacles and useful tools. *Australian Universities Review, 55*(1), 17–26.

Gill, R. (2009). Breaking the silence: The hidden injuries of neo-liberal academia. In R. Flood & R. Gill (Eds.), *Secrecy and silence in the research process: Feminist reflections.* London: Routledge.

Hamilton, C., & Maddison, S. (Eds.). (2007). *Silencing dissent: How the Australian government is controlling public opinion and stifling debate.* Sydney, AU: Allen and Unwin.

Hardt, M., & Negri, N. (2011). *Commonwealth.* Cambridge, MA: Belknap Press.

Harney, S., Moten, F. (2013). *The undercommons: Fugitive planning & black study.* Oakland, CA: AK Press.

Hobsbawm, E. (1973). Peasants and politics. *Journal of Peasant Studies, 1*(1), 3.

Junor, A. (2004). Casual university work: Choice, risk, inequity and the case for regulation. *The Economic and Labour Relations Review, 14*(2), 276.

Klein, N. (2015). *This changes everything: Capitalism vs. the climate.* New York: Simon & Schuster.

Kropotkin, P. (1974). *Fields, factories and workshops tomorrow.* London: Freedom Press.

Lang, J. (2013). The Lorax's dilemma. *The Chronicle of Higher Education*, 25 November. Retrieved from http://chronicle.com/article/The-Loraxs-Dilemma/143243/

Lynd, S. (2012). *Accompanying: Pathways to social change*. Oakland, CA: PM Press.

Macintyre, S. (2007). Universities. In C. Hamilton & S. Maddison (eds.), *Silencing dissent: How the Australian government is controlling public opinion and stifling debate*. Sydney, AU: Allen & Unwin.

Mackenzie, M. (2014). The ethics of casual teaching contracts: How we are all implicated in selling out academia and exploiting our students, *Duck of Minerva*, 13 January. Retrieved from http://duckofminerva.com/2014/01/the-ethics-of-casual-teaching-contracts-how-we-are-all-impli cated-in-selling-out-academia-and-exploiting-our-students.html

Maisto, M. (2013). Adjuncts, class and fear. *Working Class Perspectives*, September 23, 2013. Retrieved from https://workingclassstudies.wordpress.com/tag/maria-maisto/

Martin, B., Baker, C. M. A., Manwell, C., & Pugh, C. (eds.). (1986). *Intellectual suppression: Australian case histories, analysis and responses*. Sydney: Angus and Robertson Publishers.

Marx, K. (1992). *Capital: Volume 1: A critique of political economy*. London: Penguin Classics.

May, R., Strachan, G., Broadbent, K., & Peetz, D. (2011, 4–7 July 2011). *The casual approach to university teaching; time for a re-think?* Paper presented at the Research and Development in Higher Education: Reshaping Higher Education: HERDSA Annual International Conference, Gold Coast, Australia.

Nocella II, A. J., Best, S., & McLaren, P. (2010). *Academic repression: Reflections from the academic industrial complex*. Oakland, CA: AK Press.

Parker, M., & Jary, D. (1995). The McUniversity: Organization, management and academic subjectivity. *Organization, 2*(2), 319–338.

Ryan, S., Guthrie, J., & Neumann, R. (2008). Australian higher education transformed: From central coordination to control. In C. Mazza, P. Quattrone, & A. Riccaboni (eds.), *European universities in transition: issues, models and cases* (pp. 171–187). Cheltenham: Edward Elgar Publishing.

Ryan, S. (2012). Academic zombies: A failure of resistance or a means of survival? *Australian Universities' Review, 54*(2), 3–11.

Schmidt, P. (November 18, 2013). Advocates for adjunct instructors think broadly in search for allies. *Chronicle of Higher Education*. Retrieved from http://chronicle.com/article/Advocates-for-Adjunct/143139/

Scott, J. (1985). *Weapons of the weak: Everyday forms of peasant resistance*. New Haven, CT: Yale University Press.

Taylor, L. (June 25, 2015). Bjorn Lomborg University funding tied to 'rational conversation' lectures. *Guardian Australia*.

Tertiary Education Quality and Standards Agency (TEQSA). (2014). Statistics report on TEQSA registered higher education providers. Retrieved from http://www.teqsa.gov.au/news-publica tions/statistics-report-teqsa-registered-higher-education-providers

Thornton, M. (2012). *Privatising the public university: The case of law*. Oxford: Routledge.

Trowler, P. (1998). *Academics responding to change—New higher education frameworks and academic cultures*. Berkshire: Open University Press.

Williams, J. (2013). The great stratification. *The Chronicles of Higher Education*, 2 December. Retrieved from http://chronicle.com/article/The-Great-Stratification/143285

Williams, R. (1989). *Resources of hope: Culture, democracy, socialism*. New York: Verso.

CHAPTER THREE

Parasites, Sycophants, and Rebels: Resisting Threats to Faculty Governance

MARK SEIS

INTRODUCTION

The greatest academic repressive threat to higher education is the normalization of the ideology of neoliberalism. Neoliberalism is a set of economic policies that privilege private ownership over the public good by emphasizing reductions in public funding for services like education and health care, the deregulation of private enterprise, and the privatization of public space. Neoliberalism's emphasis on privatization of public spaces and public wealth has led to a forty-year decline in funding for higher education and a litany of repressive measures aimed at turning public colleges and universities into for profit corporations (Badger, 2015; Cox, 2013; Giroux, 2014; Marmol, 2015; Newfield, 2008; Nocella II, Best, & McLaren, 2010; Ward, 2012). Less funding has forced most public-supported colleges and universities down the road to privatization, meaning rising tuition rates for students, fewer tenure-track faculty, and more streamlined and standardized curricula: "More incredible—and outrageous—the American Council on Education [...] predicts that if current trends hold, by 2059 state funding for colleges and universities will be reduced to zero" (Badger, 2015).

An even more disturbing trend in the realm of academic repression is that with less government funding more federal and state legislative mandates have come, requiring publicly supported higher education to fulfill neoliberal ideological requirements focused on career-based education, "seeing students as consumers, and viewing the university brand through the prism of narrow market calculation"

(Cox, 2013, p. 4). Certainly skills that will be useful in a career are important, but traditionally publicly supported liberal arts education has also included learning how to learn and how to become a morally autonomous agent (Deresiewicz, 2015). A career-based neoliberal education agenda translates as "we need more welders and less [*sic*] philosophers" as stated by Marco Rubio in a recent Republican presidential debate. This is not meant to slight welders because we need both welders and philosophers, welders who can philosophize and philosophers who can weld.

Equating state funding with fulfillment of neoliberal ideological objectives has led to the creation of a new administrative class focused on refashioning public colleges and universities to resemble the operations of for-profit corporations. This new administrative class comprised of bureaucrats and technocrats siphon off huge amounts of income from public institutions to turn them into essentially private corporate institutions with neoliberal ideological structures and agendas (Ginsberg, 2011). Members of this parasitic administrative class (Parenti qtd. in Marmol, 2015) are the instruments by which neoliberal ideological objectives are implemented, undermining the meaning of higher education in general and liberal arts in particular. These objectives can be characterized by a bureaucratic obsession with centralized power, mechanization, standardization, and endless assessment and surveillance, using market-based outcome measures. Some of the consequences of the neoliberal ideological agenda have been the demise of faculty governance, the deletion of multicultural curricula, and the ranking of academic disciplines and faculty based on their utility to the market place. Other important consequences and fallout from the neoliberal agenda are declining solidarity among faculty, the loss of tenured faculty, and skyrocketing tuition costs for students, up to 300 percent of the consumer price index from 1990 (Cox, 2013).

This chapter examines the context, process, and players of a major incident of academic repression, and the resistance to it, that took place at Fort Lewis College (FLC) in Durango, Colorado. This incident involves the usurpation of faculty governance processes by overzealous, ambitious administrators, eager to implement a neoliberal agenda, and undermine traditionally valued democratic processes. This chapter has been divided into four sections to analyze the context and players that led to this incident of academic repression. In the first section, a detailed account of the incident of academic repression is provided. This section provides the context and players subsequently analyzed in the following three sections. In the second section, the parasitic culture of college administrators is explored as it relates to the neoliberal educational agenda. The third section focuses on sycophants and the declining solidarity of faculty as neoliberal policies divide and infantilize faculty through the use of market-based evaluative measures. In the last section, the academic rebel is explored as it relates to fighting this incident of academic repression.

CASE STUDY: SHARED GOVERNANCE DENIED

On February 7, 2014, the FLC Board of Trustees (BOT) unanimously voted to change FLC curriculum from a three- and four-credit mix to an all three-credit model against the apparent will of a majority of faculty and students at the institution. This is the first time in the history of FLC that the BOT, advised by the FLC administration, has overruled the will of the faculty on matters pertaining to curriculum, violating the American Association of University Professors (AAUP)'s principles of shared governance. This vote was based on a manufactured crisis generated by the provost and president of the college.

The FLC administration, claiming to adhere to AAUP principles of shared governance, misled the BOT, faculty, and students on several counts. First, the administration convinced the BOT that the three- and four-credit mixed curriculum was such a contentious issue among the faculty that "exceptional circumstances" (the only situation deemed by AAUP to constitute a need for administrative overreach) required the administration to override faculty governance by recommending to the BOT that FLC move to a three-credit model. However, the three- and four-credit issues had already been studied, debated, and voted upon by the faculty. The faculty senate convened a task force to study the issue in April 2013. The task force surveyed all departments and received eighteen out of twenty-two responses and agreed, based on the responses, that the best way to move forward was to maintain the three-and four-credit mix.

The three- and four-credit issue has long been conflated by the administration with workload inequity issues in some of the Science, Technology, Engineering and Mathematics (STEM) disciplines because of the way lab hours/credits have been counted toward faculty workload. The task force report called for addressing workload inequities for the sciences by suggesting a two-course two-lab workload, reducing the workload for faculty in the sciences. The task force also recommended solutions for dealing with scheduling both three- and four-credit courses in a more uniform way to avoid overlap, another perceived problem with the mix of credits. The report was approved by all task force members and passed the faculty senate by 12 to 3. In a survey conducted of voting faculty members, fify-six percent overall favored keeping the mix, and among faculty who would be directly affected by the change, ninety percent favored keeping the mix. In a poll conducted by students, eighty-four percent of students surveyed believed that an all three-credit curriculum change would have negative consequences for their education.

In the face of a clear faculty and student majority against the three-credit model, the administration next put forward, what they perceived to be, four irrefutable justifications for moving the college to a three-credit model: (1) Higher Learning Commission (HLC) accreditation; (2) transferability of courses; (3) scheduling; and (4) workload inequality. In a document submitted to the

BOT by the FLC AAUP chapter each of these administrative justifications were addressed separately.

The provost repeatedly insisted that the three- and four-credit mix was put into place without approval from HLC. However, the mix had been in place for over two decades in some disciplines, without ever having raised any red flags on previous accreditation visits. The provost also claimed that a massive shift to an all three-credit model would not require approval of HLC. Both of these claims were spurious and disingenuous. Neither claim was supported by previous HLC reviews, by substantive change policies, by requirements available from the HLC's website, nor by email communications directly from the HLC. The FLC president and provost clearly misled the BOT and faculty by suggesting that moving to a three-credit model was being driven by the need to avoid added review and scrutiny by the HLC. This was obviously not true.

The next justification offered by the FLC administration was the argument that transferability required by statute that FLC must move to a three-credit model. The Colorado statutes cited by the FLC administration 23-1-108 (7), 23-1-125(1–5) as well as Colorado Commission on Higher Education (CCHE) Policy I, L do not in any way suggest that Colorado public institutions of higher learning should adopt a three-credit model. These statutes refer to the ability of transfer students to transfer unimpeded between Colorado public institutions of higher learning to ensure that students can satisfy general education requirements within sixty credits on their way to earning a bachelor's degree within the 120-credit limit. Because other Colorado colleges have some three and four-credit mix, seamless transferability does pose some challenges for students transferring. However, students transferring to FLC get full credit for every course they take elsewhere. In short, all students transferring to FLC who have completed general education courses at other institutions are given full credit for having completed those requirements. It is clear that the FLC administration was being disingenuous regarding the interpretation of the law to both the BOT and the faculty.

There is no doubt that there were some scheduling conflicts with a three- and four-credit mix as demonstrated and argued by the FLC administration. In some cases, scheduling conflicts caused students to have to enroll in slightly overlapping classes. In response, faculty proposed five different models for resolving most of these scheduling problems while maintaining a three and four-credit mix of courses. These scheduling alterations involved starting courses earlier and ending them later. Faculty members voiced no objections to adjusting their schedules to accommodate student needs. While scheduling presented challenges, it did not constitute, as the FLC administration suggested to the BOT, an "exceptional circumstance," justifying the usurpation of faculty governance and the dismantling of an entire curriculum.

the career administrators are concerned with expanding their own administrative domains, using bureaucratic structure to implement political ideology embedded in externally mandated performance criteria. Parasitic administrators are handsomely paid tools, turning public colleges and universities into well-disciplined bureaucracies. They are charged with the task of mechanizing the role of faculty so they appear more accountable using market-based outcome measures. As such, faculty attend workshops on how to construct a twenty-page syllabus (Schuman, 2014), how to develop measurable goals and course objectives, and how to create rubrics designed to assess learning in the most mechanical and superficial of ways possible. Everything is standardized: courses, content, evaluations, and the criteria used for hiring, firing, and promoting. All of this energy has been lavished on a process designed to give the illusion that it is not arbitrary or ideological—that it is merit based.

Neoliberal administrative emphasis on standardization and mechanized routines consolidates power upward in the hierarchy of the bureaucracy, undermining democratic processes of faculty control. Such a model treats all academic disciplines as being the same with respect to pedagogical practices, subject matter and evaluative processes. The rote memorization that defines much of the learning done in the sciences is different from the evaluation of moral and ethical implications of political, economic, and social systems that define learning in the humanities and social sciences. The three- and four-credit mix that FLC faculty had developed over several decades was a product of accommodating different pedagogical and learning practices unique to several disciplines. Because right and wrong answers are not readily available in many of the humanities and social science disciplines, many courses required extra time for writing, reflection, and discussion.

The three- and four-credit mix issue had been contentious at FLC on and off for many years. The issue had been brought up by previous administrations and faculty, mostly from STEM disciplines, but the issue had always been resolved through evaluative and governance processes supporting the continuation of the mix. These governance processes, which worked for decades, were sacrificed by the FLC administration who had absolutely no personal experience or knowledge of the process by which the three- and four-credit mix came into being. The administration's arguments, which were addressed by the local AAUP chapter, all had workable solutions. Why was the administration in conjunction with a minority of faculty so eager to obliterate the democratic faculty governance process?

Logic, reason, and democratic processes did not seem to satiate the overriding desire for the administration to exercise absolute power. The administration's decision to usurp faculty governance has come at a great cost to the institution with respect to faculty solidarity. The faculty is greatly divided on almost all major issues of significance with respect to the future of the college as a liberal arts institution. Morale is horribly low at least among the humanities and social sciences.

Yet another justification for moving to an all three-credit model by the FLC administration was the issue of workload inequities for faculty in the sciences. The FLC administration misled the BOT and attempted to divide the faculty by emphasizing this issue as a major point of contention among disciplines. However, faculty members across the entire campus agreed that the sciences had a greater burden when teaching three courses and two labs per semester. There was no doubt that three courses plus two labs required more preparation than three courses alone. Both the faculty-senate-created task force on the three- and four-credit mix and FLC's chapter of the AAUP supported a change to a two-course/two-lab model for faculty in the sciences. This accommodation to deal with workload issues for the sciences was a nonissue among the faculty, yet the FLC administration repeatedly misled the BOT and the faculty by conflating workload issues in some disciplines with the completely separate issue of changing the entire curriculum to a three-credit model. Forcing every discipline to operate under a three-credit model would not change the workload issue in the sciences.

It is important to emphasize that this entire process was in no way presented as a fiscally motivated decision. In fact, it will cost the college more money to make this massive transition to a three-credit model than it would to maintain the current mix of credits. A fact admitted by the administration. If the decision was not about money, then it must have been about something else.

ADMINISTRATIVE PARASITES

Today's college administrators are not the administrators of the past. Prior to the introduction of the neoliberal agenda to higher education, many college administrators came from the ranks of the faculty. Many academics called to administrative duty would serve a term of a few years and then return to their appropriate departments to serve out their careers teaching and conducting research (Ginsburg, 2011; Miller, 2012). In-house administrators had the advantage of understanding their institution's historical context. They also had a personal investment in the reputation of their institution and a sense of accountability to those they served in their capacity as administrators. Administrators operating in the preneoliberal academic institution advocated on behalf of their institutions, educating legislatures, and the public about the important roles public universities serve, their accessibility and affordability, curricula focused on intellectual content and personal identity, and a strong emphasis on sociocultural inclusion (Ginsberg, 2011; Newfield, 2016).

The new class of neoliberal parasitic administrators are not concerned with any of these ideals. Neoliberalism has changed the nature of administration. College administrations are now comprised of ambitious careerists, many hiring personal agents to scout future lucrative positions for them to pursue. Most of

But, as it turns out, this divisiveness among faculty makes the job of administering the ideological agenda of neoliberalism that much easier. Neoliberalism by nature hates unified work forces and more importantly it hates solidarity among working people—witness the union busting of Reagan and Thatcher. A divided workforce is a great context in which to further alienate individuals through the depersonalization and dehumanization found in endless bureaucratization.

One of the key advantages created by the divide-and-rule strategies of neoliberal parasitic administrators is the culture of distrust. With a divided faculty comes the childish fear and suspicions that one's colleagues do not work hard enough. Yes, there are lazy faculty, and there are lazy administrators. Neoliberalism's remedy to this problem is to create a labyrinth of surveillance measures grounded in the psychology of insecurity. In academia, we learn to live with the constant anxiety that we are never good enough. Do you use enough technology when you teach? Is your research popular and voluminous despite the fact that you teach three or four different courses per semester? Did you provide enough institutional service despite the fact that most of it is disregarded by the administration, resulting in futile, thankless wastes of time? In short, we are tired and stressed, but we are never good enough. There is nothing more politically impotent than an institution filled with anxiety-ridden academics with a perpetual sense of insecurity, forced by the neoliberal structure to act like self-promoting narcissists, attempting the Sisyphean task of appearing meaningful.

Such compromised academic environments are the fertile grounds of neoliberal parasitic administrative tyranny. Administrators know that it is difficult to exercise authoritarian rule when a class of unified people with a sense of security and dignity opposes nondemocratic rule. Bureaucracy is a great place to disguise an ideological agenda—witness the use of bureaucracy by the Nazis to execute the Holocaust (Rubenstein, 2014). Bureaucratic structures are designed to create the illusion of meritocracy and are the modern institutional tool of choice for running the corporation (not a democratic institution) and now, more so than ever, the college or university. The neoliberal administrative agenda is to use bureaucratic hierarchy and standardization to obviate the need for creative faculty engagement in pedagogy, making all academic positions repetitive and replaceable in the industrial "diploma mill" we now call higher education.

In an analogous way, the neoliberal administrator performs a similar function to that of the parasite, syphoning off valuable resources of publically supported colleges and universities to pay their over inflated salaries and to instill hegemonic forms of ideological domination aimed ultimately at the demise of public liberal arts education. Like so many parasites, these are likely to kill their host. A recent CBSNews.com article reports that skyrocketing compensation packages for upper-level college administrators at public-supported institutions of higher learning have meant that "students go deeper into debt […] and the universities rely more on low-paid faculty labor by hiring more adjuncts and fewer full-time professors" (Picchi, 2014, para. 3). Over the last forty years nationally, numbers of "administrators have risen by 85 percent and the number of staffers required to help the administrators has jumped by a whopping 240 percent" (Miller, 2012, para. 16). Nonacademic staffs are now making policy decisions about how faculty should do their jobs with respect to evaluation and assessment. Fulfilling the neoliberal ideological agenda requires a large army of administrative minions to promote and execute the marketization and bureaucratization of colleges and universities.

In October 2014, a newly elected faculty representative to the BOT at FLC noted that there were 157 tenure-track faculties in 2002, but that number had declined to a low of 122 by 2014 with little overall change in student enrollment. His report went on to explain that "if you were to meet a college employee on campus in 1970, the odds were overwhelming that you would have met a teacher (about 77%)" and if you were to meet a college employee in 2014 you would have about a 30% chance of meeting a teacher (McBrayer, October 2014). A subsequent December 2014 Board Report demonstrated that from 2008–09 to 2014–15 there has been a thirty-six percent increase in administrative staff making over $75,000, a 4.1 percent increase in staff making under $75,000, and a 6.8 percent decrease in teachers (McBrayer, December 2014). Neoliberalism is everywhere and the losers are all working- and middle-class persons who could benefit from public-supported education (Newfield, 2008).

Why was the FLC administration so eager to destroy faculty governance processes? The short answer is because they could. The FLC administration has proven that they can do whatever they want with impunity. Neoliberal administrators do not serve students and faculty; they serve an ideology. Administrators are concerned with their respective institutions only insofar as they bring them into compliance with neoliberal, externally mandated performance criteria, much of these criteria focused on preparing public-supported institutions for privatization in service to market-based demands and incentives. Ward (2012) illustrated this point well when he described the framing of the neoliberal project by corporate advocates like the Organization of Economic Cooperation and Development (OECD), which wrote in a 1987 report "university administration would need to dismantle strong forms of collegial control that made universities less manageable and replace them with strong, corporate style administrators" (p. 142).

Neoliberal, parasitic administrators are careerists and have little accountability to the faculty whom they manage because they will never return to the ranks of that faculty. Students and alumni have little awareness of who the upper-level administrators are despite their power to increase tuition, change curriculum, and frame the message and content of what they learn. Neoliberal administrators have captured their Boards of Trustees. How can else one explain the skyrocketing cost of higher education, which is directly correlated with the exponential growth of the parasitic administrative class? Most BOT members are business people who lack significant knowledge of the inner workings of higher education, specifically curriculum and faculty governance. There is little oversight from legislatures, which have normalized the neoliberal agenda (Cox, 2013) and expect the handsomely rewarded parasitic administration to implement the agenda. Even the so-called accreditation officials are in on the neoliberal project as this anonymous quote from a higher education accreditation official demonstrates "higher education today should be understood more as 'a strategic investment of resources to produce benefits for business and industry by leveraging fiscal and human capital to produce a direct, immediate and positive return on those investments'" (Ginsberg, 2012, p. 174).

SYCOPHANTS

The demise of the faculty governance process could not have happened without the assistance of a minority of faculty willing to please, serve, and flatter the administration. Neoliberalism practiced in the work place changes the ethical framework by which people interact with each other. When incessant evaluation and assessment permeate the work place, then a psychological dependency on externalized authority creates infantilized employees (Verhaeghe, 2014). Infantilized employees are the product of heavily regulated neoliberal bureaucratic structures, where thinking and acting independently and autonomously become difficult or even impossible. Infantilized employees are often jealous of those who exercise autonomy and assert their independence. When infantilized employees become aware of individuals exercising independence and autonomy, the infantilized employees seek them out utilizing authorities (in this case administrators) to punish the perpetrators. The infantilized employees seek revenge, asserting that their colleagues do not work, are lazy and need to be punished.

Part of what spurred the resentment against the disciplines at FLC that taught four-credit courses were the infantilized faculty who snooped through the hallways, reading the doors of their colleagues, scrutinizing how much time they spent in their offices. Many of us in the humanities and social sciences taught three (soon to be four) different preparations per semester and only spent three days per week in our offices. This was interpreted by some of our colleagues to mean we did not work hard enough. Anyone who is engaged in the work of social sciences and humanities knows how difficult it is to read, write, and preparation while constantly being interrupted. And, of course, there are those colleagues who have both careers and families to attend to, requiring them to work at home. It seems strange that colleagues who teach the same credit loads, conduct research and write, and serve on committees work less than other colleagues who do the same thing. This is what has happened to faculty solidarity under a neoliberal ideology focused on divide-and-rule strategies and crude forms of work quantification.

Neoliberal infantilization undermines moral agency and the ability to think independently and critically about the political and ideological substances of bureaucratic structures, creating petty and vengeful employees. The culture of neoliberalism makes possible the infantilized academic who becomes incapable of questioning power as demonstrated by this comment from one of our science professors at a public meeting: "I just don't understand why the provost would want to divide the faculty. I may be Pollyanna about it, but I just don't get it." This statement was made after the provost had diligently worked to undermine the majority will of the faculty and obliterate faculty governance. What could more clearly demonstrate how an absence of liberal arts education might serve the neoliberal agenda?

An academic culture of distrust makes possible the gross and disturbing sycophant. The sycophant is primarily concerned with unquestioning appeasement of authority in hopes of obtaining favorable advancement. With respect to the incident of academic repression presented in section one, both the senate president and faculty representative to the BOT (active during the event) qualified for the title of sycophant. They intentionally misrepresented the majority sentiment of the faculty to the BOT, emphasizing the minority position that the issue of the three- and four-credit mix was so contentious that it required the BOT to rule in the favor the minority. At the same time, the senate president was up for promotion and the faculty representative to the board was seeking a sabbatical. Their misrepresentation of the survey data and the general consensus of the faculty shocked even some of those undecided about the three- and four-credit issue. The AAUP chapter and other concerned faculty have now made it a priority to seriously vet future candidates that are supposed to represent them. The effort has paid off with respect to finding reputable representatives despite the fact that the faculty governance process has been rendered impotent.

The tragedy of this whole event is the triumph of the neoliberal agenda in dismantling collegial governance processes and destroying the solidarity of the faculty by constructing a normalized culture of distrust. Our little college now is like every other neoliberal corporatized work environment, where people are cautious to engage with one another and very suspicious of their colleagues' motives and intentions, destroying all possibilities of solidarity. Hats off to the administration for accomplishing their neoliberal goals as the renewal of their contracts made clear *power tends to corrupt and absolute power corrupts absolutely.*

REBELS

When many of the humanities and social science faculty figured out that the three- and four-credit mix was going to be used as the wedge to destroy the faculty governance process, there was an immediate response by the faculty to formulate an AAUP chapter. In fact, the statewide AAUP officials noted that we were one of the quickest formulated chapters they had ever seen. The aggrieved FLC faculty response was to utilize the long-established traditions of the AAUP, demarcating the specific roles assigned to faculty and administration in performing the operations of the university. The main crux of our AAUP chapter's argument was that curriculum design and implementation belong to the domain of the faculty. There were several tactics AAUP employed to resist the academic repression and some tactics we should have employed but did not.

1. The first action of our AAUP chapter was to resort to reason, logic, and AAUP precedent. The precedent referred to is endorsed by AAUP, the American Council on Education, and the Association of Governing Boards of Universities and Colleges and reads: The faculty has primary responsibility for such fundamental areas as curriculum, subject matter, and methods of instruction, research, faculty status, and those aspects of student life which relate to the educational process.

2. The second tactic employed was based on the assumption that faculty are professionals who have been trained in their respective areas of knowledge and are the most appropriate people to design and evaluate curriculum; our AAUP chapter prepared a ten-page response to the president's proposal to move us to a three- and four-credit mix to be presented to the BOT. The BOT ignored the document for the most part and voted with the administration's recommendations.

3. A third strategy to deal with this issue of academic repression is to maintain a viable presence. While the members of this AAUP chapter are excellent people, the majority are not radicals. That is, they are content with fighting academic repression through conventional academic discourse of argument and debate. This approach, however, has won over neither administrators nor BOT members. The AAUP chapter remains active, focusing on trying to ensure adequate faculty and student representation in key areas of curriculum. The overall morale is low, however, and the chapter has not grown since its inception.

4. A fourth tactic that should have been employed would have been to pursue unionization with the goal of an actual working contract. While this effort was discussed, ultimately there were insufficient will and effort to make it happen. A demoralized faculty certainly played a role.

5. A fifth tactic discussed but not acted on was a service strike. With the recognition that faculty input was no longer valued, there was discussion of faculty not preforming any college service until faculty governance was fully restored.

Unfortunately, more radical action seems to be waning due to neoliberal demoralization, burnout, a sense of futility, and a lack of public concern.

CONCLUSIONS

As long as the ideology of neoliberalism in higher education remains normalized, public financial support for colleges and universities will continue to dwindle and new forms of academic repression will continue. This means that the parasitic administrative class will continue to raise student tuition to pay for their corporate-styled salaries, while eliminating tenured-track faculty positions and replacing them with easy-to-exploit adjunct faculty. Disciplines not quantifiably advancing marketplace objectives and values will be eliminated or financially marginalized. This has already happened to modern languages and ethnic studies programs and has begun to affect other humanities and social science programs. The consequences of continuing this pursuit are the loss of real critical thought and an inability to evaluate economic, political, and social systems of power. We are losing our ability to identify the meaning of morality, ethics, and democratic processes of decision making with respect to the public good.

What is happening in higher education is an ideological war. The publically supported college and university is one of the greatest accomplishments of American society. As corporate influence creeps into academia through the artificially created funding shortfalls endemic to neoliberal politics, the publically supported college and university are dying a slow and painful death. To illustrate this hegemonic neoliberal takeover of the academy we need go no further than the generous contributions of the Koch foundation:

> Florida State University (FSU) was one of the foundation's earliest grantees. A $6.6 million award [...] was paid after an agreement between the foundation and FSU economics department was hammered out. The contract stipulated that five faculty would be hired to teach "The Value of Free Enterprise," with oversight by an advisory board chosen by the Kochs. The AAUP notes that the board not only gave the foundation authority on hiring, but also allowed it to "review the work of professors to make sure they complied with the objectives and purposes of the foundation" [...] many argued that this was a gross infringement of academic freedom, *the administration* seemingly had no qualms about accepting the donation (Badger, 2015).

Badger (2015) went on to note that there are many other campuses being funded by the Kochs and other like-minded companies who wish to promote "the moral foundation of capitalism." Industries with agendas have been funding science and engineering programs for years, and it should come as no surprise that they are not neutral on the runaway neoliberal train.

Without a radical challenge to the root of neoliberalism as a viable ideology for education, the day is fast approaching when we will be teaching based on the mandates of our corporate sponsors only. This lecture is brought to you by [...].

REFERENCES

Badger, E. J. (2015). As public funding of universities dwindles, faculty are unionizing. Retrieved from http://www.truth-out.org/news/item/34102-as-public-funding-of-universities-dwindles-faculty-are-unionizing

Cox, R. W. (2013). The corporatization of higher education. *Class, Race and Corporate Power*, 8(1), 1–17. Retrieved from http://digitalcommons.fiu.edu/classracecorporatepower/vol1/iss1/8

Deresiewicz, W. (2015). The neoliberal arts: How college sold its soul to the market. *Harper's Magazine, 331*(1984), 25–32.

Ginsberg, B. (2011). *The fall of the faculty: The rise of the all-administrative university and why it matters.* New York: Oxford University Press.

Giroux, H. A. (2014). *Neoliberalism's war on higher education.* Chicago, IL: Haymarket Books.

Marmol, E., Hill, D., Maisuria, A., Nocella, A. J., & Parenti, M., (2015ba). The corporate university: An e-interview by Emil Marmol with Dave Hill, Alpesh Maisuria, Anthony Nocella, and Michael Parenti. *Critical Education, 6*(19). Retrieved from http://ojs.library.ubc.ca/ index.php/ criticaled/article/ view/185102

McBrayer, J. (2014). October board report. Retrieved from https://www.fortlewis.edu/...Reports/Faculty-Report-BOT-100114.pdf

McBrayer, J. (2014). December board report. Retrieved from https://www.fortlewis.edu/Portals/.../December-2014-Board-Report.pdf

Miller, N. (2012). The corporatization of higher education. *Dissent Magazine.* (Fall) Article 1. Retrieved from https://www.dissentmagazine.org/article/the-corporatization-of-higher-education

Newfield, C. (2008). *Unmaking the public university: The forty-year assault on the middle class.* Cambridge, MA: Harvard University Press.

Newfield, C. (2016). What are the humanities for? Rebuilding the public university. In G. Hunter & F. G. Mohamed (Eds.), *A new deal for the humanities: Liberal arts and the future of public education.* (pp. 160–178). New Brunswick, NJ: Rutgers University Press.

Nocella II, A. J., Best, S., & Mclaren, P. (Eds.). (2010). *Academic repression: Reflections from the academic industrial complex.* Oakland, CA: AK Press.

Picchi, A. (2014). Why students should be wary of college leaders' high pay. Retrieved from http://www.cbsnews.com/news/why-students-should-be-wary-of-college-leaders-high-pay/

Rubenstein, R. L. (2014). The cunning of history: Bureaucratic domination and the Holocaust. In R. Heiner (ed.), *Deviance cross cultures: Construction of difference* (pp. 287–293). New York: Oxford University Press.

Schuman, R. (2014). Syllabus tyrannus: The decline and fall of the American university is written in 25-pages course syllabi. Retrieved from http://www.slate.com/articles/life/education/2014/08/college_course_syllabi_they_re_too_long_and_they_re_a_symbol_of_the_decline.html

Verhaeghe, P. (2014). Neoliberalism has brought out the worst in us. Retrieved from http://www.theguardian.com/commentisfree/2014/sep/29/neoliberalism-economic-system-ethics-personality-psychopathicsthic

Ward, S. (2012). *Neoliberalism and the global restructuring of knowledge and education.* New Brunswick, NJ: Routledge Press.

Part II.
Resisting

"Man that school shit is a joke
The same people who control the school system control
The prison system, and the whole social system
Ever since slavery, nawsaying?"

—DEAD PREZ

"The learning process is something you can incite, literally incite, like a riot."

—AUDRE LORDE

CHAPTER FOUR

On Identity Politics, *Ressentiment*, and the Evacuation of Human Emancipation

CAMILA BASSI

The tradition of all the dead generations weighs like a nightmare on the brain of the living.
—KARL MARX

The late modern liberal subject quite literally seethes with *ressentiment*.
—WENDY BROWN

INTRODUCTION

At the UK-based *National Campaign Against Fees and Cuts* (NCAFC) annual conference, held at the University of Birmingham Students' Union on November 23, 2013, I spoke on a panel titled "Privilege, Intersectionality and Fighting Oppression." In preparation for my talk, I had assumed no prior knowledge on the audience's behalf so as to make my intervention as accessible as possible. My basic introduction of Marxism therein was to illustrate both its intersectionality and its distinct perspective on exploitation and resistance. One of the other panel speakers stated during the discussion that I had "made an assumption that everyone in the room was at the same level," and that "the use of high convoluted language by people who are able to read theory" is a "privilege" and is therefore "oppressive" and "exclusionary." She frustrated that in such discussions (about privilege and intersectionality?) people (in general?) "refuse to shut up about Marx." She pushed an anti-intellectualism and an anti-Marxism which troubled me, since there was no reflection on such questions, simply indictments. Moreover, she appeared to be angry with me and that puzzled me because I had kept my contribution respectful of other positions. I wondered then, how emotionally healthy and politically useful is an anger that forestalls open thought and exchange?

On May 1, 2014 (International Workers' Day), I attended a session titled "Intersectionality: Checking Our Own Privilege" at the launch event of the *Free University of Sheffield*. The (African American) woman leading the session problematized an image used by the (white) organizers to advertise the event: an image that she described as Black African children holding a free-education poster. This was, she said, "an ignorant appropriation." The (white) audience sat in an awkward moment of silence, looking concerned by their accidental but privileged appropriation of an image of the unprivileged. I (a British Indian) was one of the two nonwhite participants in the room; the other, of course, was the session leader. I spoke up, "while we must be sensitive to the temporal and spatial specificities, and therein the lived experiences, of such images, there is also something universal here." The session leader replied with incredulity, "what could you possibility think you had in common with the people in the image?" I suggested, "the universal struggle for free education, and also perhaps, the universal struggle for free health care, and the universal struggle for independent trade unions." There was no reply, just another moment of awkward silence. At the end of the session, I left with the impression of a politics wherein no one can speak for anyone else, resulting in naval-gazing entanglement.

The academic repression I proceed to discuss in this chapter is that by a neoliberal wave of identity politics in the form of intersectionality and privilege theory. It is a repression of self by self, which precludes connection, bypasses freedom, and generates *ressentiment*. I explore a specific case study of the political deadlock between a current of radical feminists and a current of transgender and transsexual activists, both with wider sympathizers, which has played out on social media and across university campuses. I also offer a general theoretical and practical call for dialogue between left-wing academics and students in the hope that we can, once again, collectively aspire for freedom.

WHERE DID FREEDOM GO?

In *States of Injury* political scientist Wendy Brown (1995) observed that in the era of late modernity, as the bleak reality of a contorted Marxism is framed against the sunshine of liberalism, progressives have chosen to pursue a form of freedom which is based on state-managed economic justice and private liberties.

Furthermore, "'freedom' has shown itself to be easily appropriated in liberal regimes for the most cynical and unemancipatory political ends," such that:

> the dream of democracy—that humans might govern themselves by governing together—is difficult to discern in the proliferation of [...] claims of rights, protections, regulations, and entitlements (Brown, 1995, p. 5).

Brown does not dispute the importance of rights, protections, regulations, and entitlements, but rather she asks, beyond this what is our dream of freedom? She defends the explanatory power of Marxism in seeing the question of freedom *vis-à-vis* social relations, which are "implicitly declared 'unpolitical'—that is, naturalized—in liberal discourse" (Brown, 1995, p. 14). In other words, genuine freedom cannot be found in state (re)distribution. Here it is helpful to understand the important distinction Marx makes between "political emancipation" and "human emancipation," which can be found in his essay *On "The Jewish Question"* (1843/1977) that was part of a debate with the left Hegelian Bruno Bauer. Marx's discussion is not *per se* a consideration of the Jewish condition but a critique of political emancipation in order to expose the relationship of political emancipation to human emancipation.

Marx (1843/1977) acknowledged the "great [...] real, practical" progress of political emancipation, that is, liberal rights and liberties (p. 47). However, on its limits, he argues that whilst the capitalist state abolishes in its own way the distinctions of class, birth, profession, and education—by declaring them "to be unpolitical differences"—it allows them "to have an effect in their own manner" (p. 45). What is inherent in political emancipation, Marx spells out, is *a gap* between human beings as—ideally—public members of a universal state or "citizens," and—materially—private, egoistic members of civil society or "bourgeois." As such, humankind leads a twofold existence: "a heavenly one and an earthy one" (Marx, 1843/1977, p. 46). Private rights are innately "bourgeois" and the basis of the separation of human beings from one another:

> Man [*sic*] was [...] not freed from religion; he received freedom of religion. He was not freed from property; he received freedom of property. He was not freed from the egoism of trade; he received freedom to trade (Marx, 1843/1977, p. 56).

Marx deplored the debasement of theory, art, history, nature, and human relations by religion, property, commodities, and commerce; he deplores the bartering of women, "[t]he species-relationship itself," as "an object of commerce!" (1843/1977, p. 60). This debasement, he contends, is the exile of human beings' communal essence. Marx foreseen human liberation as the eradication of the aforementioned gap, in other words, the freedom of human beings is contingent not merely on political emancipation but on human emancipation, which necessitates the abolition of capitalist social relations.

Returning to Brown's *States of Injury*, she astutely remarks that the Right's ability to capture a discourse of freedom for its own ends, alongside the tendency of progressive politics to abandon the socialist project on the basis of its supposed failure (*apropos* Stalinism), has led in academia to:

> developments in philosophy and in feminist, postcolonial, and cultural theory [that] have eroded freedom's ground. For many toiling in these domains, "freedom" has been swept onto the dust-heap of anachronistic, humanistic, androcentric, subject-centred, and "Western shibboleths" (1995, p. 18).

So while Marxism desires human emancipation from capitalism, Brown (1995, p. 61) asks:

> to what extent do identity politics require a standard internal to existing society against which to pitch their claims, a standard that not only preserves capitalism from critique, but sustains the invisibility and inarticulatedness of class—not accidentally, but endemically? Could we have stumbled upon one reason why class is invariably named but rarely theorized or developed in the multiculturalist mantra "race, class, gender, sexuality"?

Bringing forward Brown's argument, it is worth considering the context for the present-day popularity of privilege theory and intersectionality.

IDENTITY POLITICS AND SELF-SUBJUGATION

Privilege theorist pioneer McIntosh (Rothman, 2014) stated:

> what I believe is that everybody has a combination of unearned advantage and unearned disadvantage in life [...]. We're all put ahead and behind by the circumstances of our birth. [...] In order to understand the way privilege works, you have to be able to see patterns and systems in social life, but you also have to care about individual experiences. I think one's own individual experience is sacred. Testifying to it is very important [...].

The basic premise of privilege theory is that wherever there is an oppressive structure—capitalism, patriarchy, white supremacy, heteronormativity, and so on—there is both an oppressed group of people and a privileged group of people (who, consciously or not, benefit from that structure). Interlaced with privilege theory is the notion of intersectionality: that we are all privileged by some structures of oppression and burdened by other structures of oppression, thus our privileges and our oppressions intersect. At a macrolevel, race, gender, and class, for example, are seen as "distinctive yet interlocking structures of oppression" (Collins, 1993, p. 26), whereas "the notion of intersectionality describes microlevel processes—namely, how each individual and group occupies a social position within interlocking structures of oppression" (Collins, 1997, p. 74). Moreover, in a matrix of domination, "[e]ach individual derives varying amounts of penalty and privilege from the multiple systems of oppression which frame everyone's lives" (Collins, 1990, p. 230). By lacking full awareness of our privileges and their intersectionality, the reasoning goes, we are politically divided and weak, and whilst we cannot be held responsible for the structures of oppression that impart privilege upon us, we do have a choice in how we respond to our privilege, for instance, to our whiteness, our maleness, our straightness, our ableness, our cisness, etcetera.

The origins of privilege theory and intersectionality can be traced to the theoretical framework of identity politics in the 1980s and 1990s, which developed amid labour movement defeats and the expansion of the neoliberal project of free-market capitalism (including free trade, deregulation, privatization, and austerity) during the Thatcher and Reagan years. In Britain specifically, the government policy of multiculturalism in the 1980s and 1990s (popular with leftist local councils) furthered the notion of discrete "ethnic" identities from which gains could be made by state accommodation. And from 1998, marketization began in the higher education sector with the introduction of tuition fees (The Dearing Report, 1997). By the late 1980s and 1990s, second-wave feminism had given way to third-wave feminism—whose theory was very much influenced by academic postmodernism and identity politics. Third-wave feminists Kimberlé Crenshaw (1991) and Patricia Hill Collins (1990) developed the concept of intersectionality in the early 1990s. Both also drew on earlier second-wave feminist discussions by Black feminists in the United States. In 1977, the Boston-based Black lesbian feminist *Combahee River Collective* (1977) advanced the concept of "simultaneity," and stressed the importance of personal identity: "We believe that the most profound and potentially most radical politics come directly out of our own identity, as opposed to working to end somebody else's oppression."

The elephant in the room *vis-à-vis* the identity politics of intersectionality and privilege theory is Marxism. Collins (2000, p. 287) dismissed the "radical [Marxist] left" as saying: "If only people of colour and women could see their true class interests […] class solidarity would eliminate racism and sexism." There can be no denying an element of truth to this claim. What's more, dominant sections of the revolutionary Marxist left have a damning record of pandering to racism, sexism, and homophobia for organizational gain (Bassi, 2013a, 2013b, 2013c). But abandoning altogether the explanatory power of Marxism leaves us short on the question of how to achieve social change. Intersectionality applies a generalized cultural and economic understanding of class alongside other registers of oppression such as gender and sexuality (Heaphy, 2011; Taylor, 2011). I question what might be lost in its implicit redefinition of class, *qua* classism, when thinking through the nature of oppression and exploitation, and the means of resistance; class, after all, is not primarily a structure of oppression but a systematic relation of exploitation (Bassi, 2010). Given also that racism, sexism, homophobia, and transphobia, for instance, are individually distinct forms of oppression with individually distinct relationships to capitalism, which include specific and universal features, the danger with intersectionality lies in it sliding into a conceptual collapse through its kaleidoscopic, intersecting structures of oppression, and in it nullifying universality while in pursuit of specificity (Bassi, 2016). In privilege theory, people tend to talk about "white supremacy" rather than "racism," but the former carries no explanatory power over the latter: white supremacy falls short in being able to analyze and politically respond to anti-Irish racism, antigypsy racism, and anti-Semitism, for example. And the emphasis on personal testimony (remember, as McIntosh states, "one's individual experience is sacred") overrides the possibility for any universal truths. The net effect is "no way out" *vis-à-vis* resistance.

Marx (1843) made plain in *On "The Jewish Question"* that the route to real freedom lies in social relations not rights alone. Brown's astute point on the lack of theorizing of class in the multiculturalist mantra resonates especially well in the present-day privilege theory and intersectionality mantra. Is it not time to name and call out once more what is, in reality, the relinquishment of the dream of freedom as humans governing themselves by governing together? Present-day identity politics is based on unchanging status—as privilege theorist Kimmel (2013, p. xxv) asserts, "[o]ne can no more renounce privilege than one can stop breathing"— rather than a dynamic understanding of human consciousness through human history. Society is viewed as a seesaw: you are up there because I am down here, and you are up there because you weigh me down. It is a personalized dual camp distortion of social relations, "me versus you" (with various intersectional combinations), that breeds resentment and is devoid of class politics. Ultimately, freedom has become dangerously lost in the contradiction of identity politics. As Brown (1995) observed:

> politicized identities generated out of liberal, disciplinary societies, insofar as they are premised on exclusion from a universal ideal, require that ideal, as well as their exclusion from it, for their own continuing existence as identities (p. 65).

She develops Nietzsche's concept of *ressentiment* to explain how the desired impulse of politicized identity to "inscribe in the law and other political registers its historical and present pain" forecloses "an imagined future of power to make itself" (Brown, 1995, p. 66). What one has instead of freedom then is the production of *ressentiment*:

> *Ressentiment* in this context is a triple achievement: it produces an affect (rage, righteousness) that overwhelms the hurt; it produces a culprit responsible for the hurt; and it produces a site of revenge to displace the hurt (a place to inflict hurt as the sufferer has been hurt) (Brown, 1995, p. 68).

We are left with an effort to anaesthetize and to externalize what is unendurable. I turn now to this chapter's case study: a toxic war between a current of radical feminists and a current of transactivists, both of which with wider layer of sympathizers. This is a war that has played out on social media and across university campuses and which has impeded connection, circumvented freedom, and bred *ressentiment*.

PRIVILEGE PRODUCTION OF IMPASSE: THE CASE OF THE DEADLOCK BETWEEN RADICAL FEMINISTS AND TRANSACTIVISTS

In February 2015, a letter titled "We cannot allow censorship and silencing of individuals" was published in *The Observer*, signed by several academics and feminist and LGBT activists; it identifies:

> a worrying pattern of intimidation and silencing of individuals whose views are deemed "transphobic" or "whorephobic." Most of the people so labeled are feminists or profeminist men, some have experience in the sex industry, some are transgender. […] "No platforming" used to be a tactic used against self-proclaimed fascists and Holocaust-deniers. But today it is being used to prevent the expression of feminist arguments critical of the sex industry and of some demands made by transactivists. The feminists who hold these views have never advocated or engaged in violence against any group of people. Yet it is argued that the mere presence of anyone said to hold these views is a threat to a protected minority group's safety. You do not have to agree with the views that are being silenced to find these tactics illiberal and undemocratic. Universities have a particular responsibility to resist this kind of bullying.

As important background to this letter, two high-profile public confrontations are worth noting. The first relates to the radical feminist Julie Bindel. In 2012, the National Union of Students' (NUS) LGBTQ Campaign passed a motion of no platform against Bindel for her alleged transphobia. Bindel had made offensive comments in relation to transsexual people in a 2004 piece for *The Guardian*, which she later apologized for as "misplaced and insensitive" (Bindel, 2007). The NUS motion included the sentence: "Conference believes that Julie Bindel is vile" (Deacon, 2014). The history of NUS's no platform policy relates specifically to fascism, and debate on no platform has tended to centre on the question: while fascists (given the direct physical threat they pose) must be no platformed, should one, and indeed can one, no platform racists? In this context, the no platforming of Julie Bindel is extraordinary, as she joined a list that includes Al-Muhajiroun, the British National Party, the English Defence League, and Hizb-ut-Tahrir—fascistic political forces that incite violence. In autumn 2014, Bindel was due to speak at the University of Sheffield Students' Union on her book *Straight Expectations*, but a week before she was due, the student management banned her (Deacon, 2014). A year later, in autumn 2015, Bindel was invited by the Free Speech and Secular Society, at the University of Manchester Students' Union, to partake in a debate titled "From Liberation to Censorship: Does Modern Feminism Have a Problem with Free Speech?" Once again, she was banned by the student management. The students' union women's officer stated in defense of the decision that this "is not about shutting down conversations or denying free speech; this is about keeping our students safe" (Palmer, 2015).

The second high profile public confrontation was the backlash generated from an article titled "Seeing Red" in the *New Statesman* in 2013, written by the journalist and feminist Suzanne Moore. In the article, Moore (2013) argued against austerity and for those who are hardest hit by austerity—women—to be angry and to resist:

> It's not just the double shift of work and domestic duties that women do. There is now a third shift—we must keep ourselves sexually attractive forever. [...] The cliché is that female anger is always turned inwards rather than outwards into despair. We are angry with ourselves for not being happier, not being loved properly, and not having the ideal body shape—that of a Brazilian transsexual. We are angry that men do not do enough. We are angry at work where we are underpaid and overlooked. This anger can be neatly channeled and outsourced to make someone a fat profit. Are your hormones okay? Do you need a nice bath?

A significant reaction followed this publication against Moore's alleged transphobic reference to "a Brazilian transsexual" (an implicit reference to the model Lea T). This was a vitriolic row between, in the main, radical feminists and transactivists, which was played out on social media and in the press, and included Moore herself temporarily resigning from Twitter, apologizing for a "throwaway" comment, and stating "I am not your enemy" (Wynick, 2013).

Cultural theory academic Sara Ahmed (2015), in retort to *The Observer* (2015) letter "We cannot allow censorship and silencing of individuals," contended in a blog post titled "You are oppressing us!":

> Politics is rarely about one good and one bad side, nor about innocence on one side and guilt on the other. But politics is also messy because power is asymmetrical. [...] Transphobia and anti-trans-statements should not be treated as just another viewpoint that we should be free to express at a happy diversity table. There cannot be a dialogue when some at the table are in effect or intent arguing for the elimination of others at the table. [...] The presentation of transactivists as a lobby and as bullies rather than as minorities who are constantly being called upon to defend their right to exist is a mechanism of power. Sadly this letter is evidence that the mechanism is working. [...] Racists present themselves as injured/under attack/a minority fighting against a powerful antiracist lobby that is "busy" suppressing their voices. We can hear resonance without assuming analogy.

Contrary to Ahmed (2015) here, Brown (1995) stressed that while we must recognize that "[s]ocial injury such as that conveyed through derogatory speech becomes that which is 'unacceptable' and 'individually culpable,'" it actually "*symptomizes deep political distress in a culture*" (p. 27, my emphasis). One day after the *The Observer* letter was published, signatory and English classics academic Mary Beard (Lusher, 2015) reported:

> Last night I went to bed wanting to weep […]. It was the relentless pummeling of attack on the basis of extraordinary loaded, sometimes quite wrong, readings of the letter. The complaints fall into several categories. (1) I am an appalling transphobe. (2) I am a bit past it, a poor old lady who hasn't quite got the issues straight, bless her. (3) I have been duped by the transphobes, because I am a nice person really. I was not signing up to an attack on the transcommunity.

Another signatory, human rights activist Peter Tatchell (Lusher, 2015), stated:

> I've received about 5,000 messages attacking me. The volume and vitriol of the attack has been almost unprecedented in forty-eight years of human rights campaigning. I'm shocked. I have supported the transgender freedom struggle for forty years. But I have been accused of trying to silence transpeople and called "an advocate for oppressors." The letter was about freedom of speech and includes no attack on transrights. When I signed the letter I didn't know who else was going to sign it. Now I am being condemned by the McCarthyite tactic of guilt by association.

Here we see in action the aforementioned triple feat of *ressentiment*: the production of an affect (a rage and a righteousness) that overwhelms a hurt, a culprit who is responsible for the hurt, and a site of revenge to displace the hurt; all of which temporarily anaesthetize and externalize the hurt but demolish any potential for political coalition.

The radical feminist and transactivist deadlock is the privilege production of impasse, and a symptom of acute political distress in which freedom has been abandoned for *ressentiment*. On the one hand, we have a camp of people insisting that those born into biologically male bodies carry privilege regardless of their identification as women—privilege over women who have an entire lived experience of being women and of its related oppression. On the other hand, we have a camp of people arguing that there are those who are cisgendered (whose gender aligns with their sex at birth) and who carry cis power and privilege—privilege over those who have a lived experience of being transgendered (whose gender doesn't align with their sex at birth) and of its related oppression. In a neoliberal wave of identity politics, the politicized identification of personal bodily experiences, and the struggle to trump or negate such bodily experiences in a battle over power asymmetry, effectively lets power off the hook.

Privilege theory activist McKenzie (2014) prescribed four ways to push back against one's privilege: one, relinquish power; two, don't go (she uses as an example woman-only events that exclude transwomen); three, shut up; and four, be careful what identities you claim ("consider," she says, "how your privilege [...] gives you access to claim identities even when your lived experience does not support it"). The irony that McKenzie advocated a "no turning up" protest against the radical feminist exclusion of transwomen from women-only spaces is that radical feminists are employing their own argument against claiming identities when lived experience does not correspond. Crucially, McKenzie's prescription encapsulates how a politics that promises to allow a plethora of voices to be heard is in actuality the opposite, a *ressentiment*-seethed silencing: I speak, you shut up; you cannot know my pain; your experience is incomparable to my suffering. The impasse between radical feminists and transactivists is just this, a silencing, either of transactivists or of radical feminists or of a wider layer of sympathizers on either side, on both sides, or on neither side.

Instructively, in an effort to bring peace to the so-called "border wars" between butch lesbians and female-to-male transsexuals, gender and queer theorist Halberstam (1998) noted that "many subjects, not only transsexual subjects, do not feel at home in their bodies" (p. 148) and insists on taking into account the wider neoliberal, political economic context:

> Because body flexibility has become both a commodity (in the case of cosmetic surgeries, for example) and a form of commodification, it is not enough in this "age of flexibility" to celebrate gender flexibility as simply another sign of progress and liberation (Halberstam, 2005, p. 18).

Halberstam (2005) remarked:

> In mainstream gay, lesbian, and trans communities in the United States, battles rage about what group occupies the more transgressive or aggrieved position, and only rarely are such debates framed in terms of larger discussions about capitalism, class, or economics (p. 20).

"[T]ransgressive exceptionalism," "a by-product of local translations of neo-liberalism," has become "the practice of taking the moral high ground by claiming to be more oppressed and more extraordinary than others" (Halberstam, 2005, pp. 19–20). Halberstam's (2005) notion of transgressive exceptionalism chimes with the work of Brown (1994) on wound culture as a contemporary form of Nietzschean *ressentiment*, in which, as Cadman (2006) puted it, "current forms of 'identity politics' become 'attached' to destructive modes of their own subjection" (p. 140). The political challenge we are left with is: how do we support the struggle for political emancipation by and for transactivist movements worldwide, while demanding open space to critically understand and debate the construction of gender, and to forge alliances for future human emancipation?

FINDING OUR WAY BACK TO FREEDOM

The chasm Marx identified between human beings as, on the one hand, citizens of a universal community and, on the other hand, private, alienated, egoistic individuals of a civil society, is reflected in the contradiction of a neoliberal wave of identity politics considered and critiqued in this chapter. Halberstam (2005) is correct in seeing the identity politics problematic as, in part, a failure of the academy itself:

> The rehearsal of identity-bound debates outside the academy speaks not simply to a lack of sophistication in such debates, but suggests that academics have failed to take their ideas beyond the university and have not made necessary interventions in public intellectual venues (p. 20).

Brown (1995), going further still, recognized academic developments in philosophy and in feminist, postcolonial, and cultural theory as foreclosing any kind of socialist project for human emancipation on the basis of the failure of Stalinism, which is crudely subsumed into Marxism in general. Our journey back to the dream of freedom requires us as academics making a case for supplanting a politics of "*I am*"—which closes down identity, and fixes it within a social and moral hierarchy—with a politics of "*I want this for us*" (Brown, 1995, p. 75 [my emphasis]). If we fail to help make this happen, we will remain locked in a history that has "weight but no trajectory, mass but no coherence, force but no direction," thus stagnated in a "war without ends or end" (Brown, 1995, p. 71). I end with ten tactics for challenging the academic repression of identity politics:

1. To positively engage in the aspects of intersectionality and privilege theory that strengthen and enrich more traditional forms of class politics, for example, by taking into account and reflecting upon the specific experiences and intersectionalities of oppressions.
2. To challenge the aspects of intersectionality and privilege theory that effectively fix human identity and detach human identity from evolving material conditions of existence.
3. To expose and explore the elephant in the room of intersectionality and privilege theory, i.e., Marxism, in order to critically assess its insight into the relationship between political emancipation and human emancipation.
4. To call upon academics to engage with the politics on their university campuses and in student activist circles.
5. To organize teach-ins and reading groups between academics and their students on political theory and issues.
6. To forge alliances between labor movement struggles and individuals and groups striving for social justice via identity politics.

7. To learn the history of past alliances between labor movement struggles and individuals and groups striving for social justice through identity politics in order to understand the potential of an intersectional class politics. For example, by examining the case of the 1984–1985 *Lesbians and Gays Support the Miners* group, as documented by the film *Pride*.
8. To identify and develop collective campaigns on pressing political issues, such as for the full and decent provision of social housing, including the safeguarding of those most vulnerable to abuse by landlords in the private rental sector, transgender and transsexual people.
9. To foster dialogue and debate on the nature of oppressions and exploitation, and the means to resistance and social change.
10. To forge a politics that is attuned to both specificities and their connections to universal struggles for democracy, freedom, and social change.

REFERENCES

Ahmed, S. (2015). You are oppressing us! *Feminist killjoys*. Retrieved from http://feministkilljoys.com/2015/02/15/you-are-oppressing-us/

Bassi, C. (2016). What's radical about reality TV? An unexpected tale from Shanghai of a Chinese lesbian antihero. *Gender, Place & Culture*, 23(11), 1619–1630.

Bassi, C. (2010). 'It's new but not that new': On the continued use of old Marx. *Feminist Legal Studies*, 18, 69–76.

Bassi, C. (2013a). Towards an honest history: The case of the militant tendency. *Anaemic on a Bike*. Retrieved from https://anaemiconabike.wordpress.com/2013/07/04/towards-an-honest-history-the-case-of-the-militant-tendency/

Bassi, C. (2013b). Further excavation of the militant tendency. *Anaemic on a Bike*. Retrieved from https://anaemiconabike.wordpress.com/2013/08/19/further-excavation-of-the-militant-tendency/

Bassi, C. (2013c). Sexist and misogynistic ridicule is NOT decent class analysis. *Anaemic on a Bike*. Retrieved from https://anaemiconabike.wordpress.com/2013/08/21/sexist-and-misogynistic-ridicule-is-not-decent-class-analysis/

Bindel, J. (2007). My trans mission. *The Guardian*. Retrieved from http://www.theguardian.com/commentisfree/2007/aug/01/mytransmission

Brown, W. (1995). *States of injury: Power and freedom in late modernity*. Princeton, NJ: Princeton University Press.

Cadman, L. (2006). *A genealogy of biopolitical contestation during the reform of the Mental Health Act (1983)*. DPhil: University of Sheffield.

Combahee River Collective Statement. (1977). Retrieved from http://circuitous.org/scraps/combahee.html

Crenshaw, K. (1991). Mapping the margins: Intersectionality, identity politics, and violence against women of color. *Stanford Law Review*, 43(6), 1241–1299.

Deacon, L. (2014). Sheffield SU and NUS ban on Julie Bindle—an affront to free speech, our intellectual freedom and an insult to students. *Huffington Post*. Retrieved from http://www.huffing tonpost.co.uk/liam-deacon/julie-bindel-ban_b_6081224.html

Halberstam, J. (1998). *Female masculinity*. Durham, NC: Duke University Press.

Halberstam, J. (2005). *In a queer time and place: Transgender bodies, subcultural lives*. New York: New York University Press.

Heaphy, B. (2011). Gay identities and the culture of class. *Sexualities, 14*, 42–62.

Hill Collins, P. (1990). *Black feminist thought: Knowledge, consciousness and the politics of empowerment*. Cambridge, MA: Hymen.

Hill Collins, P. (1993). Toward a new vision: Race, class, and gender as categories of analysis and connection. *Race, Sex & Class, 1*(1), 25–45.

Hill Collins, P. (1997). On West and Fenstermaker's 'Doing Difference.' In M. R. Walsh (Ed.). *Women, men and gender. Ongoing debates* (pp. 73–75). New Haven, CT: Yale University Press.

Kimmel, M. S., & Ferber, A. L. (2013). *Privilege: A reader*. Boulder, CO: Westview Press.

Letter. (2015). We cannot allow censorship and silencing of individuals. *The Observer*. Retrieved from http://www.theguardian.com/theobserver/2015/feb/14/letters-censorship.

Lusher, A. (2015). Transgender activists target Peter Tatchell and Mary Beard after free speech letter. *The Independent*. Retrieved from http://www.independent.co.uk/news/people/transgender-activists-target-peter-tatchell-and-mary-beard-after-free-speech-letter-10050155.html

Marx, K. (1843/1977). On 'the Jewish question'. In D. McLellan (ed.). *Karl Marx: Selected writings* (pp. 39–62). Oxford: Oxford University Press.

Marx, K. (1852/1977). The Eighteenth Brumaire of Louis Bonaparte. In D. McLellan (ed.). *Karl Marx: Selected writings* (pp. 300–325). Oxford: Oxford University Press.

McKenzie, M. (2014). 4 Ways to Push Back Against Your Privilege. *BGD*. Retrieved from http://www.blackgirldangerous.org/2014/02/4-ways-push-back-privilege/

Moore, S. (2013). Seeing red. *New Statesman*. Retrieved from http://www.newstatesman.com/politics/2013/01/seeing-red-power-female-anger

Palmer, E. (2015). 'Transphobic' feminist Julie Bindel banned from Manchester student union talk on free speech. *International Business Times*. Retrieved from http://www.ibtimes.co.uk/feminist-julie-bindel-banned-manchester-student-union-talk-free-speech-1522670

Rothman, J. (2014). The origins of 'privilege': An interview with Peggy McIntosh. *New Yorker*. Retrieved from http://www.newyorker.com/books/page-turner/the-origins-of-privilege

Taylor, Y. (2011). Sexualities and class. *Sexualities, 14*, 3–11.

The Dearing Report (1997). Retrieved from http://www.educationengland.org.uk/documents/dearing1997/dearing1997.html

Wynick, A. (2013). 'Threatening, ignorant and nasty': Suzanne Moore leaves Twitter over transgender row. *Mirror*. Retrieved from http://www.mirror.co.uk/news/uk-news/suzanne-moore-apologises-to-transgender-community-1533986

Cutting Class: On Schoolwork, Entropy, and Everyday Resistance in Higher Education

CONOR CASH AND GEOFF BOYCE

INTRODUCTION

Education is a ubiquitous category in political and development discourses, variously discussed as a panacea for social disorders; a one true church of enlightenment; the means for advancement for the disadvantaged; and an as-of-yet unrealized system for optimum socialization. In the United States, and much of the Western colonial world, education is pursued through the institution of schooling, which encloses learning within a system of centralized meritocratic administration, requiring continuous assessment, evaluation, and policing that incentivizes specific norms of behavior and penalizes those unable or unwilling to comport to these norms. For these reasons, this chapter argues that rather than an exogenous force threatening the institution (Del Gandio, 2013; Hodge, 2013), or a deviation from an historical norm (Giroux, 2010), repression is foundational to the academy and constitutes one of its primary functions within capitalist modernity.

This position is founded on the assertion that schoolwork is an exploitative labor process for both the instructor and the student—its object the production not of an educated populace but of productive and compliant subjects. For the student, it is at once an unpaid labor process adding value to future labor power (Cleaver, 2004); a disciplinary process in which habits of mind and body are cultivated (Foucault, 1979); and a sorting process that identifies readiness for work (Caffentzis, 1980). We therefore argue that regardless of the content presented, the thorough performance of our duties as instructors is a conservative process with a conservative goal. For this reason, leftist efforts to redirect pedagogical content and structure toward critical and emancipatory ends must be approached with caution and weighed against the institutional imperatives listed above and the everyday conditions these generate.

Our argument does not end here, however. In conclusion, we assert that the fundamental struggles arising in and circulating through schools are the struggles around day-to-day material and social conditions and cannot be fully appraised or amplified outside of this framework. For those of us working within educational institutions and concerned with combating austerity and building political power, we must identify and revalue activities that we categorize as *everyday resistance* as starting points for articulating struggles within the educational system (and class society more generally)—toward more free-time and self-direction, less discipline, and indeed, ultimately, the abolition of schooling.

CONTEXT

To provide some insight into the context in which the authors have formed the positions argued below, we live and work in Arizona, a state that former-*Daily Show* host Jon Stewart has called the "the meth-lab of democracy." Since 2008, Arizona has suffered comparably the second worst fiscal crisis in the nation (following Nevada). As in California, Michigan, Wisconsin, and many other states, the treatment of choice for municipal and state budget challenges has been the imposition of austerity on public services, including (especially) the education sector. The impact upon students and workers in public universities has been severe. In Arizona, where the state constitution mandates that higher education "be as nearly free as possible" (Article XI, Section 9), in-state tuition at the University of Arizona (UofA) has grown from $5,275 in FY2008 to $11,523 in FY2016—a 118% increase in less than a decade (University of Arizona, 2015). According to the University's strategic plan, during a similar period, total degree cost is projected to have grown from $48,800 in 2005 to $77,990 in 2015. This is in addition to the state government reducing tuition waivers provided to graduating high school seniors by the popular AIMS (Arizona's Instrument to Measure Standards) scholarship from a full tuition waiver to twenty-five percent of the cost of attendance at state universities. Accompanying these tuition hikes are several changes in labor practices imposed by the University administration, including layoffs of administrative staff; privatization of service work (such as on-campus janitorial and IT services); a dramatic shift toward part-time adjunct instruction and increased graduate student teaching loads; and the development of an in-house temporary agency dubbed the UofA "Talent Network," where laid-off full-time benefits-eligible employees can be rehired for their old jobs as temporary workers, losing seniority, vacation and sick pay, pension support, and related benefits.

In the context of a nationwide assault on the wages and political power of workers in the education sector, university employees, students, and advocates have often attempted to defend education by deploying a discourse that paints it as a necessary public good that allows democracy to function (Butler, 2009; Giroux & Giroux, 2004). As university administrators utilize state-mandated austerity as a means to reduce the University's wage bill and increase the workload for university employees, even purportedly radical initiatives attempting to articulate the class dimensions of this crisis have advocated against budget cuts at the state level while ignoring the imposition of crisis in the workplace (McDonnell, 2009). For example, in Arizona's K-12 system, where teachers are amongst the lowest paid in the country and seniority has been rescinded after three consecutive years of layoffs (roughly 5,500 in 2009 alone), public-sector unions, including the Arizona Education Association, mobilized in the spring of 2010 to support a one percent sales-tax increase—once again to "save education" (Wynn, 2009; www.yeson100.com, 2010).

Yet, while some radical, class-oriented analyses have sought to defend the university as the "last great commons" (Harvie, 2004; www.beneaththeu.org, 2010), we wish to argue the opposite: that public education at the K-12 and university level is not worth saving on its own merits. To echo teaching assistants Casas-Cortes and Cobarrubias (2006), rather than an independent ivory tower, the university should be understood as a site of production "crisscrossed by intense relations of power" (pp. 123–124). As such, defending education is only important inasmuch as the educational system is the site of labor and struggle for nearly all Americans under the age of 18, the approximate 6.2 percent of the U.S. workforce involved as teachers, faculty, and support staff in K-12 and higher education (U.S. Bureau of Labor Statistics, 2015), and the roughly 20.2 million college and university students enrolled in academic year 2015 (National Center for Education Statistics, 2015). Throughout the labor regime of schooling, one may encounter class struggles over wages and control of working time between actors situated at every level of the institutional hierarchy. Therefore, what is important in struggles around education is not funding as such, but control over wages, costs, and the labor process (including the content of curriculum) exercised by those who work and learn in these institutions. Although education may certainly encompass valuable and desirable opportunities and objectives, we fundamentally maintain that the interests of educational institutions are not necessarily the interests of those working within them (whether understood as students, staff, or instructors), and indeed the two interests should be generally understood as opposed.

EDUCATION AS A LABOR PROCESS AND DISCIPLINARY REGIME

The self-discipline and acceptance of authority that correspond to a willingness to engage in waged work is one of the major social variables mediated through formal education. If we accept Marx's dictum that capitalism is first-and-foremost a system that imposes waged labor (Marx, 1990), then school is a primary site whereby individuals' cooperation with and performance of such labor is both disciplined and adjudicated for future employers. In the Marxian schema, only human labor power, or the ability to perform work, is capable of producing surplus value (and thus profit). Human labor is highly variable in its utility and intensity, as are the volume and kinds of commodities it takes to recreate the body's capacity and willingness to work from one day to the next. These are politically determined qualities around which massive struggles play out that have significant effects upon the profits of the individual capitalist and upon the circulation of capital as a whole (Cleaver, 2004). In keeping with the above, an over-riding ambition of capitalist planners has been the production of what Gramsci (1971) called "rational demographic composition" (p. 281)—through the establishment of base habits, skills, and disciplines amongst (ideally) laboring populations. Since the middle of the ninteenth century, a preferred mechanism for accomplishing this task in industrializing societies, following base expropriation of the means of production and more violent expressions of cultural genocide, has been through public and compulsory education (Freire, 2003; Gatto, 2000; Giroux, 2001; Hooks, 1994; McLaren, 1999).

For this reason it is useful to separate education as an emancipatory objective—as a question of becoming "more fully human in the process of achieving freedom" (Freire, 2003, p. 49)—and education as it is generally practiced within state-sanctioned educational institutions (e.g., schools). Central to our argument is the assertion that the two have very little to do with one another. The schooling we administer, and more generally the regime of credentialing, is in practice an enclosure of learning which adds "prejudice and guilt to the discrimination which a society practices against some of its members and compounds the privilege of others" (Illich, 2000, p. 33). In this sense, we might think of schooling as a contemporary complement to the criminal justice system—each enacting a distribution of status and opportunity that is applied to constrain or improve future conditions of labor and vulnerability to state violence.

For the student, institutionalized schooling represents an unpaid labor process in which the commodity produced is his or her own abstract labor power, with attributes and work habits that make it suitable for employment and reproduce class divisions along lines of race, ethnicity, gender, and sexuality. Such value-added labor power responds to discipline, expects surveillance, and accepts hierarchical mediation. In his ethnography of working-class English school boys, Willis (1976) neatly summed up the articulation between abstract labor power and schooling: "Concrete labour power is important not for its intrinsic or particular contribution but for its withdrawal of the potential negative: it will not interrupt or disrupt production" (p. 136). In other words, while the "educated" individual might not always do what she/he is told, she/he is intended to rarely do the unexpected. At the college level, where future administrators and tech-nocrats are trained and evaluated, it becomes fundamentally important to ensure that people will accept responsibility for carrying out nonsensical, dangerous, or otherwise foolish tasks with which they disagree (Caffentzis, 1980). This is accomplished through busy-work, enforcement of attendance policies, and the logic of grading.

Within this process, we, as instructors, act as the foremen/women of the classroom, assigning rewards or punishment for the quality and quantity of labor performed (as well as the compliance and conformity to norms of behavior during the labor process itself—this is especially true for instructors in K-12 education—see Langhout, 2005). If school is a disciplinary apparatus for the imposition of work, the wages of that work are manifest specifically in the form of grades, which act as a tool for the evaluation of the labor performed, a means of exerting social pressure around such performance, and finally a direct tie to future financial compensation. Those who are most capable and most willing to accept the arbitrary imposition of schoolwork are rewarded with the possibility of higher wages in the future through a more advantageous and privileged posi-tion in the labor market.

Thus, through grading, education as a qualitative practice and objective is devalued in favor of a disciplinary system of rewards and punishments. Caffentzis (1980), writing for the *Midnight Notes Collective*, suggested that the degree of suc-cess of this system on a laboring population can be measured through the concept of entropy—whose rate is measured as the proportion of available energy in a population relative to the quantity of (objectified) labor actually appropriated from it. Within this system, workers represent the basic unit of analysis: "eternally ener-getic, crafty, obedient, cowardly, insolent, revolting, but always in a motion that is the only source of work, development, *surplus*" (p. 261). Our job as educators is critical to maintaining the rate of entropy as advantageous to capital, sorting high-from low-entropy students toward the constitution and maintenance of as com-pliant and productive (that is, low entropy) a workforce as possible under existing conditions. This is to say that our primary function is not merely to add value to the labor power of the working class through the application of productive skills, but also to render it governable by producing gradation and hierarchies within it, sorting it for future employers.

EVERYDAY RESISTANCE AND SCHOOLING

People in subordinate positions oftentimes engage in activity that indirectly challenges and evades discipline and attempts to minimize the performance of coerced and exploitative labor. As Scott (1992) argued, regardless of intentionality this activity should be understood as manifestly political—and indeed it may do more to shape relations of discipline and administration than does overt political activity. There are direct, reciprocal connections between everyday forms of resistance and more visible strikes, riots, and protests (Kelly, 1996; Watson, 1971). Critics of the everyday-struggle framework tend to emphasize the fragmented, seemingly isolated nature of its associated activities; however, this ignores the extent to which there is a necessary complicity between coworkers in many forms of everyday resistance that suggests not only the cooperative nature of seemingly disorganized actions, but also the extent to which these produce forums for the development of more massified political action. Everyday resistance is visible in the beginnings of the Indian *gherao* (Dasgupta, 1992), Chinese labor riots (Marks, 2010), and the urban riots that occurred in the United States in the 1960s/1970s (Piven & Cloward, 1976)—each case forcing concessions on wages and social spending.

It is commonplace for students to suffer trying to meet the manifold expectations placed upon them. At the same time, they are no strangers to a litany of everyday resistance practices, employing strategies such as absenteeism, tardiness, diversions in the classroom, disrespect of authority figures, and otherwise goofing off to lessen the unpleasant aspects of schooling. Students utilize physical space and knowledge generated from many years of negotiating power in the classroom to deploy these strategies with as few negative repercussions to themselves as possible (Langhout, 2005; McFarland, 2001). Some of the most obvious examples of the ways that these struggles manifest in the classroom include constant efforts to half-ass the work that is assigned, or to get away with refusing it altogether (indeed, it is not uncommon for instructors to cynically combat this by assigning more work than is reasonable, with the calculation that only a fraction of it will actually be performed). Cheating and plagiarism are, likewise, efforts to transform the work/wages ratio, while more collective forms of action include social pressure against "brown-nosing" and any response to an effort to compel participation that manifests with too much enthusiasm (Mcfarland, 2001). How many of us have asked a question to a classroom that surely knows the answer, only to be met with silence and blank stares?

If we accept the arguments so far presented—e.g.—(1) the classroom is a site of everyday struggles between students and instructors over wages (grades) and conditions of labor; (2) our labor under capitalism is primarily performed upon the future productive labor power of our students; (3) the repercussion of the successful completion of our work is the (re)production of socially average labor; and (4) socially average labor is the central element in the uninterrupted functioning of capitalism—then perhaps it is possible to allow this work discipline to slip, by doing a bad job, identifying and allowing high-entropic habits, practices, and sentiments to play out more openly amongst students/workers and instructors (discussed further). We offer this line of thinking as an alternative to traditional conceptions of radical or progressive pedagogies, and contend that it offers opportunities for intervening in discourses at their base, nullifying work speed ups with little risk, and allowing for lecture and class time to be turned toward subject matters that are more directly relevant and less alienating for both instructor and students.

PROBLEMATIZING RADICAL AND PROGRESSIVE PEDAGOGIES

We are expressly attempting to articulate an alternative to what have been variously referred to as radical, critical, or activist pedagogies. Various progressively aligned pedagogies seek to identify and challenge systems of oppression; to empower students to be critical thinkers; and to encourage students to participate in activism. We feel that when deployed within the institutional constraints of our classrooms these formulations frequently suffer from a particular set of narcissistic assumptions and a lack of reflexivity: A professor's perception of a lack of critical thinking skills among their students may be no more than a self-satisfied reflection on the privilege and necessity of his or her station. Further, it is important to make the assertion that the suppression of critical thinking can be better understood as the forcing of critical speaking and acting underground by a disciplinary process that closely polices and regulates students' movements and statements beginning at a young age. The conceit that a single college course consisting of an admonishment to think critically will undo more than a decade's worth of discipline is foolish and destined to fail, as is the supposition that raising consciousness is an adequate measure to address structural racism and poverty. Schooling doesn't banish these problems—it is an essential part of their reproduction.

While pedagogical styles may vary, the economy of these styles (for the most part) tends to remain the same. Work (study) is performed for a wage (grade), and insufficient or inadequate work is penalized. Progressively aligned pedagogies usually do little to challenge these labor relations, and often instead reinforce the most disempowering conventions of leftist position and practice. For students and teachers alike, the trajectories of alternative pedagogies are delimited by institutional norms and initiatives that operate principally to maintain one's position within institutional hierarchies. Conflicts within the institution are thus mediated, delayed and displaced to prevent work stoppages and other sorts of widespread refusals. At the same time, progressively aligned pedagogies often summon activism as a desirable category of activity, and frequently present participation in organized campaigns and nonprofit advocacy organizations as the correct site for committed political struggle. As observed by Andrea Smith (2007) in her introduction to *The Revolution Will Not be Funded*, the historical professionalization of organizing and advocacy in the United States occurred in the aftermath of waves of mass action in the 1960s/1970s, and often served to defuse the initiative of communities and groups engaged in struggle. This is similar to the institutionalization of unions in the United States following the labor insurgency of the 1930s (Brecher, 1977). Concessions granted to these movements came packaged with mediating bodies that institutionalized formerly unmanageable class struggles, transforming struggles into class deals that incorporated them into the logics of capitalist accumulation and state governance.

We feel there is a good basis in history for abandoning our attachment to these avenues of political participation. The role of the activist and the organizer—institutionally enshrined through unions, nonprofits, and electoral politics—has historically been to mediate class struggle by shifting the venue of dispute from the site of shared exploitation to bureaucratic mechanisms of redress (Brecher, 1997; *Incite!*, 2007; Piven & Cloward, 1976). These institutions defuse initiative, monopolize legitimacy (by representing people through professional advocates), and temper militancy in order to maintain their position as representatives. Their function has been to defuse and harness site-specific struggles, turning them toward institutional ends.

In 1972, Vaneigem famously wrote "[p]eople who talk about revolution and class struggle without referring explicitly to everyday life, [...] such people have a corpse in their mouth" (p. 7). Vaneigem's point is that it is in our daily social interactions where we must locate the composition of state and capitalism. The suite of activities that are generally referred to as "political activism" usually appear outside the scope of everyday life, and at a scale that is unapproachable. Esteva and Prakash (2001) illustrated this point in a discussion of the general Agreement on Tariffs and Trade, or GATT, trade agreements:

> GATT or the World Bank are emblems, symbols or paradigms [...] they are unbeatable at the abstract level. [...] To identify the implications of GATT everywhere, to be fully aware of what it means in specific local struggles is extremely useful. [...] Here, local struggles can make them irrelevant at the localized level; and an accumulation of localized struggles may well produce a new set of arrangements (p. 21).

Connecting this to the classroom, our experience as students and as instructors is that exhortations to engage in activism and attempts to teach toward social change generally offer austere and distant conceptions of the political. Chatterton, while discussing his attempts to teach activism, shared a student's reaction to the subject matter: "he felt he was not up to the task of social change: [...] why am I not participating fully in such activities? I'm being selfish and conscious of it […] will I do more in the future? I don't know. It takes brave people (with power) to make a difference. I don't feel brave enough to step out of my normal lifestyle" (Chatterton, 2008, p. 435). Chatterton's students are reacting to the altruism, self-sacrifice, and hard work that seems to be required of them to create social change. The sort of concerns and self-doubt being expressed, far more than the cop-outs of a selfish college student bound for private sector employment, seem to be a reaction to the actual work regime of the nonprofit and advocacy sectors, where wages and workloads are negatively correlated. In light of the work regime of the educational sector and the current political and fiscal landscape of neoliberal austerity, the continued banishment of political action to mediating bodies contributes to our own disempowerment.

TEACHING TOWARD ENTROPY

An accumulation of localized struggles producing a new set of arrangements (of the type summoned by Prakash and Esteva (2008)) is what we advocate. We feel that this can only be accomplished through valuing everyday forms of struggle, and indeed everyday concerns, above our concerns with an (abstract) institutional landscape. If we emphasize these more prosaic activities as political, then it becomes possible to argue that there are myriad, dispersed struggles not only against the austerity regime being imposed on public education in the current fiscal and economic crisis, but also to the regime of schooling itself. Instead of aiming at more-or-less abstract economic structures or formal policies, these struggles are typically day-to-day disputes over practices around coursework, grades, and attendance policies.

Indeed, these have shaped much of our experience as university instructors. We typically spend more time assigning and managing grades than we do preparing or delivering course material. More often than not, when students come to visit us at office hours, this is directly related to negotiations over grading. Many of the complaints and grievances that we often hear students make have to do with the quantity of work imposed and with the kind of treatment and interaction that students have with instructors. This is typical of boss/worker relationships—it is bad enough having a shitty, boring job that consumes the best hours of your day, without also having a boss who is an asshole.

What we have in mind is a strategy we'd like to call *teaching toward entropy*. To offer just one example, an underappreciated tactic that instructors use against the speed up of the work regime involves what is essentially doing a worse job at sorting our students, something that—although in most cases inadvertent—has nonetheless been a steady trend across higher education, with the national average of grade point averages growing from 2.9 in 1992 to 3.11 in 2007 (Rojstaczer, 2010). Various causes have been suggested for this phenomenon, from the pressure on students to succeed to inflated expectations and feelings of entitlement (Rojstaczer & Healy, 2010). We would add another: as workloads increase and teaching is increasingly automated, it becomes increasingly difficult as instructors and teaching assistants to provide the kind of individual care that a thorough sorting of performance would require. In the face of constant, everyday efforts by our students to transform the work/wage ratio in their favor (discussed previously), the path of least resistance for instructors (e.g., the least work intensive) is to cede, individually and collectively, to this pressure. Thus, in the aggregate, as our labor regime is sped up, university instructors are turning out an inferior product.

From an institutional perspective this trend presents all kinds of challenges, not the least of which is the degree of reliability that graded performance provides for employers, graduate programs, fellowships, etc. Of course, it must be acknowledged that grade inflation is not always and altogether benign. Some forms of grade inflation may augment the differentiating, hierarchy-reproducing qualities of education by privileging the already privileged. We refer here to such practices as buying test papers, fraternities and sororities that save and reproduce exams, the intentional inflation of grades in elite and professional programs and schools, etc. At the same time, these practices do considerable damage to the purposes of formal education, because some workers are effectively counterfeiting their credentials, feeding into the entire cycle of business fraud, financial manipulation, etc., that have become so endemic to late capitalism. Here we wish to avoid a normative evaluation, except to recognize the axiom that every form of resistance can lead to the reification of social and economic hierarchies, just as every "solution" to capitalist crises inevitably leads to further and deeper contradictions.

Discussing everyday resistance as a form of political activity with students turns attitudes and practices everyone tends to engage in (and everyone gets told to feel bad about) into legitimate and rational responses to an unpleasant situation—and is a surprisingly effective vehicle for discussing power relations and power effects in the context of everyday life. This can be pursued in the following ways.

1. Facilitating frank conversation about the disciplinary, normalizing, and legitimizing dimensions of the educational apparatus, and the unpleasant or damaging ways that associated pressures structure students' lives.
2. Sublimating and recuperating the sensual aspects of alienation (immediatism, indolence, substance abuse)—exploring the utility of these rather ubiquitous compulsions for capital, and their function within a psychic economy.
3. The fostering of class resentment—a task that is easily accomplished at many public universities, where there are broad disparities in levels of access

and privilege. These should be strategically denaturalized, and tensions that arise should be discussed without an ameliorative agenda.

4. Enacting grading metrics with diminished or alternative performance variables, while fostering social pressure that spurs participation. When students take their responsibility to have a respectful and intelligent discussion with their peers more seriously than their obligation to complete coursework (or even to earn a passing grade), we may in fact improve our overall pedagogic outcomes.

5. Encouraging spontaneity, horizontal thinking, and versatility as habit and inclination.

6. Doing away with or disregarding as much busy work as possible. Instructors can even discuss with students the reasons for waiving requirements (e.g., because you're already overworked and things are easier for everybody that way; because such requirements are arbitrary and there are clearly better, less alienating things to do with one's time).

7. Highlighting and validating everyday forms of resistance in the classroom, as a way of unpacking the disciplinary behaviors of hierarchical institutions (something with which students are inevitably familiar). Certainly as a job skill, the ability to critically understand bureaucracies in order to undermine them, avoid their scrutiny and maintain an appearance of productivity are more valuable than being barely conversant with one or another obtuse social scientific theory.

8. Diverting lectures and class time to discussion of issues on campus and dynamics affecting students' lives—e.g.—policing, racial tensions, individual pressures to perform, conflicts in dorms, shitty interactions with bosses or professors (but we repeat ourselves), anxiety about postgraduation employment, student debt, and tuition hikes. These are issues that students are almost universally concerned about and generally eager to discuss. And they provide an immediate frame of reference for unpacking racial and class hierarchies and affirming everyday, spontaneous and insurgent forms of resistance.

Although by no means an exhaustive list, we have found that the above tactics tend to denaturalize the classroom and produce a refreshingly honest and open learning environment. As an instructor, it is easy to be frank about the work relationship you are involved in with your students. People may not know Marxism, but they know that they don't like coerced or alienating labor. In our experience, most students are more than willing to admit that they are pursuing credentials above all other things, and that the majority of schoolwork is not worth performing for other than punitive reasons. Were we to pay attention to what Scott (1992) called the hidden transcripts (e.g., the quiet but persistent forms of subterfuge, evasion, and resistance) that circulate among our students—and even our own suppressed beliefs and desires—it is likely that we would find that such attitudes are both commonplace, explicit and perfectly reasonable. The work relationship of the classroom is nowhere more apparent than in the ways students justify the performance of otherwise meaningless work by reminding themselves that it's just a hoop they have to jump through to find optimal employment later.

CONCLUSION

In closing, we have argued that those of us concerned with social justice and confronted by austerity budgeting in the educational sector have often deployed education as an extremely mystifying cornerstone of progressivism. In doing so, we ignore the immediate, everyday class dynamics at play within the current crisis and assist in the further structural adjustment of our everyday lives.

Accepting a class analysis, we submit that there is no way to understand the changes being imposed through the current crisis and its academic industrial complex except as attacks on working class power, on our control over our labor, on our wages, and finally as a speed up in the labor regime. Yet despite this assault, the massive decomposition that neoliberal restructuring is meant to accomplish *vis-a-vis* the working class can always be met with recomposition, and myriad opportunities promise to develop as this process unfolds. Recognition of our class position as both foremen and workers within the education process is a step toward developing strategies of resistance that can be shared and generalized within and across this position and enacted without mediation.

What we are arguing, essentially, is for the recognition of the common and everyday nature of class struggle within the academy, struggles that already define our work relationships and should be recognized as doing so. Class struggle isn't somewhere else—it operates between students and instructors, just as it operates between instructors and our bosses and employees and university administrators. We do not need to teach our students to engage in class struggle but instead to ally with them and help to draw out and legitimize the practices, beliefs, etc., that already operate in resistance to work and authority.

Of course, the above does not exhaust the need or opportunity for the composition of class insurgency. In Tucson, we have been supporters and participants in organizing, walkouts, protest, and other forms of direct action led by middle and high school students to defend ethnic studies curricula against racist attacks by the local school board and the state government. Across the country, insurgent efforts by students to escalate racial conflict on campus in order to increase the power and representation of oppressed groups (including, recently, the heroic involvement of Black football players at the University of Missouri) offer another inspiring example. We are encouraged by the growing movement among students, parents, and teachers in K-12 schools to refuse standardized testing and assessment. Finally, of course, the organized efforts of teachers, graduate students, adjunct instructors, and part-time staff to improve their wages and working conditions deserve our unconditional support.

But we must at the same time avoid the temptation to view the dynamics that play out in our classrooms as somehow removed from or unrelated to the conflicts described previously. Because although the institutional power relationships between students and teachers are unequal, our cooperation with this inequality is the most crucial element of our labor power that we can withhold from the work regime. In the context of both domestic and global austerity agendas, we should recognize these inequalities as a source of exploitation for all involved; their maintenance as a structural barrier to the development of free, unalienated activity and shared understanding (read: learning); and their negation as a movement toward far better conditions of life.

REFERENCES

Arizona State Constitution. Retrieved from http://www.azleg.gov/const/Arizona_Constitution.pdf

Brecher, J. (1977). *Strike!* Boston, MA: South End Press.

Butler, J. (2009). Save California's universities: The promise of affordable higher education is dying. The University of California's students and faculty demand answers. *The Guardian*, Sunday 4 October. Retrieved from http://www.guardian.co.uk/commentisfree/cifamerica/2009/sep/30/california-university-berkeley-budget-protest

Caffentzis, G. (1980). The work/energy crisis and the apocalypse. Retrieved from http://www.midnightnotes.org/pdfapoc16.pdf

Casas-Cortes, M., & Cobarrubias, S. (2006). Drifting through the knowledge factory. In E. Biddle, D. Graeber, & S. Shukaitis (eds.). *Constituent imaginations: Militant investigations, collective theorization* (pp. 112–126). New York: AK Press.

Chatterton, P. (2008). Using geography to teach freedom and defiance: Lessons in social change from 'autonomous geographies'. *Journal of Geography in Higher Education, 32*(3), 419–440.

Cleaver, H. (2004). *On schoolwork and the struggle against it.* New York: Treason Press.

Dasgupta, S. K. (1992). *West Bengal's Jyoti Basu: A political profile.* New Delhi: Gian Publishing House.

Del Gandio, J. (2013). Arrests and repression as a logic of neoliberalism. In A. J. Nocella II, & D. Gabbard, (Eds.). *Policing the campus: Academic repression, surveillance, and the occupy movement* (pp. 3–14). New York: Peter Lang.

Esteva, G., & Prakash, M. S. (2001). *Grassroots postmodernism: Remaking the soil of cultures.* New York: Zed Books.

Foucault, M. (1979). *Discipline and punish: The birth of the prison.* New York: Random House.

Freire, P. (2003). *Pedagogy of the oppressed.* New York: Continuum International.

Gatto, J. T. (2000). *The underground history of American education: A school teacher's intimate investigation into the problem of modern schooling.* Oxford: Oxford Village Press.

Giroux, H. A. (2001). *Theory and resistance in education: Towards a pedagogy for the opposition.* Westport, CT: ASOR Books.

Giroux, H. A. (2010). Higher education after September 11th: The crisis of academic freedom and democracy. In A. J. Nocella II, S. Best, & P. McLaren (Eds.). *Academic repression: Reflections from the academic industrial complex* (pp. 92–111). Oakland, CA: AK Press.

Giroux, H. A., & Giroux, S. S. (2004). *Take back higher education: Race, youth, and the crisis of democracy in the post-civil rights era.* New York: Palgrave Macmillan.

Gramsci, A. (1971). *Selections from the prison notebooks.* United States: International Publishers.

Harvie, D. (2004). Commons and communities in the university: Some notes and some examples. *The Commoner* 8. Retrieved from www.thecommoner/uk.org

Hodge, D. W. (2013). Policing college campuses: Race, social control and the securitization of college campuses. In A. J. Nocella II, & D. Gabbard (eds.). *Policing the campus: Academic repression, surveillance, and the occupy* movement (pp. 29–38). New York: Peter Lang.

hooks, b. (1994). *Teaching to transgress: Education as the practice of freedom.* New York: Routledge.

Illich, I. (2000). *Deschooling society.* London: Marion Boyars Publishers.

INCITE! Women of Color Against Violence. (2007) (eds.). *The revolution will not be funded: Beyond the non-profit industrial complex.* Boston, MA: South End Press.

Kelly, R. D. G. (1996). *Race rebels: Culture, politics and the black working class.* New York: Free Press.

Langhout, R. D. (2005). Acts of resistance: Student invisibility. *Culture and Psychology, 11*(2), 123–158.

Marks, B. (2010). Living in a whirlwind: The food/energy/work crisis of 2008–09. In Team Colors (eds.). *Uses of a whirlwind: Movement, movements, and contemporary radical currents in the United States* (pp. 255–268). Oakland, CA: AK Press.

Marx, K. (1990). *Capital, volume 1.* New York: Penguin Classics.

McDonnell, T. (2009). Students, faculty rally for solidarity. *Arizona Daily Wildcat,* 25 September. Retrieved from http://wildcat.arizona.edu/news/students-faculty-rally-for-solidarity-1.529525

McFarland, D. A. (2001). Student resistance: How the formal and informal organization of classrooms facilitate everyday forms of student defiance. *The American Journal of Sociology, 17*(3), 612–678.

McLaren, P. (1999). *Schooling as a ritual performance: Towards a political economy of educational symbols and gestures.* New York: Rowman & Littlefield.

National Center for Education Statistics. (2015). Fast facts. Retrieved from https://nces.ed.gov/fast facts/display.asp?id=372

Piven, F. F., & Cloward, R. (1976). *Poor people's movements: Why they succeed, how they fail.* New York: Vintage Books.

Prakash, M. S., & Esteva, G. (2008). *Escaping education: Living as learning within grassroots cultures.* New York: Peter Lang.

Rojstaczer, S. (2010). GradeInflation.com: Grade inflation at American colleges and universities. Retrieved from http://www.gradeinflation.com/

Rojstaczer, S., & Healy, C. (2010). Grading in American colleges and universities. *Teachers College Record* 4 March. Retrieved from http://www.tcrecord.org/content.asp?contentid=15928

Scott, J. C. (1992). *Domination and the arts of resistance: Hidden transcripts.* New Haven, CT: Yale University Press.

Smith, A. (2007). Introduction. In INCITE! (eds.). *The revolution will not be funded: Beyond the non-profit industrial complex.* Boston, MA: South End Press.

U.S. Bureau of Labor Statistics. (2015). "May 2014 National Occupational Employment and Wage Estimates." Retrieved from http://www.bls.gov/oes/current/oes_nat.htm#00-0000

University of Arizona. (2015). 2015–2016 estimated cost of attendance. Retrieved from https://finan-cialaid.arizona.edu/undergraduate/2015-2016-estimated-cost-attendance

Vaneigem, R. (1972). *The revolution of everyday life*. Retrieved from http://www.snake.orconhosting.net.nz/books/THE%20REVOLUTION%20OF%20EVERYDAY%20LIFE.doc

Watson, B. (1971). Counter-planning on the shop floor. *Radical America*. May–June, 1–10.

Willis, P. (1976). *Learning to labour: How working class kids get working class jobs*. New York: Columbia University Press.

Wynn, M. (2009). Teacher layoffs. *The Arizona Republic* 20 April 20. Retrieved from http://www.azcentral.com/news/articles/2009/04/20/20090420teacherlayoffs.html

CHAPTER SIX

Owning Curriculum: Megafoundations, the State, and Writing Programs

ERIK JUERGENSMEYER AND SUE DOE

The problem is that placement into an extra section of composition causes the student to be on the wrong horse on the carousel, to miss the ring, and be off the road map to success. FYC is usually the prerequisite to all major courses, so this is a major inefficiency from the point of view of administrators watching the assembly line [...] They don't see students as having different needs, so they don't value programs that try to address those needs.

—J. EDLUND *(2016, PARA. 3)*

The US university, long touted as embodying the democratic principles of academic freedom and the free exchange of ideas, can be a dangerous place [...] for a rhetorician to teach and practice the political arts of democracy.

—M. J. BRAUN *(2011, P. 137)*

Nearly all stages of education are encountering challenges brought on by the academic-industrial complex. Stories of intimidation, excessive oversight, program and position eliminations have abounded for some time (Feldman, 1999; Giroux, 2007; Yee, 2011). Why? Why are such aggressive tactics used on the stewards of future generations of thinkers and citizens? Are we merely collateral damage of the machinations of ideological complexes? Does our position on the front lines of new ideas simply make our exposure to a barrage of fire unavoidable? Or, do thinkers and educators pose the greatest risk to those who threaten our democratic ideals because our workplace is a place where informed individuals think and collaborate and generate ideas that lead to change? Because we are groups of citizens occupying a place where a range of actors—community members, students, faculty, staff—freely unite to combat repression? The following details a space where faculty members at two different institutions have watched their discipline and curriculum undergo significant changes brought on by the corporatization of education. It investigates the roots of the repression, details collaborations that challenge democratic approaches to education, and offers strategies for reclaiming our roles in controlling the curriculum that we feel is best for fulfilling our goals as teachers of critical thinking and educators of citizens.

Academic repression is nothing new to teachers of rhetoric and composition and especially writing program administrators: oftentimes, writing program administrators (WPAs) are coerced into mandating standardized curricula that succumb to a variety of external outcomes and priorities. As first-year writing courses are often located within general education systems, countless voices often attempt to control content specific to the disciplines of rhetoric and composition. This is especially relevant in schools where neoliberalized administrations view writing and rhetoric not as disciplines of their own but as basic skills to simply be taught to students early in their academic careers so they can efficiently move through their disciplines in order to quickly graduate and enter the workforce (Scott, 2009; Welch, 2008). The shift to administrative policies that triumph expediency and are often accompanied by streamlining is best described by Nocella II, Best, and McLaren (2010) in their introduction to *Academic Repression: Reflections from the Academic Industrial Complex*:

> [B]y the 1980s and 1990s, universities and society as a whole were becoming increasingly corporatized, marketized, and globalized. Acting like capitalists committed to the tyranny of the bottom line, universities began the cut-and-slash tactics that Reagan took to social programs in the 1980s, for a profitable enterprise cannot have excess costs, and labor expenses must be minimized. The dynamic that led to the restructuring of universities along corporate lines stemmed from aggressive neoliberal policies. [...] As universities implemented the neoliberal model, and economic realities became more pressing, particularly in the global economic crisis of 2008, universities, like automobile industries and other businesses, continued a trend of downsizing that led to replacing tenured and full-time faculty with part-time, adjunct, and contingent instructors viewed contemptuously as an army of cheap surplus labor (pp. 82–83).

The trends of cutting excess costs, minimizing labor, and general downsizing are a day in the life of many writing faculty. Moreover, because those who primarily teach first-year writing courses—graduate student teachers and nontenured instructors—have little job security and are unable to stand up to the hijacking of their discipline, administrative bodies have even more control over a group of faculty who dare not challenge the decisions. For those few tenured writing instructors (usually serving as WPAs), this creates even more pressure to advocate for colleagues and challenge the restructuring.

One place in which the neoliberal hijacking is most present is in curricular oversight. WPAs are especially familiar with the concept of policed pedagogy explained in Socha's (2013) "Policed Pedagogy: Controlling and Dominating Classrooms, Curriculum, and Courses." Detailing the lack of curricular ownership especially experienced by community college writing instructors, she explained,

> Policed pedagogy, a specific type of academic repression, refers to teaching under external repressive and controlling conditions and influences. Policed pedagogy can take one of three forms: (1) by administration dictating curriculum, lesson plans, methods, physical place of instruction (i.e., online, in the classroom, or hybrid) and materials used; (2) by law enforcement, military or other armed agencies through physical intimidation and coercion; and (3) through propaganda campaigns seeking to instill fear and stigmatization in faculty, staff, and/or students (p. 40).

Whereas all three of these examples are relevant to the types of oppression taking place in the new corporatized postsecondary learning environment we are currently experiencing, it is the first form we find the most troubling as we struggle to control our curriculum from local and state agents.

Arguably, the inexorable march toward state-controlled pedagogy has been fomenting for decades, propelled by the publication of sanctioned reports such as the 1983 *The Nation at Risk: An Imperative for Educational Reform,* which called into question the condition of U.S. education generally, and Rudolf Flesch's (1955) *Why Johnny Can't Read* and *Newsweek*'s (1975) "Why Johnny Can't Write." In Colorado, where we live and work, increasing involvement of the state in matters of higher education was ushered in through passage of the Student Bill of Rights, aka the King Bill in 2001, which assured transferability of general education courses across higher education institutions through *assessable shared competencies.* The originating legislative act, HB 01–1263, required Colorado colleges and universities to develop graduation plans for all students, which are essentially contracts between students and institutions guaranteeing that sixty credit hours will complete the associate's degree and 120 credits hours the bachelors. HB 1263 thus ushered in state-mandated outcomes among general education courses and across institutions. Each course became associated with a regulated set of competencies and content criteria that would presumably make it possible for students to switch schools within the state without suffering academic penalty—a seemingly legitimate objective. Yet the effect was to homogenize and deauthorize local control over curricula that might otherwise address institutional and demographic differences. In the Colorado example, the rhetorical strategy of masking control of curricula, or the policing of pedagogy, as the beneficent arm of the state looking out for its citizens against an educational system run amok (characterized as poor stewards of public monies and perhaps also dangerous, liberal think tanks) is over a decade old. Ironically, the arm of the state was extended by the same conservative forces that traditionally argue for decreased involvement of the state but which apparently are needed when managing university faculty—thus offering direct challenge to the value and integrity of disciplinary expertise and those who claim it.

By 2015, a decade and a half after the Student Bill of Rights was enacted and a decade after Colorado institutions became largely compliant due to the transfer problem largely being solved through extensive statewide review processes, a new stage of compliance was ushered in, this one moving more fully and aggressively into assessment, as called for in the original legislation. Once again the alarm was sounded—a process we find ourselves deep in the middle of. We believe that this regional history reflects trends and processes occurring across the country, bolstered in part by the nationalizing of K-12 curriculum through the Common Core, a preschool to twelfth grade initiative, wherein students are presumably being prepared for college or career.

THE RISE OF MEGAFOUNDATIONS

Effects from the 2006 Report on the Future of Higher Education (aka the Spellings Commission) are still being felt. As many know, it created a dark cloud over postsecondary education and furthered a narrative that describes colleges and universities as entities depriving students of the "skills and knowledge to become economically competitive agents" thanks to "faculty [who] didn't understand what was necessary to achieve this purpose" (Adler-Kassner, 2012, pp. 119–120). The backlash resulting from these accusations has been quite powerful, especially in regards to who has become involved in curriculum design. According to Adler-Kassner (2012), numerous organizations have now become heavily involved and created structures that complicate who determines student readiness and coursework appropriate to that readiness. For example, one such organization, the American Legislative Exchange Council (ALEC), has begun to draft influential legislation and articulation agreements that restrict the number of courses faculty and institutions can deem necessary for certain students (Adler-Kassner, 2012, pp. 120–121). Resulting from this legislative work, institutions have become increasingly pressured to participate in structures such as the Voluntary System of Accountability that seek to hold institutions publicly accountable by comparing them to neoliberal standards of efficiency and expediency. Serving as an umbrella for such postsecondary assessments as the Collegiate Learning Assessment (CLA), the Collegiate Assessment of Academic Proficiency (CAAP), and the Educational Testing Service Assessment Proficiency Profile, the Voluntary System of Accountability controls the measures for identifying students' readiness and ultimately determines which students should take which courses. Such control would not have been possible had it not been for the intense lobbying efforts of the new face in higher education decision making—organizations such as the Lumina Foundation, "the country's largest private foundation focused solely on improving higher education" that has extended its grasp by establishing "roots in the private student loan industry" (Hensley-Clancy & Baker, 2014, para. 2, 11).

Additionally, and complementary to the loan industry, robust efforts are underway to advance a college completion agenda that promises a college diploma in as short a time as possible—what we think of as the accelerate-to-graduate initiative. Such approaches are hailed as strategies for reducing tuition costs and associated student loan debt. Under this scheme, a notion known as Prior Learning Assessment has gained traction. Students are granted credit in as many alternative ways as possible—lowered Advanced Placement (AP), International Baccalaureate (IB), and Cambridge International scores, concurrent or dual enrollment in high school courses awarding college credit, College-Level Examination Program (CLEP), transfer credit for the first sixty credits from virtually any source calling itself "postsecondary," workplace and military credit for on-the-job skills that are deemed "college equivalent," and international agreements in which curricula is broadly construed as transferable even when language proficiency is unassessed by local entities.

Writing for the *San Francisco Bee* and arguing for a renewal of public funding of state colleges and universities, Gubernat (2014), a faculty member in the California State University system, argues that instead of responsible public funding, what is springing up are "silver bullet" solutions that prioritize efficiency and economy over quality. Such efforts win favor with publics who point to "low graduation rates and long times to get a degree as the major culprits" preventing the timely matriculation of students and sustainable budgetary models on college campuses (para. 3).

Unfortunately, the publics who often support such neoliberal solutions to postsecondary education are influenced by a small handful of foundations that represent a majority of the lobbying. One such foundation, Complete College America, has put forth a powerful agenda set to improve time to graduation and completion, a push that—in writing studies—has been dubbed the *war on remediation* (Nabi, 2012). Strategically, this effort has been "focused mainly on state policy leaders, governors, legislators, and boards of higher education" and has sought to drastically reduce the number of remedial courses offered in postsecondary education in an effort to decrease the amount of time one spends in school (Walters, 2012, para. 2). Accompanying the legislative push comes a natural system of rewards and punishments tied into funding that have created a system of "pressure-punitive funding" that leaves schools and especially faculty with very few choices (Walters, 2012, para. 3).

Some states, like Florida, have taken this pressure very seriously, making remedial coursework voluntary for students—"It's up to the students to decide if they need them" (Hefling, 2014, para. 14). These trends are very troubling. Whereas faculty used to be able to apply disciplinary expertise to determine appropriate coursework for students, we are losing the ability to make such decisions, which only hurts students in the long run. And, many of us in writing know who has the most to lose from such changes: "Those who are the least prepared for college stand the most to lose from policies that push students quickly into college-level classes […] those students tend, disproportionately, to be minority and poor" (Mangan, 2014, para. 2). Of course, prior to reaching this point, K-12 students are already in a precarious spot as their mandated curriculum is already making important choices for them.

The Common Core is one such example of curricular decision making at the K-12 level that is sponsored by foundation support and subjected to business values; Lemming (2014) laid out the genealogy of this most recent educational reform. Sponsored by yet another megafoundation—the Bill and Melinda Gates Foundation—Common Core was endorsed by former Secretary of Education Arne Duncan, who piloted many of the ideas when he was superintendent of the Chicago Public Schools. Newkirk (2013) described the relationships between those who constructed the standards and those who benefitted from their sale as unseemly, saying, "It is a fundamental principle of governance that those who establish the guidelines do not benefit financially from those guidelines" (p. 1) and yet, as Newkirk points out, it was the two major testing agencies, the College Board and ACT that wrote the standards and then produced the testing mechanisms adopted to assess performance on them. Newkirk also described the Common Core as a "triumph of branding" (p. 1). He said: "The standards are portrayed as so consensual, so universally endorsed, so thoroughly researched and vetted, so self-evidently necessary to economic progress, so broadly representative of beliefs in the educational community—that they cease to be even debatable" (p. 1).

Seeking to prepare students in consistent ways across the United States for either higher education or careers and work, the Common Core features strong accountability measures that are tied to educational outcomes. These outcomes reflect a regressive politics, according to Lemming who says that "[s]upporters of the Common Core claim that the document's strength lies in its economic potential. If students are prepared adequately for college and careers, they will be able to transition more easily to the workforce and will be effective, competent contributors in growing a strong, national economy" (p. 14). These approaches, Lemming argues, reinscribe a form of colonialism directed toward Fordist definitions of success:

> Since the writers of the CCSS English Language Arts have chosen to privilege a Western, hegemonic discourse, all other knowledge from non-dominant discourses are essentially devalued, making them easy to Other. The knowledge associated with non-dominant discourses then has no power in literacies and discourses reinforced in public schools (p. 105).

Failure to perform under Common Core, assessed through the Partnership for Assessment of Readiness for College and Careers, or PARCC, exam, can result in failing teachers and failing schools (continuing the legacy of No Child Left Behind wherein penalties, terminations, and school closures are the consequence of nonconformity). To incentivize broad compliance with such threat, federal funding was tied to participation through a competitive process known as "Race to the Top." The vast majority of states chose to participate in this "race" due to the ubiquitous fiscal woes being suffered by the states, particularly in terms of education funding. As Lemming points out, the Gates Foundation awarded a quarter of a million dollars to any state that applied for the award "as long as they could prove that they agreed with the Foundation's philosophy on education" (p. 10) and then offered considerably more to "winning" states. We submit that it is not accidental that the current accountability trend and focus on economic markets extends across all levels of public education and is deeply tied to corporate interests.

EXTENDING CONTROL: HOW OUR STATE CONTRIBUTES TO THE PROBLEM

When it comes to succumbing to the pressures of megafoundations and controlling curriculum, the State of Colorado Commission on Higher Education (CCHE) and the Department of Higher Education (CDHE) have consistently implemented mandates that follow suit with megafoundations' agendas and limit faculty control of curriculum. One such example can be seen in the recent revised value assigned to Advanced Placement (AP) test scores—a move that clearly limits faculty ownership of content and curriculum. During the summer of 2015, the state mandated a change in the credits high school students receive from their AP test scores: whereas in the past, faculty were able to determine what a score of 3 or 4 or 5 on the English Language and Composition portion of the AP exam would represent, we now are obligated to follow uniform state standards. For example, in the past, we determined that, based on our departmental outcomes and expectations, which are driven by local needs, as well as broad knowledge of writing curriculum, an AP score of 4 or 5 should count as an elective course but should not exempt a student from taking a core writing course. However, thanks to Agenda Item V, A of the CCHE's May 8, 2015 meeting, a policy was created to "assist students in achieving their goals and the state in achieving Commission Master Plan

Goals 1 & 3 to increase degree completion and close achievement gaps" (p. 1). Of course, the policy could not be unique to different schools within the state system so "credits earned at one public institution will be accepted in transfer and apply to equivalent general education requirements at any receiving public institution and to unify equivalently applied cut scores for major and elective credit to the greatest extent possible," making it even more difficult for faculty to have a say in the process (p. 1). In order to justify its decision making, the CCHE refers to a usual suspect: "Colorado is not alone in this endeavor. The Lumina Foundation (2014), one of the main national organizations assisting states to achieve their goals, has as its own goal for the year 2025 to have 60 percent of Americans hold a college degree, certificate or other high-quality postsecondary credential" (p. 2). Apparently, conforming to the Lumina Foundation and the desire to graduate more students rank more importantly than faculty knowledge of student needs and curriculum. Of course, when faculty protested such a mandate, they were quickly rejected by local administrations.

Another example of this overreach can be seen in how the state of Colorado addresses remedial education—another move that stripped faculty of its say in curricular decisions. In the past, based on knowledge of student preparation and interest in student success, writing faculty created a variety of remedial courses for both reading and writing skills as well as different credit structures for certain students. Faculty identified new ways to help underprepared students, such as creating "stretch" courses that expand instruction beyond one semester to certain underprepared students. However, such efforts conflicted with the agenda to graduate as many students as quickly as possible. In an effort to eliminate practices that slow a student's graduation, the CDHE put forth a plan for streamlined remediation, dubbed Supplemental Academic Instruction (SAI). This plan mandates that all remediation takes place as a corequisite at the same time as nonremedial courses, essentially creating a smaller, studio-type course that accompanies an anchor course. In some institutions, such a policy has to the elimination of other remedial courses and stretch courses—curriculum that writing specialists deemed appropriate for the needs of certain students. This has especially been the situation at one of our institutions where fifty percent of the remedial and 100% of the stretch offerings have been eliminated at the same time the SAI courses were put in place. Of course, when faculty attempted to challenge the curricular hijacking, they were overridden by local administration, who claimed that the State would simply not accept alternative approaches.

To inform faculty of their mandate, the CDHE first distributed a document entitled "Core Principles for Transforming Remedial Education: A Joint Statement" (2012), coauthored by several organizations including Complete College America and Jobs for the Future, a nonprofit organization funded by— you guessed it—the Lumina Foundation. This informational brochure argued that "the assessment and placement process [used to put students in remedial courses] is too often an obstacle to college success" and "the academic focus of remedial education is too narrow and not aligned with what it takes to succeed in programs of study" (pp. 3–4). Clearly, these organizations view faculty decisions over placement and curriculum as *obstacles* to expediency. Following these claims, the authors provide very little research—they cite only one study that justifies their view. In advocating for the elimination of remedial writing courses, they also delegitimize the writing discipline and argue for a curriculum that ignores unique disciplinary content in writing: "With its one-size-fits-all curriculum, remedial education does not provide solid academic preparation for the programs of study most students pursue" (p. 4). Here, writing instruction is devoid of disciplinary content that is designed by writing specialists but instead merely exist as a means of getting students immediately into their programs of study, with the hopes of increasing their time to graduation.

Yet another instance where external agencies, bureaucrats, and administration have stripped faculty ownership from curriculum comes from the current push for standardized outcomes. In the state of Colorado, general education courses that count as guaranteed transfer courses (for some schools, this applies to 100% of the general education curriculum) must conform to a series of criteria and competencies. In the past, these standards were established by faculty from almost all institutions who participated in faculty-to-faculty discussions—biannual meetings and countless email conversations that fostered constructive dialogue about curriculum. As participants in these meetings, we took part in numerous conversations that were designed to revise the core competencies and criteria. Because composition courses are at the core of general education, usually under the larger category of a written communication component, these conversations were incredibly important to us. Naturally, we sought to contribute to the conversations and provide disciplinary expertise to the administrators and assessment coordinators who facilitated the conversations.

One such way we sought to contribute to the conversation was to inform participants of ideas established by writing specialists in our faculty-led national governing organization—the Council of Writing Program Administrators (CWPA). The CWPA has designed, vetted, revised, and articulated a series of outcome statements and frameworks for identifying core skills in postsecondary writing instruction. This seemed like a perfect fit, but not surprisingly, the CDHE chose to ignore these and wholeheartedly adopt others. Both authors have advocated repeatedly for the use of the CWPA outcomes statements at statewide meetings where faculty are supposed to be able to influence administrative decision making, yet, even with support from other colleagues, these pleas have been ignored. Instead, we are now adopting the American Association of

Colleges & Universities Liberal Education and America's Promise, or LEAP, outcomes and rubrics. Rather than deepen student learning, the competency and criteria simplify learning and restrict faculty autonomy. Even though a group of faculty officially "participated" in the "creation" of the outcomes and are encouraged to adapt them to specific contexts that fit into standardized assessments, our experience has been incredibly top-down. Beyond restricting faculty autonomy, these outcomes also restrict state autonomy as such regularized outcomes and rubrics are components of a larger attempt to regularize course content with that of other institutions in our multistate region. Conveniently, LEAP outcomes are part of the Western Interstate Commission for Higher Education's Interstate Passport Initiative that hopes to align higher education institutions within the entire Western region:

> While the overarching goal of the project is simple—to eliminate unnecessary repetition of academic work after students transfer—the ramifications of this goal are profound. The Passport is designed to improve graduation rates, shorten time to degree, and save students money. It can also strengthen existing articulation agreements and help institutions in continuous improvement efforts. All of the Passport elements have been designed by faculty, registrars, institutional researchers, and academic advisors (para. 1).

In all of these situations, the CDHE bypassed faculty input and pushed through an agenda that controls our curriculum and limits our ability to create curricula that we feel is necessary for student learning.

FIXING THE PROBLEM

Gene Sharp's (1973) highly influential 198 Methods of Nonviolent Action provided an arsenal of nonviolent weapons that empowered citizens to overthrow dictators and end tyrannies. To this day, these tactics are being used across the globe to create change. Partitioned into three sections—nonviolent protest and persuasion, noncooperation, and nonviolent intervention—these means of nonviolent struggle and nonviolent direct action have been extremely significant strategies for countless disempowered peoples—people fighting against a variety of faces of oppression and repression. Similarly, yet paling in comparison with Sharp's classic, we propose three categories of tactics to hopefully empower educators to enact change: legislative and legal, local and national, and streetline, in the belief that while connections between tyranny and educational oversight might seem hyperbolic, nothing less than democracy itself is at stake when control over education and curriculum are threatened. We therefore argue for a grassroots effort to take back curriculum and urge educators at all levels to get involved in the ways that follow.

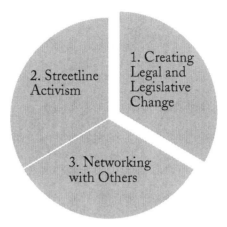

1. Get involved in state and national level legal cases and legislative bills challenging this repressive takeover of higher education. We must join the conversations early and often, questioning the reasons behind the mandates and demonstrating the effects on student learning and faculty knowledge of student learning. Both of us have spent countless hours collaborating on ideas, lobbying colleagues, and travelling across the state to meetings in order to have a say in the important discussions that can drastically affect our curriculum. Serving as regional leaders on various task forces has also helped add legitimacy to our voices as we seek to stop the policing of our curricula.

2. Fight against top-down curricular mandates and push back through activism such as speaking out, boycotting, protesting, rallies, sit-ins, teach-ins, strikes, walkouts, blockades, and banner drops. The more we communicate our experiences and concerns for student learning, the better off we are. However, such communication needs to be grounded in evidence. We need to explain that other forms of curriculum are available. What are our best practices? As Walters (2012) explains,

> Too many academics spend too much time whining about legislators. That's not only unproductive, it's also wrong. The fact is that, with surprisingly few exceptions, state legislators are intelligent, hard-working, thoughtful, and moral individuals who want to help people and improve the economy; they would never deliberately do anything to the contrary. They're buying into the completion agenda primarily because it's all they're hearing. That's the heart of higher education's challenge today. […] Attacking the attackers provides needed balance, but it certainly doesn't solve the problem (para. 24).

3. Get involved in the national and international conversations around academic repression. Unions, student movements, and organizations like the Campaign for the Future of Higher Education (http://futureofhighered. org/) have already laid the foundation to combat external pressures for fair

pay and benefits along with affordable education and by making arguments similar to those in this chapter:

> Graduation rates, in isolation, appear to be gaining ascendancy as the national measure of higher education success. [...] A more fruitful direction would recognize that educational success, like human health, is a complex systemic process. [...] For higher education to flourish, all our leaders—in government and in education—must avoid the lure of reductionist measures and simplistic goals that will foster a false sense of progress now but bitter disappointment at the results in the future (Principles, 2011, para. 27–28).

The Campaign argues for affordable, high-quality higher education that is democratically accessible and reflects the input of its constituencies, particularly the voices of the faculty, staff, and students and "not just administrators, politicians, foundations and think tanks" (About/Contact, para. 2). The Campaign decries the accountability and efficiency trends that are focused on increasing graduation rates and accelerating matriculation without evidence-based research to back up these approaches. Figuring strongly into the Campaign's agenda is Gary Rhoades, Head of the Department of Educational Policy Studies & Practice, Professor and Director, Center for the Study of Higher Education at the University of Arizona, and former General Secretary of the American Association of University Professors in Washington, D.C. Rhoades has denounced the diminution of faculty into *the managed professional* in today's higher education setting. Rather than setting curricular and institutional governance agendas themselves, faculty in new systems of shared governance are largely in the service of top-heavy administrations. This must change.

4. Control the conversation through writing scholarly work, social media, press releases, interviews with the media, and creating handouts and brochures to give out to the public. The more legislators and lobbyists make basic claims about our content, the more we need to do damage control and regain the public's confidence in our work (Hesse, 2012). Writing scholars, for example, have begun to concretely articulate exactly what encompasses our discipline. Relying on the framework of threshold concepts (Meyer, Land, & Baillie, 2010), we are mapping out the core principles of our discipline in order to help external audiences better understand what we do. For example, articulating ideas such as "writing is a social and rhetorical activity" and "writing is (also always) a cognitive activity" can help external audiences better understand our discipline (Adler-Kassner & Wardle, 2015). Moreover, such frames can help combat the current overreliance on outcomes and student assessment and allow us to better shape our curricula

and assessment of student learning by avoiding standardized outcomes and rubrics (Estrem, 2015).

MOVING FORWARD

Hopefully, the information we have provided can help us both communicate the changes taking place in the name of a more efficient approach to education and help us regain control of our curriculum. By providing these tactics and detailing ways to use them, we—along with the other contributors in this book—want to advance an ongoing conversation and concretize a plan of action to challenge academic repression.

REFERENCES

Adler-Kassner, L. (2012). The companies we keep or the companies we would like to try to keep: Strategies and tactics in challenging times. *WPA: Writing Program Administration, 36*(1), 119–140.

Adler-Kassner, L., & Wardle, E. (Eds.). (2015). *Naming what we know: Threshold concepts of writing studies.* Logan, UT: Utah State University Press.

Braun, M. J. (2011). Against decorous civility: Acting as if you live in a democracy. In Kahn, S. & Lee, J. (Eds.). *Activism and rhetoric: Theories and contexts for political engagement* (pp. 137–146). New York: Routledge.

Campaign for the Future of Higher Education. (2012). Retrieved from http://futureofhighered.org/

Campaign for the Future of Higher Education. (2012). About/Contact. Retrieved from http://futu reofhighered.org/about/

Campaign for the Future of Higher Education. (2011). Principles. Retrieved from http://futureof highered.org/principles/

Charles A. Dana Center, Complete College America, Education Commission of The States, Jobs For the Future. (2012). Core principles for transforming remedial education: A joint statement. Retrieved from http://www.jff.org/publications/core-principles-transforming-remedial-educa tion-joint-statement

Colorado Commission on Higher Education. (2015). Agenda Item V, A. Retrieved from http:// highered.colorado.gov/CCHE/Meetings/2015/may/may15_va.pdf

Colorado Commission on Higher Education. (2014). Supplemental academic instruction. Retrieved from https://highered.colorado.gov/Publications/Policies/Current/i-partw.pdf

Complete College America. (2014). Four-year myth: Make college more affordable. Retrieved from http://completecollege.org/wp-content/uploads/2014/11/4-Year-Myth.pdf

Edlund, J. (2016, August 25). Elimination of WPA position at NJCU (Electronic mailing list message]. Retrieved from https://lists.asu.edu/cgi-bin/wa?A0=WPA-L

Estrem, H. (2015). Threshold concepts and student learning outcomes. In L. Adler-Kassner & E. Wardle (Eds.). *Naming what we know: Threshold concepts in writing-studies* (pp. 89–104). Logan, UT: Utah State University Press.

Feldman, J. (1999). *Universities in the business of repression: The academic-military-industrial complex in Central America*. Brooklyn, NY: South End Press.

Flesch, R. (1955). *Why Johnny can't read—And what you can do about it*. New York: Harper & Row.

Giroux, H. A. (2007). *University in chains: Confronting the military-industrial-academic complex*. New York: Paradigm.

Gubernat, S. (2014). Viewpoints: California's higher education systems need more cash, not more catchwords." *San Francisco Bee*. Retrieved from http://www.sacbee.com/opinion/op-ed/article2604792.html

Hefling, K. (2014). Colleges are trying to fix remedial programs. *Huff Post College*. Retrieved from http://www.huffingtonpost.com/2014/04/14/college-remedial-programs_n_5148803.html

Hensley-Clancy, M., & Baker, K. (2014). How a private foundation with student loan ties became a force in higher education. *BuzzFeed News*. Retrieved from http://www.buzzfeed.com/molly hensleyclancy/how-a-private-foundation-with-deep-ties-to-the-student-loan#.qe2oXkao8

Hesse, D. (2012). Who speaks for writing? Expertise, ownership, and stewardship. In J. Rich & E. D. Lay (Eds.). *Who speaks for writing: Stewardship in writing studies for the 21st century* (pp. 9–22). New York: Peter Lang.

Lemming, M. C. (2014). *A Burkean Analysis of the common core state standards: Revealing motive by analyzing the agent-purpose ratio and critiquing the standards with a postcolonial lens*. (M.S. thesis). Retrieved from http://hdl.handle.net/10217/82515

Mangan, K. (2014). Push to reform remedial education raises difficult questions for college. *The Chronicle of Higher Education*. Retrieved from http://chronicle.com/article/Push-to-Reform-Remedial/145817/

Meyer, J. H. F., Land, R., & Baillie, C. (eds.). (2010). *Threshold concepts and transformational learning*. Rotterdam, Netherlands: Sense Publishers.

Nabi, S. (June 19, 2012). Complete College America declares war on remediation. Retrieved from http://www.educationdive.com/news/complete-college-america-declares-war-on-remediation/35692/

National Commission on Excellence in Education. (1983). *A nation at risk: An imperative for educational reform*. Retrieved from http://www2.ed.gov/pubs/NatAtRisk/index.html

Nocella II, A., Best, S., & McLaren, P. (Eds.) (2010). *Academic repression: Reflections from the academic industrial complex*. Oakland, CA: AK Press.

Newkirk, T. (2013). Speaking back to the common core. Retrieved from https://www.heinemann.com/shared/onlineresources/E02123/Newkirk_Speaking_Back_to_the_Common_Core.pdf

Scott, T. (2009). *Dangerous writing: Understanding the political economy of7 composition*. Logan, UT: Utah State UP.

Sharp, G. (1973). *The Politics of nonviolent action*. Boston, MA: Porter Sargent.

Sheils, M. (1975). Why Johnny can't write. *Newsweek*. Retrieved from http://disdblog.com/wp-content/uploads/2012/12/sheils_johnnycantwrite.pdfhttp://disdblog.com/wp-content/uploads/2012/12/sheils_johnnycantwrite.pdf

Socha, K. (2013). Policed pedagogy: Controlling and dominating classrooms, curriculum, and courses. In A. J. Nocella II & D. Gabbard (eds.). *Policing the campus: Academic repression, surveillance, and the occupy movement* (pp. 39–53). New York: Peter Lang.

Spellings, M. (2006). Test of leadership: Charting the future of U.S. higher education. Jessup, MD: U.S. Department of Education—Education Publications Center.

Student Bill of Rights (aka the King Bill). Colorado House Bill 01–1263. (2001). Retrieved from http://highered.colorado.gov/academics/transfers/Bills/hb1263.pdf

Walters, G. (2012). It's not easy: The completion agenda and the states. *Liberal Education, 98*(1), 34–39. Retrieved from http://www.aacu.org/publications-research/periodicals/its-not-so-easy-completion-agenda-and-states

Welch, N. (2008). *Living room: Teaching public writing in a privatized world.* Portsmouth, NH: Boynton/Cook.

Western Interstate Commission for Higher Education. (2015). Interstate Passport Initiative. Retrieved from http://www.wiche.edu/passport/home

Yee, J. (Ed.). (2011). *Feminism for real: Deconstructing the academic industrial complex of feminism.* Ottawa, Canada: The Canadian Centre for Policy Alternatives.

Part III.
Reclaiming

"The hottest places in hell are reserved for those who, in times of great moral crisis, maintain their neutrality."

DANTE

"The time has come to reclaim the stolen harvest and celebrate the growing and giving of good food as the highest gift and the most revolutionary act."

VANDANA SHIVA

Bureaucratic Stifling of Students and Faculty: Reclaiming College and University Campuses

LAURA L. FINLEY

INTRODUCTION

I consider myself an activist, as in addition to my teaching and writing, I am involved in numerous community and campus-based initiatives to address structural and institutional violence and to promote a more peaceful and just world. As an educator, I see one of my primary roles as a university professor to be introducing students to the many ways they can take action on social issues. I do my best to share with my students' information about these issues and to model for them the diverse tools available to activists. I find my students to be interested and excited, and invariably when I share with them some of my own "projects," many jump to get involved. Others are already passionate about something and seek only the mentoring that I can provide.

Unfortunately, too often I have found that university administrators stifle both faculty and student activism. This stifling occurs in a variety of ways, but it basically comes back to the imposition of excessive rules, policies, and procedures. Essentially, bureaucracy gets in the way, and interested students and faculty members either struggle to navigate it the best they can or, I think more frequently, decide that it isn't worth their time. Underlying the bureaucracy are, well, far too many bureaucrats. The bloat of administrators in higher education is nothing short of disturbing and serves to eat up funding, time, and resources that can and should be devoted to activities that benefit students.

This chapter provides insights into the degree to which campus bureaucracy dissuades and undermines student and faculty activism. Drawing on personal experience, the experiences of students with whom I have worked, and examples from other campuses, the chapter highlights the rules, policies, and procedures that make it challenging to engage in campus-based activism. At the root of the problem, I argue, is the increasing number of bureaucrats on campuses whose positions allow or even require them to control activities that should be freely allowed. This is reflective of the growing influence of neoliberalism in higher education. Developed by economists Hayek, Friedman, and others, neoliberalism is an ideology that places the free market as the organizing center of all human life (Harvey, 2005). According to neoliberalists, the profit-seeking corporation should be the model for all institutions, as it is considered the epitome of efficiency (Connell, Fawcett, & Meagher, 2009). Neoliberalists generally favor deregulation and privatization, as the goal is to "minimize government" and thus to allow the free market economy to drive as much of the economy and society as a whole as is possible. Neoliberals generally reject the notion that governments should be providers or even overseers of equality and social justice, instead arguing that it is competition and personal responsibility that allow people to achieve (Giroux, 2004). Slaughter and Leslie (1997) referred to the growing neoliberal influence on higher education as "academic capitalism." Academic capitalism is broadly defined as "the involvement of colleges and faculty in market-like behaviors," and these behaviors have seemingly been increasing over the past twenty years (Slaughter & Rhoades, 2004, p. 37). In all,

> Rather than providing space for intellectual thought and worldly experience, the academy has become an adjunct to corporate profit. The average college campus is ground zero for licensing agreements; construction contracts; outsourcing of bookstores, vendors, concessions and food, laundry, traveling and printing services; corporate sponsoring of buildings, events, speakers, and campus programs; patenting of intellectual property rights; and corporate funding, ownership and direct influencing of research. Such corporatization transforms students into customers, teachers into workers, administrators into CEOs and campuses into market populations (Del Gandio, 2010, para. 4).

The chapter concludes with a brief assessment of what can be done.

RULES, RULES, AND MORE RULES...

While campuses are supposed to be one of the last bastions of free speech, my experience has been that they are often far from it. This is not because students and faculty are disinterested but instead because colleges and universities make it increasingly difficult to actually exercise the rights to speech and expression.

In general, I oppose "free speech" zones, as I feel as though the entire campus should be one. But, in cases like mine, where there is no free, safe, and accessible space at all, a designated zone would surely be an improvement. Staff members have told faculty and students that if they were to use what would appear to be an ideal space in the central portion of campus for a protest or program, the immediate reaction would be to call public safety to stop them. The organization Foundation for Individual Rights in Education (FIRE), and Lukanioff (2012), who works for FIRE, have noted that campuses today stifle free speech by severely limiting the spaces in which it is allowed. In his book *Unlearning Liberty: Campus Censorship and the End of American Debate*, Lukianoff (2012) noted the devastating effects of depriving students of their right to free speech, "an environment that squelches debate and punishes the expression of opinions, in the very institution that is supposed to make us better thinkers, can lead quickly to the formation of polarized groups in which people harbor a comfortable, uncritical certainty that they are right" (p. 9). Even if one does not personally experience censorship, the fear that any kind of public dissent might result in punishment will inevitably have a chilling effect on public speech (Lukianoff, 2012). Ali Cohen, an education major at Coastal Carolina University, held up a sign that articulated the need for time and space to speak freely during a campus rally: "Free speech all the times. Not just when admin says when, where, what about," while the opposite side of the sign read, "#BlackLivesMatter. And I should not be facing charges for writing that [...] in chalk" (Brown, 2014).

In order to even host a group or club meetings, students and faculty on my campus must use a web-based reservation system. Staff in Conference and Events Services receive these requests and must approve them prior to any publicity (formal or informal) about the meeting or event. This is already less than ideal, as it means nothing can occur spontaneously. Worse, the system is terrifically slow, perhaps because the staff members in the department are overwhelmed although surely there are other factors. So, many times, I have planned events on campus only to have to reschedule or to have them be poorly attended because the system of reserving space and marketing events is so slow. I have had to pass up on opportunities to bring renowned guests to our campus because I cannot receive confirmation that a space is available.

On several occasions, I have received confirmation that a room I requested was reserved for me only to find some other group had also been told they could use it at the same time. On other occasions, I have arrived to find the space locked. The event then gets started late and we all stand around awkwardly while waiting for someone with a key to open the space. Many times I have been embarrassed in front of guests I have invited while we stand outside of the allotted space, waiting for someone to provide us access. Further, since my campus, and perhaps others, has no common calendar that is accessible to everyone, we often find that we have scheduled events at times when there are competing programs, thus decreasing the attendance for all of them.

Recently, several faculty and staff members from different areas of campus collaborated to host a day-long peace event, in honor of the UN International Day of Peace. This free event is in its fifth year, and each year students alone or in entire classes attend workshops on various forms of violence, on peacebuilding, and peace education. This year the day was to culminate in a deliberative dialogue on police and community relations, and local media was expected. Unfortunately, the events services people forgot to rearrange the meeting room during lunch, as they had promised, so I/they had to interrupt the speaker just prior to the dialogue to move chairs and tables around. I happened to be leading that workshop, and twice we were asked to move our chairs to a corner of the room while another portion was set up. The organizers of that portion of the day felt terrible, and this frenzied and chaotic situation was far from ideal, especially when guests to the campus and media were arriving. Organizers were upset afterward, and surely many will think twice before taking on this extra work only to meet with such inefficiency.

FUNDRAISING OVER EDUCATING

For example, at my university, similar to others, we celebrated our seventy-fifth anniversary, and thus planned a series of events throughout the year. These celebrations are traditions that aid in fostering repressive practices as well as intellectual value, such as prioritizing branding generalized missions over pedagogy and student achievements. Moreover, oftentimes such annual celebrations include a black-tie gala that resembles corporatization and elitism, usually excluding faculty and students. The fundraisers are discussed as dinners and gatherings of alumni, but in actuality are classist traditions of Western education. Consequently, these events take precedence over teaching and community engagement. The seventy-fifth anniversary celebrations at my institution are the excuse provided this year for how difficult it is to reserve meeting or event space on campus. Evidently, pretty much every sizeable room was reserved in case a seventy-fifth event were to take place. Clearly commemorations like these are important, but it would seem as though a calendar of speakers and major events would have already been developed and thus any room not being used would now be listed as available.

In addition to the issue of finding space for activities on campus, faculty and students were told via email and reminders channeled through our Department Chairs that we must advertise any and all events through our Marketing Division. Those who have tried to advertise events on their own have received less-than-pleasant phone calls and emails reminding them that this is the function of Marketing. Marketing has increased their reach over the last few years, requiring that virtually any initiative that faculty or students want announced in any way be handled through their office, but they have not been able to handle this workload efficiently. In fact, because so much of their time is being spent this year on some seventy-fifth anniversary events, faculty and staff were told that they could not actually take on any other marketing requests. So, while we are told we cannot market our own events, we are now told that they won't be able to do it either. Again, the priority is clearly to support elitist celebrations over activism on campus. Even prior to this, I have submitted requests for marketing events and programs, only to receive such a slow response that the marketing materials come out the day before or even the day of an event. This is not exactly an effective way to get students on campus to attend events and programs, let alone to alert the community. Even when I have provided the text and images I want to use, the individuals in charge of marketing typically rewrite them and find new images, which is a waste of not only my efforts and precious time but theirs as well.

Additionally, all flyers about meetings, events, and programs must be approved by staff in Student Affairs. This is true regardless of whether they have any role in it. If we choose to post materials in a bootleg fashion, inevitably they get removed and someone from Student Affairs issues a less-than-pleasant phone call or email reminding us of the policy. Those who have no "official" affiliation with a student group or organization essentially cannot get approval to post notice of their initiatives. My campus is not alone in this. For example, a 2012 *Huffington Post* story details how a student at Rock Valley College (Illinois) was stifled by bureaucratic policies (Kingkade). Dominic Celletti, a criminal justice student, ultimately filed a lawsuit against Rock Valley College because they prohibited him from posting a flyer on a campus bulletin board. The flyer was far from subversive; it merely reminded his peers to read the Constitution. Celletti had even contacted administrators in Student Life to get permission to post the flyers and was told that he could only use two bulletin boards because he was not affiliated with a recognized student organization. Cellitti posted the flyers elsewhere, then university officials removed them. He tried to appeal to the Board of Trustees, to no avail.

Student groups that do not have "official" status have little power on my campus. They are not eligible for funding support, cannot reserve university vans to transport students to events or activities, are prohibited from posting signage of any sort, and cannot even reserve meeting space. Since the "official" status seems to be the only real way to go at this university, one would think it would be a pretty simple designation to receive. That is not the case, however, as excessive bureaucracy again stands in the way.

One of my students experienced this bureaucratic stifling as she attempted to start a new group on campus. She wanted to start a "She's the First" club, which supports girls' education in countries where many are denied access to schooling.

College student chapters help raise funds to support the selected girls. This student and I, along with a few others who were interested, met to brainstorm what we might like to do on campus, and then she decided to contact the office in charge of registering new student groups to begin the application process. Each time she thought she was done with the required paperwork, something else was added. Before they can even begin, student groups are to have an advisor, a constitution, officers, and documentation of membership. Not exactly easy before you are allowed to advertise the group!

Another student group seeking official status applied last spring but, at the start of the fall 2015 semester, still had not been contacted about their application. They wanted to take part in the fall welcome activities for new students so that they could recruit members, but without official status they were prohibited from participating. They finally learned that with staff turnover in the Division of Student Affairs, their application and basically been misplaced.

"TOO POLITICAL"

A fall 2013 incident on my campus highlights the curtailing of activism deemed to be "too political" by bureaucrats. Some colleagues and I had arranged for Floridians for Alternatives to the Death Penalty (FADP) and Amnesty International USA (AIUSA) to provide training to interested students on community organizing for a death penalty abolition campaign. We brought in two death row exonerees and local activists, and, upon receiving the training, the students were to work with us to promote abolition on campus and beyond. When we learned that Florida Governor Rick Scott had scheduled an execution shortly after the training, these students wanted to hold a vigil on campus. They didn't want anything really elaborate, merely a speak-out session in front of the University's peace pole. Because we wanted to attract attendees beyond our small group, we submitted a request to our marketing division to make an announcement on the intranet. We hit a wall there. Evidently, the person in marketing who received the request thought this activity was "too political," and, rather than seeking clarity about the event from the organizers, went directly to the university president. The Director of Campus Ministry went to bat for us, noting how abolition is a key part of the doctrine of the Adrian Dominican Sisters who founded the institution, and we were thus allowed to go ahead. We were informed, however, that we could not market the event to anyone off campus, nor could we inform local media about it. The minimal and delayed marketing surely prevented many from attending. Further, the debacle sent a powerful message to students, staff, and faculty organizers: clearly there is a significant disjuncture between the social-justice mission the university claims to have and its willingness to actualize it.

Another group of student activists at my university experienced a similar blocking of their "political" activity. The group had once been officially recognized, but as leadership changed due to graduation, it missed a reapplication date and lost its status. They also got the run around as they sought to reapply, and so this group of committed social justice proponents decided to eschew official status and stay an informal club. Despite the fact that Student Affairs should have no oversight of this group's activities because it offers them no support, the group went ahead and checked in with those administrators when they wanted to plan an action on the Day of Silence, October 18, 2014, to honor those who have been marginalized and abused for their sexual orientation or other identities. Their plan was to kick off a campaign called "Don't Wait 'til We're Dead," with the intent of honoring youth instead of demonizing, marginalizing, and silencing them. They told leaders their plan: to carry a coffin around the perimeter of campus silently. They would fill it with a variety of statistics about youth which they planned to distribute as they walked around campus. Despite getting verbal support from those administrators, when the students' actions gathered a large following that was clapping for their initiative, they were told they did not have the right to conduct such an action on campus because they were not an official club. When the student leaders explained that they had sought and received prior approval, they were reprimanded and told to disperse. The primary leader of the group was asked to meet with the administrator in charge of student organizations. He was told that this would be a one-on-one meeting, but instead, that individual invited six other colleagues; the student leader was clearly outnumbered as these seven administrators repeatedly told him his leadership was inappropriate and threatened that he could lose his position as a Resident Assistant. The student told me he felt intimidated, harassed, and silenced, and couldn't see what was wrong with their action nor why a university allegedly committed to social justice would want to curtail student activism.

This fall, several faculty and staff members at my university wanted to organize some type of activity in solidarity with the Black Lives Matter movement. When a new staff member sought approval from her boss, she was told to avoid that language, as it was "too political," and instead she could do something about "all lives matter" or more simply, peace and love. We chose to persist in a small affair, like we did with the death penalty action, rather than do nothing or do something that completely whitewashes the nature of the movement.

While in the previously mentioned cases we all persisted and navigated the bureaucracy, too often faculty and students fear reprisals for their activism and thus decide against it. Both students and faculty can suffer even when they are not actually involved, just presumed to be. Starr (2010) recounted that when students he had never taught engaged in a confrontation with an administrator. They were still discredited as being "his" students because administrators believed all campus activism somehow involved him. They were even speaking on behalf of an organization of which he had no part. Faculty like Starr (2010) have expressed concern that being seen as too political or too radical can jeopardize the chance for retention and promotion, despite the quality of one's teaching or scholarship, which inhibits many. Colleagues may be hesitant to offer support for their peers' activism due to fear of guilt by association, as was the case when University of Colorado sought to punish Ward Churchill. Colleagues at his campus and others across the nation failed to back him, claiming that his words were "unwise" even when many had made similar comments (Starr, 2010). Those who did stand up were demonized in media and by administrators. The dangers of a fearful faculty are huge. As Giroux (2014) explained, "A weak faculty translates into one governed by fear rather than by shared responsibilities, one that is susceptible to labor-bashing tactics such as increased workloads, the casualization of labor, and the growing suppression of dissent. Demoralization often translates less into moral outrage than into cynicism, accommodation, and a retreat into a sterile form of professionalism" (pp. 16–17).

It's not just faculty who face sanctions for their "political" activity. Valdosta State President Ronald M. Zaccari expelled student T. Hayden Barnes for publicly protesting the administration's decision to spend $30 million of student fees to construct a set of parking garages that were environmentally hazardous. FIRE filed a lawsuit on Barnes' behalf that resulted in the overturning of his expulsion and the early retirement of Zaccari, but the fear that this incident may have instilled in other students cannot be accurately measured (Kahn, 2010).

TOO MUCH WORK, TOO LITTLE TIME

Teaching load increases this fall (with no additional pay) have served to dissuade faculty activism. Faculty members like myself who work with student groups to help bring a variety of events and programs to campus are simply tapped out, our time already overdevoted, our emotional state frazzled, and our morale depleted. We are not only teaching the additional class, but are also still responsible for advising some twenty students as they pursue their degrees in a timely fashion, being actively involved with campus committees, engaging in professional development, and being productive with our scholarship. I personally have two major initiatives I have historically coordinated and am trying to do them again this year despite the challenges, but it would be far easier if I just opted out.

The same is true for students. Most of my students are taking a full course-load while balancing at least a part-time job. Many have families or significant others, and a lot commute lengthy distances to campus. Long-time activist Thomas Hayden has maintained that students today are so worried about how they will pay for school and whether they will get a job afterward to pay their loans that they have little time for activism (Martin, 2010). Some have even called college today a form of indentured servitude. Giroux (2014) explained that "crippling debt plus few job prospects in a society in which individuals are relentlessly held as being responsible for the problems they experience leaves little room for rethinking the importance of larger social issues or the necessity for organized collective action against systemic injustice" (pp. 67–68). Further, Giroux (2014) noted that:

> Under this economic model of subservience, there is not future for young people, there is no time to talk about advancing social justice, addressing social problems, promoting critical thinking, cultivating social responsibility, or engaging in noncommodified values that might challenge the neoliberal world view (p. 58).

In sum, students, who are busy trying to pay for their schooling are overworked and want to be assured that their efforts will be rewarded with paid employment. As such, they are more likely to demand an education that will sustain the neoliberalist, corporatized model. Harried professors who too are overworked may find it is easier to provide such an education, rather than a more transformative approach.

IT'S ALL ABOUT THE MONEY, MONEY, AND MONEY

Clearly some of the most effective activist campaigns involve very little funding support, as grassroots groups get creative when they develop and implement campaigns for peace and justice on shoe-string budgets. That being said, few are entirely free. Most colleges and universities severely limit or prohibit funding for faculty or staff activism, allotting it only for presenting professional conferences. I have been denied funding, even when I presented multiple times at a conference, because it was more activist oriented. Worse, resources for student activists are almost nonexistent. On my campus, the Student Government Association (SGA) distributes funding to official student groups upon their request. While these are all good-hearted student leaders, the processes for submitting requests that were put into place by bureaucrats, not students, are cumbersome. First, a group must submit a request to an SGA Senator, who then must craft a "bill" to usher through the SGA for the funding request. This process takes weeks if not more, which might not be suitable for the activity. Some requests are excluded because they don't suit the politics of the students and their advisor. Mostly, student groups don't really know what to do, don't want to deal with all the red tape, and thus at the end of the year, monies remain in SGA's account.

One of the biggest initiatives I coordinate on my campus is called the College Brides Walk. It is a dating and domestic violence awareness-raising event that reaches some 1,200 people annually, many of whom are not from campus but from local schools or groups. Because it is cosponsored by a group of representatives from other campuses and not specifically a club or department at my university, I have always had to front the money for the event and then the funds that were raised through our Grants or Institutional Advancement Office are reimbursed to me. Every year I have waited many months to be reimbursed large sums. In one case, it took four months to receive over $4,000, while this past year it was only after seven months and some more pointed emails to administrators that I was reimbursed the almost $1,500 I was owed. Further, each year the university has raised less money for this, leaving me and the other organizers to find our own sources of funding. We have indeed done so, but it is sad that an event of this magnitude, which continues to receive positive local, state and even national media coverage, cannot be funded in a far better way. Clearly, student groups are unlikely to be able to front the monies needed for their activism.

It is not that funding for all things is scarce at colleges and universities today, however. The growth of bureaucracy has been clearly documented. In 2009, U.S. universities employed more than 230,000 administrators, an increase of sixty percent since 1993. This is a rate ten times the growth of tenure-track faculty members, according to the U.S. Department of Education. A study conducted in 2010 by Greene, a professor of education at the University of Arkansas, found that, at 198 of the leading U.S research institutions, spending on administration rose faster than did funds for instructors and for research (Hechinger, 2012). Lukanioff (2012) noted that, since 1992, the "most conspicuous component" in the rise in cost of higher education is the increased salaries of top administrators and the growth in the number of people employed as campus administrators. Thus "students are not paying for an exponential increase in the quality of their education, but rather for a massive increase in campus bureaucracy" (Lukanioff, 2012, p. 73). The increase in administrators has resulted in dramatically different administrator-student ratios. Even schools claiming to be struggling with budget crises hire hosts of administrators and staffers annually. As Ginsberg (2011) noted,

> As a result, universities are now filled with armies of functionaries—vice presidents, associate vice presidents, assistant vice presidents, provosts, associate provosts, vice provosts, assistant provosts, deans, deanlets, and deanlings, all of whom command staffers and assistants—who, more and more, direct the operations of every school. If there is any hope of getting higher education costs in line, and improving its quality—and I think there is, though the hour is late—it begins with taking a pair of shears to the overgrown administrative bureaucracy. Before they employed an army of professional staffers, administrators were forced to rely on the cooperation of the faculty to carry out tasks ranging from admissions to planning. An administration that lost the confidence of the faculty might find itself unable to function. Today, ranks of staffers form a bulwark of administrative power in the contemporary university. These administrative staffers do not work for or, in many cases, even share information with the faculty. They help make the administration, in the language of political science, "relatively autonomous," marginalizing the faculty (para. 6).

This is definitely the case at my university. While enrollment is down and faculty have been asked to take on additional classes, departments have even smaller budgets for events, and adjuncts have been let go, new bureaucrats who garner much higher salaries than I have been hired across various divisions. While money for professional development remains forever in peril, bureaucrats in some divisions are allowed to upgrade their hotels at conferences, on the university's dime. And, while much of the growth has been in Institutional Advancement, which is tasked with raising funds for the campus, the monies raised by these individuals so far (at least as far as I can tell) barely cover their own salaries, much less support a quality education for students.

At my campus and I imagine many others, activism that might in any way challenge or threaten a donor is a big no-no. Given the increasing corporate funding of higher education, it can be difficult to engage in activism that challenges the companies that financially support a college or university. Conservative billionaire Charles Koch actually funded seven universities in 2005; in 2014, the number was 250 (UnKoch my Campus, n.d.). As Levinthal (2014) explained, the conservative Koch brothers have so much influence through their funding that "The campus of Koch Brothers Academy spans a nation" (n.p.). In 2012, two of the six private charitable foundations the Koch brothers control and personally fund combined to give colleges and universities more than $12.7 million, according to an analysis by the Center for Public Integrity, using Internal Revenue Service tax filings (Levinthal, 2014). This cash was spread among 163 colleges and universities in forty-one states and was in addition to the tens of millions the Koch brothers donated in past decades. George Mason University alone received nearly $8.5 million from the Kochs.

Of course these monies come with strings attached. Although the universities deny that Koch funding has altered the education they provide, those claims are clearly dubious. For example, "the Charles Koch Foundation in 2011 pledged $1.5 million to Florida State University's economics department, a contract between the foundation and university stipulated that a Koch-appointed advisory committee select professors and conduct annual evaluations." Greenpeace argued that professors in Koch-funded departments are involved in climate science denial, despite their academic credentials and even their previous positions on the issue (UnKoch my Campus, n.d.). Giroux (2014) pointed out that BB&T Corporation gave a $1 million donation to Marshall University's business school but required that at least one course use Ayn Rand's *Atlas Shrugged*. Slaughter and Leslie (1997) referred to the growing neoliberal influence on higher education as "academic capitalism," which is broadly defined as "the involvement of colleges and faculty in market-like behaviors," and these behaviors have seemingly been increasing over the past twenty years (Slaughter & Rhoades, 2004, p. 37). In all,

Rather than providing space for intellectual thought and worldly experience, the academy has become an adjunct to corporate profit. The average college campus is ground zero for licensing agreements; construction contracts; outsourcing of bookstores, vendors, concessions and food, laundry, traveling and printing services; corporate sponsoring of buildings, events, speakers, and campus programs; patenting of intellectual property rights; and corporate funding, ownership and direct influencing of research. Such corporatization transforms students into customers, teachers into workers, administrators into CEOs and campuses into market populations (Del Gandio, 2010, para. 4).

At my campus a few years ago, students were denied the opportunity to engage in activism that administrators argued would have threatened a donor. The Alternative Spring Break group was headed back to South Florida from a service trip to New Orleans when they heard about an action being planned in Lakeland, Florida. In solidarity with the Coalition of Immokalee Workers (CIW), the action was against the Florida grocery chain Publix, whose headquarters are in Lakeland. It was a march intended to get representatives from Publix to sign an agreement guaranteeing better wages and working conditions for the farmworkers, who almost exclusively pick the tomatoes they sell in their stores. CIW has successfully negotiated these agreements with several other corporations, including Yum Brands, which owns Taco Bell, Kentucky Fried Chicken, and A & W. These students had previously studied the work of CIW as a form of nonviolent activism and wanted to join the march. When the group's chaperone called to inform her supervisor, she was told they could not participate. They were in a university van and thus he explained, it would appear to be officially sanctioned by the university. They were told that they could drive the four hours back to the university and return on their own if they chose. Obviously, that was unlikely to happen.

CONCLUSION

While the situation on college and university campuses today is less than ideal, I remain hopeful. Rather than the claims of narcissism and apathy about today's college students, I see great energy and excitement to make change.

1. Faculty and staff can help students navigate the structural barriers noted herein, and, more importantly, can work collaboratively to challenge them.
2. Faculty, staff, and students can raise their voices about unnecessary or exceedingly cumbersome procedures, inappropriate curtailing of free speech, and repression of academic freedoms. Using the power of faculty and student governments, as well as articles in the student newspaper, social media, and other tried and true activist techniques like sit-ins, a critical mass of voices opposing bureaucratic stifling can indeed make change"

3. Faculty, staff, and students can demand information about how funds are devoted on the campus. Even at a private institution like mine, some degree of transparency should be expected. Such data can help catalyze movements to reallocate funding so that it better serves students.

REFERENCES

Del Gandio, J. (2010, August 12). Neoliberalism and the academic-industrial complex. *Truthout*. Retrieved from http://truth-out.org/archive/component/k2/item/91200:neoliberalism-and-the-academicindustrial-complex

Finley, L. & Concannon, K. (2015). Conclusion. In L. Finley & K. Concannon (Eds.), *Peace and social justice education on campus: Faculty and student perspectives*, (274–286). Newcastle, UK: Cambridge Scholars.

Ginsberg, B. (2011, September/October). Administrators ate my tuition. *Washington Monthly*. Retrieved from http://www.washingtonmonthly.com/magazine/septemberoctober_2011/features/administrators_ate_my_tuition031641.php?page=all

Giroux, H. (2014). *Neoliberalism's war on higher education*. Chicago, IL: Haymarket.

Hechinger, J. (2012, November 14). Bureaucrats paid $250,000 feed outcry over college costs. *Bloomberg*. Retrieved from http://www.bloomberg.com/news/2012-11-14/bureaucrats-paid-250-000-feed-outcry-over-college-costs.html

Kingkade, T. (2012, September 21). Dominic Cellitti suing Rock Valley College for denying his poster space on campus bulletin boards. *Huffington Post*. Retrieved from http://www.huffingtonpost.com/2012/09/21/dominic-celletti-suing-rock-valley-college_n_1904137.html?utm_hp_ref=student-activism

Levinthal, D. (2014, March 27). Inside the Koch Brothers' campus crusade. *The Center for Public Integrity*. Retrieved from http://www.publicintegrity.org/2014/03/27/14497/inside-koch-brothers-campus-crusade

Lukanioff, G. (2012). *Unlearning liberty: Campus censorship and the end of American debate*. New York: Encounter Books.

Martin, C. (2010). *Do it anyway: A new generation of activists*. Boston, MA: Beacon.

Saunders, D. (2007). The impact of neoliberalism on college students. *Academia.edu*. Retrieved from http://www.academia.edu/8451398/The_Impact_of_Neoliberalism_on_College_Students

Slaughter, S., & Rhoades, G. (2004). *Academic capitalism and the new economy: Markets, state, and higher education*. Baltimore, MD: The Johns Hopkins University Press.

Slaughter, S., & Larry, L. (1997). *Academic capitalism: Politics, policies, and the entrepreneurial university*. Baltimore, MD: The Johns Hopkins University Press.

Starr, A. (2010). Academic repression. Retrieved from http://amorystarr.com/academic-repression/

UnKoch my Campus. (n.d.). Retrieved from http://www.unkochmycampus.org

Reclaiming Campus as an Event Site: A Comparative Discussion of Student Resistance Tactics

RYAN THOMSON

"We're not calling for a free university, but a free society. A free university amid a capitalist society is much like having a lecture hall inside a prison."
MONTREAL, QUEBEC—NOV. 22, 2012 GLOBAL EDUCATION STRIKE BANNER

INTRODUCTION

The following essay is in essence a tactical review of a radical tactics initiated by a wide variety of autonomously assembled pupils seeking education free from economic cost, oppression, and coercive interference, however, collectively defined and locally implemented. From building occupations, to teach-in's, to book bloc and the unlimited student strike, a tactical legacy has clearly (re)emerged over the past decade. This is not intended to be a comprehensive encyclopedia of student rebellion (Altbach, 1989; Burg, 1998; DeGroot, 1998); it instead focuses on the tactical evolution of student movements as means for resisting repression. The chapter has three sections: the first reviews relevant preexisting work on student resistance, the second overviews a cross-national study with an emphasis on present ongoing struggles emerging within the United States, and the third concludes with a series of take away points for aspiring affinities.

This discussion would not be possible if it were not for the continued work of the International Student Movement communication platform and corresponding collective of participants dedicated to spreading news of student action in addition to coordinating global waves of protest each semester. It is from this single news source that a cross-national discussion of student movements and their responses to repression are made possible. These stories have been communicated in a variety of manners ranging from personal exchanges, communiqués, translated solidarity emails, livestreams, focus groups, and early morning Internet Relay Chat chatroom discussions. It is from these engagements and corresponding research that the following essay was compiled in hopes of aiding in the recognition of the larger global student movement and its various dynamics. I speak only for myself and not on behalf of any group, ideology, or singular cause. Nor does the following discussion intend to illustrate the entire history of the last ten years in a new, singular light. In emphasizing certain events over others, all historical work runs the risk of imposing a one-dimensional view of the world. Thus, it is important to keep in mind that the emergence of the present wave of actions/tactics be locally contingent and complex.

CAMPUSWIDE TACTICS

The current wave of austerity which has swept through academia has exhibited common consequences for higher education policy. In most instances, reform is synonymous with budget cuts and the privatization of educational infrastructure. These neoliberal scholastic reforms have inspired an opposition of workers, students, and contingent faculty. Around this same time period, new tactics emerged from the 2006 occupations of Le Sorbonne in Paris, France, and the Polytechnic University of Athens, Greece. These campus movements often exist in relation to repression from state actors (whether by campus police or paramilitary). Repression differs not only in form but also in severity throughout the world. The following cross-national case study seeks to compare student resistance tactics for combating political exclusion and repression. In-depth interviews and student communiqués served as the primary methods for the collection of content. Findings suggest that successful student movements provoke a policy representative of a larger social struggle with the student identity broadly defined. A steady escalation of tactics is crucial for avoiding exclusion while organizational legitimacy must be maintained (typically through an assembly or congressional model) for these social performances to take on the necessary political dimension capable of challenging the targeted policy reform. Additionally, strong interpersonal associations and *"power in numbers"* are reoccurring concepts among student organizers.

It was not until personally attending the "Transnational Student Congress" (a sort of quasistudent international) in Marburg, Germany during the fall semester of 2014 that the violence opposing the intersectional struggle for access to publically funded education became a serious personal concern. The congress was promoted through the International Student Movement platform and managed to bring together students from a variety of countries including those from the global South (such as Bolivia, the Congo, Sri Lanka, and Nepal), which is frequently neglected in Western student discourse. It was absolutely appalling to meet a dozen fellow young people from different countries who all shared in similar narratives such as being assaulted by police, tear-gassed, unlawfully detained, shot at, or had loved ones "disappear" for their activist participation. This harsh realization was further complicated by the realization that a number of students were detained at the border of their home countries for simply trying to attend the congress. In order to contextualize the present dynamics surrounding student resistance and corresponding acts of repression, it is helpful to first discuss what has already been established by others. In particular, three distinct subliteratures help inform the subsequent cross-national discussion. These include historical review of the student resistance tactics, a discussion of recent racial justice demonstrations throughout the United States, and conclude with a look forward for this tactical approach.

The ongoing struggle surrounding the forty-three missing students in Ayotzinapa, Mexico reflects a dynamic commonly found throughout other parts of the world—students as agents of rebellion and targets of repression. Temporal ruptures within the fabric of social reproduction have historically maintained a certain air of spontaneity about them. Such improvisations are often experienced as an assertive creativity and strategic optimism which revives the poetic aspiration of dialectical negation. Student rebellion, as a specific theatrical segment within the larger global anticapitalist/social justice movement, is certainly no different. It is difficult to articulate this experimental element or how it relates to the student organizational culture central to the mobilization and escalation of contentious performances. The failure of present student institutions (student governments), their bureaucratic tendencies toward cooptation, and immense differences in the reception of student engagement further complicate a linear interpretation of contemporary historical events.

It is within a larger context that the most recent #FeesMustFall, #Occupy-UGC, # IUSFSLmassivemarch, #ConcernedStudent2015 actions, and the ongoing wave of student occupation movements throughout Latin America (Brazil, Uruguay, and Paraguay) among others can be discussed as independent segments of a global student phenomenon. In the words of Savard and Charaoui (2013), "In the global context of the commodification of education, youth and students everywhere are becoming increasingly conscious of the need to organize as a means to defend education as a social right" (p. 3). These numerous branches of the student struggle simultaneously present narratives of both vicious acts of political repression and temporary collective triumph. There is no hierarchy of achievement for campus organizers, simply a want to escalate for-free emancipatory education.

This drive roughly translates into a utilitarian exploration of tactics that aim to disrupt both class as well as conventional consumer practices.

The current wave of austerity which has swept through academia has exhibited common consequences for higher education policy and set the stage for the present tactics. In most instances, reform is synonymous with budget cuts and privatization of educational infrastructure. These neoliberal scholastic reforms have inspired an opposition of workers, students, and contingent faculty (Adrum & Roksa, 2001). It was around this same time period that new tactics emerged in March 2006 with occupations of Le Sorbonne in Paris, France (in combination with trade union strikes by the General Confederation of Labor) followed shortly thereafter by the Polytechnic University of Athens, Greece later that summer. As articulated by the Greek student occupiers,

> We deny evaluation and intensification of our student (or not) work […]. We should not care if and when we are going to find a job. It should not be our problem. We demand a wage for all of us […]. In order to bring to close the occupied university with the rest of the city, we need to make the whole city live like the occupied university. Let's block the streets, where human and non-human commodities circulate […]. Let's celebrate wildly the re-appropriation of our time" (Group Against Work, 2006, pp. 67–68).

Similar aspirations were found among the French students and youth throughout the Banlieues who mobilized in opposition to the First Employment Contract (CPE) which would have made it easier to fire anyone under the age of twenty six during their first two years at a job. The destabilizing effects of austerity upon those with unstable working conditions, particularly among marginalized youth (commonly referred to as "the precariat"), makes them a "dangerous class" according to liberal economists (Standing, 2014). This strain of thought is recurrent within campus movements (despite occupying a relative position of privilege), so much so Giulio Calella (2011) referred to the university as "The Factory of the Precarious Worker" in his history of the contemporary Italian student movement. This emphasis was also found within the U.S. occupations that soon followed.

The 2008–2009 school year brought the arrival of these new tactics to the United States with occupations sweeping the University of California (UC) system and reoccurring occupations New York City (NYC). The *New School in Exile* authored *University Occupations* (2009), one of the most comprehensive zine's to date on the topic tracing their militant approach back to Paris 1968. During the following 2009 summer, the California State University (CSU) Trustees passed a twenty percent fee hike which resulted in a UC systemwide one-day strike on September 24th by faculty, students, and staff—the largest in UC history (Solomon & Palmieri, 2011). An open occupation was convened at CSU Fullerton's Pollak Library the following week with rallies, dance parties, blockades, sit-ins, and occupations following in quick succession. In perhaps the most popular essay from the movement, the "Communique from an Absent Future," the authors proclaimed, "The crisis of the university today is the crisis of the reproduction of the working class, the crisis of a period in which capital no longer needs us as workers" (Research and Destroy, 2009, p. 9). Throughout the wave of occupations and demonstrations, the California students maintained a conscious effort to direct their primary emphasis to the contemporary student as a future precariat laborer.

It was not until 2009 that the Bologna Accords would serve as a lightning rod for students throughout Europe. These unified interests in opposing EU legislation also laid the groundwork for what would grow into the International Student Movement Platform. The occupation at the Faculty of Humanities and Social Sciences at University of Zagreb illustrated the success of the general assembly/occupation approach before spreading to twenty other faculties in eight other Croatian cities (see Bezinovic's *Blokada*, 2009). At this point, large-scale demonstrations and occupations had become normalized throughout many Western countries (Barnhardt, 2014). The addition of highway blockades (rather than symbolic buildings) were also becoming increasingly common following the success of the tactic during the Bologna Accord demonstrations. Tactics were advanced significantly in 2010 with the arrival of Book Bloc in late November when Italian politician Silvio Berlusconi's education reform incited demonstrations/occupations of the thirty largest campuses. These demonstrations were followed weeks later by Day X demonstrations throughout England. Images of the ransacked Tory Party HQ Milbank Building in many ways represented the arrival of youth rebellion within Western media.

The final tactic to be integrated was the provincewide 2012 Unlimited Student General Strike in Quebec which, in over a six-month period, successfully blocked all classes before materializing into a popular revolt against the Charest regime (Mehreen, Bonin, & Hausfauther, 2015). In addition to providing a contemporary example of full-scale mobilization, the Quebec Student Movement (QSM) added a unique feature to their preexisting approach. The 2012 strike was unique not only because it achieved the "general status" (indicating it spread extensively throughout numerous academic institutions) but more so because it added "unlimited" which connoted that the strike would last an indefinite time period, something which had not been achieved in a formal capacity by an association before then. These different actions often times occur in dialectical relation to administrative/police behavior. Often times these acts of violence garner even larger numbers of support from students who would have otherwise not participated in such a demonstration.

The development of this militant set of tactics has emerged with a Western focus and in doing so has largely neglected additional activist responses which have emerged in the face of violent repression elsewhere throughout the world. Of all the different actions which have been successfully implementing educational budget cuts, the "long march" has largely been neglected within Western organizing approaches despite being a success in the face of some of the worst educational circumstances in the world. More specifically, students from throughout the Philippines, India, and Sri Lanka (Inter University Student Federation (IUSFSLmassivemarch—March For Free Education from Kandy to Colombo)) have coordinated a number of walking demonstrations over dozens of miles over a number of days. These tactics have maintained all the enthusiasm of occupation while vocalizing accessibility and quality of education issues within public spaces.

STREETLINE TACTICS

In late 2014, the Autonomous Students of UC Santa Cruz convened a General Assembly which issued a call for "*96 Hours of Action Against Police Murder & Tuition Hikes.*" For those in attendance, it was immediately obvious that these two issues are inseparable components within the grander movement to create a more socially just community. Put simply, decreasing accessibility to education, systemic racial oppression, student debt, the persistent threat of incarceration, and police brutality cannot be discerned as separate issues within the precarious livelihoods presently being experienced by much of the sizeable millennial cohort and more generally throughout Communities of Color. These facts of life effectively correspond to restrictions in social mobility thus creating an increasingly favorable landscape for antisystemic discord both on and off campus. This confrontational dialogue, which materialized in the wake of the successive acquittals of the murderers of Trayvon Martin, Mike Brown, and Eric Gardner (and numerous other acts of police brutality and state repression), is by no means reliant upon or in any way bound to campus spaces. However, its orators have found crowds of thoughtful participants and pockets of relatively fertile terrain in select rooms on opportune floors of the ivory tower. The following briefly discusses the emerging dynamics of Black and Brown student organizers by focusing on the substantive content, contentious performances, and realization of the (non)subject form. In doing so, these concentrated observations in no way seek to detract (or mechanistically reduce) the larger scope of the movement but rather use the opportunity to reflect upon the potentiality of campus as but one among many avenues for continued engagement.

Eastern Michigan University staged a die-in on December fifth at their Board of Regents targeting relations with the Education Achievement authority, the state-run district which has taken over fifteen Detroit public schools. In some instances, former students have begun to directly intervene in system proceedings as exemplified by the Baltimore school board die-in turned community education forum on December 15. The involvement of former students presents immense potential which has largely yet to be explored throughout much of the country. The following day another die-in took place out outside the Philadelphia district building mourning the 2013 loss of twelve-year old Laporshia Massey, who died from an asthma attack with no nurse on duty.

More recently, the dozens of considerable #ReclaimMLK vigils and demonstrations took place in metropolitan cities on January 19, 2015. Stanford students participated by using cars to blockade the San Mateo–Hayward Bridge and echoed the initial assembly demands from the Ferguson Action assembly. Various other grassroots manifestations have begun to occur in harmony of one another across college campuses such as the #KickOutTheKKK demo and countermapping effort which took place at UNC-Chapel Hill over the following week. The university campus, given its relation to the future reproduction of the labor force and economic value, maintains a complex relation to austerity in the form of budget cuts and school closures. Therefore, campus exists as both a potential event site but also as a space of conflict. Put simply, even when critical-mass contentious performances are not taking place, the institutions of education remain an opportune place for implementing these tactics.

For these reasons, the movement is not dependent upon student participation while greatly benefiting from youth involvement in the historical production of the present period. Although seldom discussed, the high school student walk outs in Boston, Baltimore, Denver, Newark, and Oakland were a historic accomplishment for young People of Color organizers despite few communities defining these actions as such (whether due to lack of continuity or failure to link the seemingly independent local news stories). The students, like the ongoing effort taking place in the Ferguson-Florissant school district (where Mike Brown was once a student), have all managed to link structural racism to a variety of complex economic issues at a grassroots level in a way which speaks volumes as to the social contradictions central to not only the institutions of higher education but also to the nation state as a whole.

The Black Lives Matter adaptation of remarkably similar tactics can be aptly understood as relatively nonviolent and horizontal "swarm" tactical model to target bottlenecks within the local circulation of capital (reminiscent of a performance described by Tilly, 2008). Like the more militant milieus within the occupy movement, sizable road intersections, highways, shopping malls, and governmental hearings have all become common targets for activist disruption. These events are site-specific and geographically grounded in logic of civil resistance to police brutality as an extension of systemic oppression. The extension of this logic extends to even greater flows of capital including all modes of freight transportation including trucking, shipping, air cargo, and freight rail. Such militant blockades have occurred but have sought to maintain a relatively solemn tone by first targeting social centers (in many instances to obtain visibility and crowd mass) before relocating to blockade. The December 2015 massive demonstration inside the Mall of America in Minnesota exhibited the potential of targeting commercial centers as a means of inciting state dialogue (mediation in the form of mass arrest). The action shared many similarities with the hundreds of vigils and die-ins which tend to seek high visibility in urban centers and have occurred within increased frequency across college campuses.

The University of California, Santa Cruz call to action was issued just days after the "Unified Students of Humboldt" commenced their occupation and rechristening of the Native American Forum building. One of the group's demands is the immediate reinstatement of the respected Lakota administrator, Jacquelyn Bolman, whom after they renamed the building following her firing at the end of last semester. Historically, the combination of winter weather, final examinations, holiday travels, and numerous other seasonal obligations tend to send student activism into a state of temporary dormancy throughout most U.S. campuses; however, this has not been the case with Black Lives Matter movement which has exhibited seasonal resiliency both on and off campus. In addition to the aforementioned actions, December observed a sizeable range of activity. This and other more recent fall racial justice movements at universities such as Missouri, Brandeis, Occidental, and Yale highlight the extent to which U.S. students organize based on race and access, a dynamic drastically different from other more homogenous cultures which primarily relies on a class orientation.

A BRIEF WORD ON ACADEMIC AND POLITICAL REPRESSION

The primary forms of repression employed by administrations are a combination of administrative and legal coercion aimed at diminishing the use of disruption tactics among students. Off campus actions, such as the Mall of America sit in or highway lockdowns during the UC's 96 Hours of Action, tend to result in formal detainment by the police, lengthy court hearings with steep legal charges (frequently necessitating the redirection of resources to legal funds). Similar outcomes are also common on campus with an additional layer of internal review regarding whether or not the student will be allowed to continue with his or her degree. However, what is frequently missed is how the role of intimidation in regulating campus space is used to limit social activity. There is perhaps no better example of this than the increasingly popular "free speech zone" designations that require students obtain a permit from administrators in order to access spaces outside a predefined area. Breaking these rules commonly results in the use of unnecessary force (i.e., beatings, detainment, and legal charges). This is equally true in Western countries (e.g., the UC Pepper-spray incident 2011) as it is elsewhere (e.g., Indian police use of live ammunition on the student strikes opposing a World

Trade Organizaton/General Agreement on Tariffs and Trade agree last year or the ongoing beatings of student crowds in Chittagong, Bangladesh).

More broadly, student representation on the vast majority of campuses is assumed by service-oriented student government structures that primarily serve as a sort of rotating figurehead who builds credentials for aspiring elites while lacking real institutional power. This is immediately felt within the marginalizing effect of bureaucracy on those seeking to create real institutional change (especially institutions which do not bother to maintain the charade of student governments). It is in this institutional context that police forces have militarized on campus to maintain control of crowds of students, whether as campus police or national paramilitary.

When students refuse to cooperate with authorities in whatever capacity, whether the forced removal of a sit in or violent clash in the streets, power is asserted through physical violence upon the student. Although similar, this spectrum of repression has been discussed by others in extensive detail, both on and off campus (Nocella II, Best, & McLaren, 2010). It is hard to articulate the brutality which occurs throughout parts of the global south. Instances such as the disappearances of student organizers in Sri Lanka and Ayotzinapa, Mexico, as well as elsewhere throughout the world, represent perhaps the most drastic form of political repression. Neglecting years of similar examples, the bloodshed perpetrated in India during the OccupyUGC campaign alone is of serious international concern. Much like those killed within the struggle of other radical social movements, whether the faces of the forty-three missing Mexican students, Alexandros Grigoropoulos in Athens, Greece, or Prosenjit Sarkar at NIT Durgapur in Nepal, India, loss of life has a way of galvanizing the participation of a critical mass. This holds true within the United States as well.

VARIATIONS IN THE ACADEMIC TERRAIN

Activism does not occur in a vacuum but rather operates within the confines/context of a particular political and commercial landscape. To illustrate this point, examine the stark differences in activist reception on neighboring campuses St. Louis University (SLU) and Harris–Stowe State (a historically Black college by U.S. description). On Columbus Day, hundreds attended the late night "Ferguson October" demonstration which was confronted by dozens of riot cops and dispersal orders before the crowd to SLU. Upon reaching the entrance, officers tried to block the march when a student commented "I am a student, I have my ID, and I have a lot of guests." The administration was unprepared for the mass of well over a 1,000 people and the officers stood down. Students were awoken by the commotion and "Out of the dorms! Into the streets!" chants as they crossed the campus with students out front with their IDs raised above their heads. Upon reaching Clock Tower Plaza, they then held a moment of silence for the recently killed eighteen-year old Vonderrit Meyers Jr. (#shaw) while drawing in hundreds of students before convening a general assembly. The group was never confronted by any additional institutional actors, pepper spray or warnings to disperse; the crowd found a place simply to assemble in mass.

While the relatively white private SLU served a temporary haven for retreat from state violence, experiences at other universities (Historically Black Colleges included) have not always been so permitting. The 2015 #ReclaimMLK actions at Harris–Stowe State University provide a unique opportunity to compare the outcomes of two similar events. The demonstration began with a march to campus and midday interfaith service. A disruption then took place at the Old Court House when demonstrators rushed the stage resulting in the administration calling for police support. Dozens of cops were then assembled in response to the crowd which had amassed outside the building immediately thereafter. In this instance, the university's hostile response to the disruption which sought to contest both the compartmentalization and cooptation of a fairly radical civil rights legacy is representative of the larger status quo within the education system. Although the SLU midnight occupation and Harris–Stowe State disruption occurred within a couple hundred feet of one another, the two situations present a stark contrast in terms of both crowd dynamics and event outcomes. In many ways, the lesson here is a simple reminder that although campus has historically provided an incubator for theoretical praxis and the adaptation of emergent tactics for confrontation, academic spaces present drastically different institutional climates for transformative action even when geographically bordering one another.

STEPS FOR LOOKING FORWARD

1. Consider the Connectedness of our Resistance
   The initial idea proposed by Traugott (1995), that similar agents within a movement (or organization) share an effective tactic has been clearly illustrated by the various autonomously assembled student collectives throughout the world. It only took a year for book bloc to spread from Italy to London and then southern UC campuses. That being said, most student efforts wither and die in the face of repression or are prevented from spreading to a systemwide level. The creation of organized affinities and heterogeneous networks requires concerted effort and often takes years. Although these present tactics are often perceived to have been developed within Western origins, we cannot neglect the spread of effective tactics elsewhere

throughout the world such as the long march first popularized in southeastern Asia.

2. Redefine the Concept of Education

The ongoing debate surrounding what constitutes "an education" is illustrated in the brief early morning exchange during the SLU midnight occupation, during which a campus security guard warned demonstrators "these kids are trying to get an education." To which a high school student replied "This is an education." As the historical conditions continue to ripen with the commercial effects of austerity, so to the likelihood of the university (once again) becoming an event site within the global class struggle. Some students, whether as precariat workers or future laborers, have begun to look upon the university landscape with hesitance and contempt that enables the development of radical critique of the academy in both substance and form. How this branch of the movement will develop is hard to say and is largely contingent upon the ability to overcome the adverse effects of repression and escalate their struggle. Given these persistent conditions, it seems unlikely that student-initiated actions will relent anytime soon.

3. Think Globally

The exploration for effective tactics has real-world implications beyond simple solidarity gestures between occupations; it effects how contentious performances are adapted and employed in the wake of repression. In the words of Thint Myat (2015), a Revolutionary Students Collective organizer from Yangon Myanmar, "we took the idea for the "free-education center" from the student squats we saw in the Netherlands and began hosting free anticapitalist education for grades eight to eleven to help spread the word. We liked the large banner's [sic] we saw from Chile and Quebec and tried to make our own while keeping our specialized flags and loud approach [...] our occupation of campus [buildings] had mixed results but we were able to raise necessary bail quickly" (Buko Congress Speech Transcript).

4. Reframe the Conversation

The mainstream political interpretation of student resistance movements is commonly reduced to a "youth problem" embedded with generational turbulence that fades when young people grow up and join the workforce. What these reductionist critiques fail to recognize is that throughout much of the world, students are viewed as intellectual workers. This perception establishes the university as an event site in its own right. More specifically, the tactics which have emerged within recent years integrate a variety of militant tactics which further escalate the struggle in wake of violent repression. When the Quebec students were faced with Law 78, the largest turnout disobeyed curfew. When the Indian students were violently beaten, a long march against fees ensued to further draw attention to the issue. Within the United States, students have often contributed to popular off-campus mass movements such as Black Lives Matter and served as accomplices to militant direct actions such as economic disruption and highway blockades. Where the next tactical breakthrough will come and how it will be adapted elsewhere throughout the world has yet to be seen.

"One World, One Struggle."

REFERENCES

Adrum, R., & Roksa, J. (2001). *Academically adrift: Limited learning on college campuses.* Chicago, IL: Chicago University Press.

Albatch, P. (1989). *Student political activism: An international reference handbook.* Westport, CT: Greenwood Press.

Barnhardt, C. (2014). Campus-based organizing: Tactical repertoires of contemporary student movements. *New Directions for Higher Education, 2014*(167), 43–58.

Bezinovic, I. (2009). *Blokada.* Documentary movie. Croatia: Restart and Factum Films.

Burg, D. (1998). *Encyclopedia of student and youth movements.* New York: Facts on File.

Calella, G. (2011). The factory of the precarious worker. In C. Solomon & T. Palmieri (eds.), *Springtime: The new student rebellion* (pp. 89–103). London: Verso Press.

DeGroot, G. (2008). *Student protests: The sixties and after.* London: Addison Wesley Press.

Giroux, H. (1999). Vocationalizing higher education: Schooling and the politics of corporate culture. *College Literature, 26*(3), 147–161.

Group Against Work. (2006). Let the occupations become time-barricades. In Inoperative Committee (eds.) (2009), *University Occupations.* Oakland, CA: 1000 Little Hammers Press.

McAdam, D., Tarrow, S., & Tilly, C. (2001). *Dynamics of contention.* New York: Cambridge University Press.

McLaren, P. (1998). *Life in schools: An introduction to critical pedagogy in the foundation of education.* Los Angeles, CA: University of California Press.

Mehreen, R., Bonin, H., & Hausfather, N. (2014). Direct democracy, grassroots mobilization and the Quebec student movement. In COLLECTIF 10 NOVEMBRE. (ed.). *This is fucking class war: Voices from the 2012 Québec student strike.* Retrieved from http://thisisclasswar.info/mehreen.html

Myat, T. (2015). *Buko Congress Speech Transcript.* Munster, Germany.

Nocella II, A. J., Best, S., & McLaren, P. (eds.). (2010). *Academic repression: Reflections on the academic industrial complex.* Oakland, CA: AK Press.

Park, J. (2014). Clubs and the campus racial climate: Student organizations and interracial friendship in college. *Journal of College Student Development, 55*(7), 641–660.

Research and Destroy. (2009). *After the fall communique.* Oakland, CA: Black Cart Press.

Savard, A., & Charaoui, J. (2013). *Organize to strike, fight to win: Quebec's 2012 student strike.* Retrieved from http://www.studentstrike.net/wp-content/pdf-version/quebecstudentstrike.pdf

Shor, I., & Freire, P. (1987). *A pedagogy for liberation: Dialogues on transforming information.* Westport, CT: Bergin and Garvey Publishers.

Solomon, C., & Palmieri, T. (2011). *Springtime: The new student rebellions.* London. Verso Press.

Tarrow, S. (1995). Cycles of contentious action: Between moments and madness and the repertoire of contention. In M. Traugott (ed.), *Repertoires and cycles of collective action* (pp. 89–116). Durham, NC: Duke University Press.

Tarrow, S. (1998). *Power in movement: Social movements and contentious politics.* Cambridge, UK: Cambridge University Press.

Tilly, C. (1986). *The contentious French.* Cambridge, UK: Cambridge University Press.

Tilly, C. (1995). Contentious repertoires in Great Britain, 1758–1834. In M. Traugott (ed.). *Repertoires and cycles of collective action* (pp. 253–280). Durham, NC: Duke University Press.

Tilly, C. (2008). *Contentious performances.* New York: Cambridge University Press.

Traugott, M. (1995). Recurrent patterns of collective action. In M. Traugott (ed.). *Repertoires and cycles of collective action* (pp. 1–14). Durham, NC: Duke University Press.

CHAPTER NINE

Interrupt, Inspire, and Expose: Anarchist Pedagogy against Academic Repression

JOHN LUPINACCI

"We apologize for the inconvenience but this a revolution."
—SUBCOMANDANTE MARCOS (IN FERLINGHETTI, 2007, P. 1)

As an urban educator and a scholar-activist committed to critically and ethically interrupting the role of education and schooling in Western industrialized culture, I have found something powerful about questioning ourselves as human beings and examining in unexpected ways our human perceptions of social and ecological relationships in connection with addressing social suffering and environmental degradation. This chapter responds to being told to be more "realistic" and shares a pedagogical example of how even in the most concrete of spaces cracks can be made, filled in, and widened. I am not alone in the line of inquiry that rethinks dominant discourses and discursive practices influencing power in relation to current regimes of oppressive ideologies that contribute to rise of neoliberalism and the academic industrial complex rooted in modernist assumptions that rationalize and justify the ongoing systemic violence of human-hetero-white-male suprem-acy. Critical theory examining these same structures of oppression in education spans decades; however, this eco-anarchic example shares a story—a pedagog-ical example—from the front lines of teaching to make cracks in the concrete assumptions about knowledge and power in the academy.

What brings this diverse work together in solidarity, through what I have been calling pedagogies of solidarity (Lupinacci & Happel-Parkins, 2015), is the recognition of powerful phenomena occurring within schools and in our society—

profoundly abusive phenomena that are violently reproducing relationships and making racism, sexism, classism, and speciesism—to name a few—seem inevitable and inescapable. The concept of *pedagogies of solidarity* is a direct nod and tribute to Freire's *Pedagogy of the Oppressed* (1993) and *Pedagogy of Freedom: Ethics, Democracy, and Civic Courage* (1998) as well as other critical and ethical contributions that empower people to not only respond to and reframe learning, but also to do so in ways that break the will of their oppressors. Specifically, *pedagogies of solidarity* intentionally draw attention to the multitude of pedagogical possibilities and the value of the diverse experimentation of teaching and learning toward diverse, decentralized, sovereign communities for all beings. Critical dimensions of these pedagogies of solidarity refer to a diversity of public pedagogical approaches that could be understood in relation to other deformations of public life under neoliberalism. Among these deformations include, but are not limited to, intensified and expanded processes of criminalization (Giroux, 2009); the rapid transfer of wealth and opportunity upward; the erosion of social identities and bonds (Bauman, 2007); and the emptying of public space and redefinition of public discourses under neoliberalism (Couldry, 2010). The various educators engaging in said pedagogies all call attention to particular relationships, practices, and discourses at work in conjunction with a common enemy—the dominant discourses and discursive practices of Western industrial culture. These educators engage in a variety of locally situated learning in support of living systems. These local and diverse pedagogies operate concurrently, sometimes separately, and in conversation with each other.

As an ecoanarchist educator in Western industrial culture, I perceive that to be in school, by situation of its location in society, means learning to function within, accept, and submit to the authority of a tremendously exploitive culture. This so-called "reality" is preparing young people for their fate in a very unhealthy and broken society. Despite this raw exposure to life for so many of us and our children, existing relationships offer not only an alternative, but also a plethora of alternatives. In life, or in the living systems within which humans exist, there are nondominant, often marginalized, stories about the abuse—stories about how living together ought to be, about what it could be, and about who and what belongs to and revels together in the what Cornel West refers to as the funk and stank of life (Mendieta, 2011). These are the stories, smells, tastes, joys, and pains that explore the potential of community and the power of a decentralized locally sovereign existence. There are voices of activism whispering, chatting, talking, rapping, dancing, singing, and sharing stories that offer alternatives to *what is* and unapologetically welcomes the reimagining of a very different society. For many students and educators, these voices call us to identify the role that education both plays and ought to play in transitioning toward socially just and sustainable communities. They call us to confront and overcome understanding our existence as human beings as so-called individuals separate from and superior to one another and all other beings and objects. Furthermore, these stories and teachings invite us to recognize how it is we make meaning through our worldviews, and remind us to recognize how it is precisely those worldviews that offer the potential for very different possibilities.

A PEDAGOGICAL EXAMPLE: POETRY, CHALK-ART, AND GUERILLA PEDAGOGY

In efforts to explore education—not schooling—that is supportive of socially just and sustainable communities, this chapter presents a close depiction of a pedagogical project to reconceptualize educational spaces through an anarchist framework (Amster, DeLeon, Fernandez, Nocella II, & Shannon, 2009; Haworth, 2012). Such an endeavor seeks to allow for both formal and informal learning designed to explore not just revolution but re-evolutions of our everyday lives, to encourage departures from hierarchically organized ways of being in order to create openings for artistically imaginative spaces in which we, as human beings in Western industrial culture, can explore situational, local, and ecologically responsive alternatives to current dominant practices rooted in authoritarian assumptions of humans as separate from and superior to all other beings. The following example not only presents insight on how repression works responsively to interruptive art, but also presents a detailed depiction of how a story from a pedagogical experiment models a dialogical learning inspired by what Weems (2013) calls "guerilla pedagogy":

> I characterize guerilla pedagogy as a form of engagement that makes use of wide range of strategies, and missives toward the aim of reterritorializing both the academy and what counts as knowledge production (p. 51).

Aligned with such a pedagogical approach inspired by guerilla pedagogy is one that interrupts, exposes, and inspires what counts as knowledge production in educational spaces. In the following example, I share how such a pedagogical experience encourages students to question deep cultural assumptions and revitalize public space, while recognizing the complex interconnected systems to which we all belong. This type of pedagogical engagement encourages subjects to explore a life disciplined by something other than "what is"—or the man-stream, white-stream, discourses of human supremacy.

Naturally, several challenges arise. How do educators engage students in counter pedagogies without becoming repressive pedagogies? Moreover, how do anarchist educators put to practice anarchic guerilla pedagogies in spaces like classrooms on college campuses? These questions illuminate that most spaces in our day-to-day lives that are reserved for learning are constituted as hierarchical schools and classrooms. This learning experiment challenges the very notion of what constitutes a learning environment—or at the very least what signifies a classroom. At the fundamental level, each lesson in a course dedicated to challenging the authority of schooling must in some way directly confront the power and control both constituted by and constituting how it is we learn *with* and *among* diverse members of our community. Further, in accordance with an antihuman supremacist objective—or the goal to recognize and commit to thinking and acting in support of interspecies equity—the coursework must interrupt human-centered and other dominant value-hierarchized assumptions about *who* and *what* can be a teacher and/or have an active voice in local decision making.

Framing the curriculum for the pedagogical example shared in this chapter is the following essential question coconstructed between the instructor and the students: "As an activist-scholar educator, how do we understand and enact an ecological perspective toward living together on Earth?" Accompanying this essential question is a set of subessential questions cocreated in class after being introduced to an EcoJustice Education framework (Martusewicz, Edmundson, & Lupinacci, 2015):

(1) What does it mean to belong?
(2) How are we both claimed by and claiming community?
(3) How do we reclaim community from discourses of exclusion and simultaneously work toward communities inclusive of all the living and nonliving members?
(4) How do we as activist educators engage in strategic pedagogical projects that challenge authoritarianism and modernity?

While such pedagogical endeavors can be understood as situational, local, and in support of living systems (Lupinacci, 2013a; 2013b), this particular snapshot of a course illustrates one particular meeting that engages in insurgent art as a way of learning to take direct action as a public pedagogy. Focusing in on the course's essential and subessential questions, each class meeting also had a set of guiding questions that could be understood as facilitating objectives for the learning each week. The guiding questions coauthored with students in the class for that particular week were:

(1) How do we engage in intergenerational learning (learning that involves people of all ages learning together from each other) aimed at reclaiming the commons?
(2) Who are our local educational philosophers?

(3) How might art play a key role in the process of recognizing, resisting, and reconstituting dominant discourses and discursive practices in our every-day lives?

Following this interruptive experience emerge new, unexpected relationships of learning that are most often missing or ignored when we only conceptualize learn-ing as framed in Western industrial assumptions about what is important and considered knowledge.

THE CURRICULUM

Each week in class after having a critical dialogue that brings into conversation perspectives from some of the required course reading—Val Plumwood's (2002) *Environmental Culture*, Carolyn Merchant's (1983) *The Death of Nature*, David Orr's (2004) *Earth in Mind*, and Vandana Shiva's (2005) *Earth Democracy*—we move the discussion from theory as a form of activism to planning for how to engage in learning that will also engage the community as we practice taking action to reclaim the commons—or the noncommodified aspects of life in the community. Classwork frequently culminates in the importance of engaging in fun, uplifting, and nourishing healthy forms of activism. While we often discuss the valuable role for the many forms of activism, this particular initiative targeted subversive strategies for intentional language use, ethical eating, and uplifting, positive interaction. In this curriculum, any action that shifts modern assumptions of social justice and sustainability required solidarity, especially among activists deeply committed to recognizing, respecting, and representing differences in order to break the will of our common oppressors—the dominant discourses and discur-sive practices of modernity.

Following a discussion on educational philosophers, selections from bell hooks' (2009) *Belonging: A Culture of Place*, Madhu Prakash's (1994) *What are People For? Wendell Berry on Education, Ecology, and Culture*, and Wendell Berry's (2012) *It All Turns on Affection*, the class engaged in a free write reflection and then group brainstorming of what constituted an educational philosopher and who or what might we, in fact, consider our teachers. With a strong focus on challenging anthropocentrism (Lupinacci, 2014), and reading selections from David Abrams' (1996) *The Spell of the Sensuous: Perception and Language in a More-than-Human World*, the class very quickly identified the importance of recognizing and lis-tening to the diverse communicative systems essentially teaching us in our local contexts.

In accordance with Orr (2004) and other environmental and place-based edu-cators (Smith & Gruenwald, 2007; Smith & Sobel, 2010; Sobel, 2004), we leave the classroom and learn in spaces where communicative systems of the more-than-human world were more likely to be heard, acknowledged, and relationships of belonging and community fostered. This spatial transition especially requires learners to relinquish human-centered assumptions in which the world becomes *our* limitless classroom. While of course it can be a massive step in the process of breaking free from the confines of the classroom, habits of authoritarian education are likely to dominate the learning spaces traditionally constituted by hierarchized assumptions of what is knowledge, who has it, and how we pass it along.

Following a close reading of ecofeminist philosopher Val Plumwood's work explaining a logic structure for centric thinking to remind us to not incorporate or instrumentalize our more-than-human kin and Merchant and Berry's work critically exposing rational thought to remind us to be appropriately critical of science, we set out to design an intergenerational learning experience that would interrupt, inspire, and expose. The following pedagogical event would interrupt dominant assumptions of who could be our teachers and where learning can take place. It would need to be inviting and filled with joy in the spirit of conviviality and solidarity. It would need to model how to organize and build a strong campaign in support of reclaiming public space and challenging authorities. Further, it would have to expose the reactions and reveal boundaries that are often very illusive and often unknown to activists. In other words, the event would need to be a relatively safe litmus test for what is possible in terms of pushing at the current parameters of what education is and moving toward a local version of what it ought to be. So with those objectives in mind, we threw what would come to be known notoriously as "the chalk party."

THE ACTION: INTERRUPT, INSPIRE, AND EXPOSE

Interrupt: Whose Knowledge?

Just outside of the education building on campus where our class met each Tuesday afternoon is a wonderful space that could be described as a grotto or a commons. The space is adorned with shrubs, trees, a small patch of manicured lawn, a row of large flat-topped cement benches and a few bolted-down round metal patio tables. With two large buildings of classrooms and offices that house the College of Education (COE) framing in two sides of the grotto, the grotto can be seen from nearby halls and offices. The public space the class referred to as the "grotto" outside of the COE had come up a few times in class as a potential spot for a learning garden and outdoor classroom, but when we asked how the space was most frequently used, we learned it was only used occasionally for an activity or discussion. While we kicked around ideas in class for how the space could be more welcoming, or what Ivan Illich (1973) characterizes as "convivial," and conducive to intergenerational learning, we agreed to interrupt the current context in which the space was used. Several people a day pass through the space, look out onto the space, occasionally stop and rest in the space, but it was observed that seldom were any of the people interacting with one another and that the space seemed prime for interrupting the everyday interactions taking place outside the COE.

Having recently participated in a poetry workshop hosted by Veronica Gaylie (2014) titled *Poetry and Bread: Writing, Roaming and Resisting Within* at the Eco-Justice and Activism conference, I decided to adapt the workshop and share the experience with the students in Environment, Culture, and Education. Students, after learning the following week's class meeting would include a poetry activity that would include listening, observing, writing, and potentially guerrilla or insurgent art, were excited and sought to connect the activity with our commitment to intergenerational learning by inviting children. While there is always a standing open invitation for students to bring children to class, we rarely engage in intergenerational activities in the college classroom, let alone in primary and secondary classrooms. Critical of the dominant educational philosophy taught in traditional education degree programs, we agreed inviting children and families interrupts dominant perceptions of teaching and learning, reclaims the grotto as a place to play and enjoy the company of one another and demonstrates the power of celebration as a form of protest and activism. So, with rough plans, we invited all the children at the preschool childcare program to join us for sidewalk chalk art and games.

Inspire: The Power and Joy of Guerilla Pedagogy

Sadly, children are often overlooked as sources of wisdom and seldom recognized as educational philosophers. With the direct intent to take serious intergenerational learning *with* and *from* children as our teachers, fifty preschool-aged educational philosophers met us in the grotto outside the educational building where half a dozen buckets of sidewalk chalk and a small group of doctoral students awaited them. The children, their adult supervisors, and invited guests of the event were instructed that the activity of the evening was to play and make art together. Equipped with handfuls of chalk sticks, they drew, wrote, shared stories, and engaged in more than simply play as they were the teaching us all to enjoy each other, the space, and to feel great about engaging in the action of leaving our mark as insurgent artists. Amidst the chaotic wonder of the grotto that spring evening, our class was instructed to observe the children artists as sources of valued teachings and to consider them as activists in the movement to understand how we might engage in intergenerational learning in support of reclaiming public space from the enclosures of everyday human adult-centered life. As the chalk covered nearly every surface possible with what looked like a mural of colors and symbols, the message was clear that something different happened in that space.

We then wrote poetry inspired from the evening's activities and discussions on interrupting dominant discourses of human supremacy. After gathering together, reciting *The Peace of Wild Things* by Wendell Berry (1998), and remembering lessons in previous course content that shared how the Situationist International (SI)—a group of social revolutionaries comprised of avant-garde artists, intellectuals, and political theorists most notable for the May 1968 insurrections in France—used graffiti to spread poetic words of insurgent art, students drafted haiku and shared that haiku embedded within the canvas of colors provided by our guest teachers—the preschool-aged educational philosophers.

After reciting examples of haiku from Matsuo Basho and graffiti from the SI, participants shared their insurgent and guerrilla poetry. The group reassembled and debriefed, and volunteers read their haiku in the unique spaces of our tapestry. As a culminating discussion point, I talked through the importance of this event as scholar-activist educators for how it also would serve as a litmus test and would most certainly reveal the boundaries and potential limitations to what is accepted, tolerated, and what is met with militarized force. The objective here is that we needed to be aware of how the children playing, the intentional use of the space for sharing nonpermanent art, and the layering of our political haiku could be seen as illegal activity on campus and that while no harm was done and conversely folks had shared space in a positive and joyful way, the power structures within which we are constituted as subjects would most definitely have disciplining responses.

Expose: "Malicious Defilement of Property."

The following morning, what was later that day to be referred to in the college of education as the "chalk incident" had been reported to campus authorities and the police were amply photographing the scene. Before noon a water truck had arrived and a team of men were flooding the grotto with a high-powered hose connected to a large reservoir on the truck, which had turned the art into what looked like a sad swamp of colors and swirling paint. Following up checking the public record Daily Crime/Fire log it appeared that at 7:44 am an officer was called to investigate "Malicious Mischief" and reported: "Officer responded for a report of someone who wrote in chalk on the sidewalks, benches, and walls in front of the Education Addition." Within the week an email with the subject line "Graffiti at the Education Addition" was sent out to inform the Dean's office who were both aware of the possible courses of action and supportive of the event. The email asked the Dean's office to be aware that a state law WAC 504-34-140 states "Neither paint, chalk, nor other marker may be used in any walkway, sidewalk, floor, or any portion of a building" and that if the issue continues they will be billed for clean-up labor and equipment. In the following Monday's edition of the *Lewiston Tribune* in the column "Blotter Fodder" journalist Ralph Bartholdt (2014) reported:

Washington State University Police responded to a call of malicious defilement of property on the college's campus. The damage was done to the side-walk—in chalk, no less. It was in front of the education department. The report did not say how far the incident occurred from the child-care center (p. 1).

The sarcastic tone of the newspaper article captured the sentiment that despite the state laws, reasonable logic finds it hard for such actions to be destructive or malicious. However, what occurred was hard to consider malicious when we confront the cultural norms of what looks like activism. When one considers that several children safely ran amok outside of the COE laughing, playing, singing, and making art, it is hard to consider these children as engaged in malicious mischief. They were not only practicing insurgent art, but also they were sharing their wisdom of how to enjoy, play, and learn together to speak up and share stories that interrupt, inspire, and expose.

CONCLUSION: EDUCATION IN THE AGE OF THE ARTIST

Such a pedagogical event sparks the question: "What comes next?" What comes from events like the chalk party or from any direct action that interrupts dominant discursive practices that silence the unrecognized voices of our community spaces? What do we do as scholar-activist educators when we are introduced to a multitude of collaborative efforts aimed at strengthening our solidarity and bringing to fruition actions that support those solidarities? When reflecting on all the potential lessons from the chalk party ranging from learning to practicing insurgent art, using poetry to interrupt and inspire, rethinking who ought to be considered our teachers, to the learning the limitations and responses from the state, we see a type of education generated by collaborative wisdom and shared among a diversity of the people, and potentially plants, animals, and insects outside in the grotto that evening. Such events, rooted in theory that manifests action, can be simply summed up using a concept Ivan Illich calls "blessings." Ivan Illich (1973), in *Tools for Conviviality*, refers to the aspects of our community we enjoy, which exist separate from economic growth. He draws our attention to the value of rediscovering the present shaped in our past as it moves out of the future's shadow. When hope in the development model of market-driven capitalism fails, he explains that communities live on because they consist of an abundance of "blessings." Blessings, in the Illichian sense, refer to the rich boon that emerges, despite free-market-monetized economies.

1. *Individualism and anticommunity* politics have cast a shadow of powerful political fear that the hard days of the present are in fact dark times. Critical of the enlightenment's grasp on poetry, Audre Lorde (2007) turns our attention to the

wisdom of women. Lorde describes the sacred knowledge of love, survival, resistance, creativity, and strength of women:

> These places of possibility within ourselves are dark because they are ancient and hidden; they have survived and grown strong through darkness. Within these deep places, each one of us holds an incredible reserve of creativity and power, of unexamined and unrecorded emotion and feeling (p. 36).

Reclaiming poetry from the luxury of the often published white cannon of poets, Lorde explains that poetry is "the revelation or distillation of experience" and for women it is "a vital necessity of our existence" (p. 37). She wrote: "Poetry is the way we help give name to the nameless so it can be thought" (p. 37). It is precisely this tradition—respectful to not appropriate Black feminism but rather to recognize and value the wisdom of such teachings—that allows for insurgent art, guerilla poetry, and messiness of not having any definite answers or specific rules for what could be creative, imaginative, and then possible. This could not be more important in the context of current times in which fear is a motivating factor in controlling and maintaining the status quo. While all too often critical scholarship tends to point us toward an epic moment in which some radical transformation in the mind is a liberating factor from the shadows of dominant regimes of power, Lorde reminds us to not run from the shadows and to reject the notion of enlightenment that tells us, I think therefore I am, and instead be in tune with "the black mothers in each of us—the poet whispers in our dreams, I feel therefor I can be free" (p. 38).

Drawing on Illich's concept of "blessings" and the wisdom of Audre Lorde in response to the imminent question of "What's Next?," it is my firm belief as a scholar-activist educator that in these dark times we can find creativity and inspiration to reclaim communities by turning our attention toward all the great things happening all around us. The noise of the children playing and the students reciting haiku—some of which were politically radical and inspired by the antiauthoritarian art of the SI—as insurgent artists together with all the planning and sharing, the teaching and learning—has been echoing through the local community like a song or a poem resonating with the hope of a radical shift to embracing the beauty of uncertainty in solidarity. The chalk party and all the similar anarchic projects aimed at disrupting what currently *is* schooling focus on the blessings and help us to recognize and learn together how to rediscover and strengthen our solidarity. The relationships within which we engage are politicized in fear, and these "blessings" offer visions of actual living in the present that will take us into sustainable futures. In other words, we have strong collaboration all around us: we just need to reclaim it and share in its abundant strength.

2. To belong and act as community representatives requires that we all *accept a shared responsibility* to the abundance of life that exists in any place, as a gift. Within that wonderful gift are the many blessings through which we share the responsibilities of existing. When asked the question "What's Next?," the answer is simple: we all join in on being poets—on being insurgent artists. We collectively share stories publically of the many blessings. We share stories publically and artistically that give voice to the voiceless. We "give a voice to a tongueless street" (p. 11) and "read between the lines of human discourse" (Ferlinghetti, 2007, p. 16). Maybe we don't all engage in what might be considered malicious mischief or in direct violation of the law, but we tell and retell the stories of hope and resilience. We tell the stories of our ancestors' poets, and how we share poetry, and how our children will share poetry together in solidarity. These stories can reclaim the language by which we communicate. And for all of us who engage in such poetry as an insurgent art, we are proclaiming to the world that we honor our responsibility to not only accept the gift of community, but also to accept the power to join in solidarity to overcome the oppression cast by these dark times.

3. We can, and arguably must, *rigorously discipline ourselves to recognize assumptions* of culturally constructed value-hierarchies playing such a dominant role in how we learn to be in this world. As scholar-activist educators—as artists— we can make the collective choice to educate each other about how the abundance of blessings present in our communities can influence our conversations and shift our language to one supportive of relationships based on mutualism and collaboration. We can, and arguably must, speak up and situate artists as leaders and artistry as a skill set that fosters the potential to transition from the Age of Enlightenment to the Age of Uncertainty—or what we might call the Age of the Artist.

4. May the artistry of insurgent artists from around the world *gain solidarity* with the movements taking place all around us and may they be spoken about, painted on walls, and sung in song publically and loudly over the dissonance of greed and individualism. May we discover that the recovery of the many "blessings" abundant in all communities lifts the heavy veil our language has cast upon us so we will no longer have to fear our communications and actions.

5. Above all learned from the chalk party and the shared wisdom in being *unapologetically utopian* in how we learn together is a new understanding of education—that just as important as every reading or paper we write is that we've got to cook and eat together, read out loud to one another, make art together, and we've got to make new friends, see old friends, and above all have fun! It's validation we are interrupting the power and privileges that repress the potential for us to imagine and bring bits of that imaginary into our lived embodied experiences.

REFERENCES

Abram, D. (1996). *The spell of the sensuous: Perception and language in a more-than-human world*. New York: Vintage Books.

Amster, R., DeLeon, A. P., Fernandez, L. A., Nocella II, A. J., & Shannon, D. (eds.). (2009). *Contemporary anarchist studies: An introductory anthology of anarchy in the academy*. New York: Routledge.

Bartholdt, R. (2014). Blotter Fodder. In the *Lewiston Tribune*. Lewiston, ID.

Bauman, Z. (2007). *Consuming life*. Cambridge, MA: Polity Press.

Berry, W. (1998). *The peace of wild things: The selected poems of Wendell Berry* (p. 30). Berkeley, CA: Counterpoint.

Berry, W. (2012). *It all turns on affection: The Jefferson lecture & other essays*. Berkeley, CA: Counterpoint.

Couldry, N. (2010). *Why voice matters: Culture and politics after neoliberalism*. London: Sage.

Ferlinghetti, L. (2007). *Poetry as insurgent art*. New York: New Directions.

Freire, P. (1993). *Pedagogy of the oppressed* (M. B. Ramos, Trans. Revised 20th Anniversary ed.). New York: The Continuum Publishing Company.

Friere, P. (1998). *Pedagogy of freedom: Ethics, democracy, and civic courage* (P. Clarke, Trans.). Lanham, MD: Rowman & Littlefield Publishers Inc.

Gaylie, V. (2014). Poetry and bread: Writing, roaming and resisting within. Presentation workshop at the annual meeting EcoJustice & Activism, Ypsilanti, MI.

Giroux, H. A. (2009). *Youth in a suspect society: Democracy or disposability*. New York: Palgrave Macmillan.

Hannah, C. (1996). Nailing Descartes to the Wall/(Liquid) Meat Is Still Murder [Recorded by Propagandhi]. On *Less Talk, More Rock* [Audio Cassette]. San Francisco, CA: Fat Wreck Chords.

Haworth, R. H. (ed.). (2012). *Anarchist pedagogies: Collective actions, theories, and critical reflections on education*. Oakland, CA: PM Press.

Hooks, B. (2009). *Belonging: A culture of place*. New York: Routledge.

Hung, R. (2008). Educating for and through nature: A Merleau-Pontian approach. *Study in Philosophy and Education, 27*(5), 355–367.

Huston, P. (1994). No where to run, No where to hide [Recorded by Gravediggaz]. On *6 Feet Deep* [Audio Cassette]. New York: Gee Street Records.

Illich, I. (1973). *Tools for conviviality*. New York: Harper & Row Publishers.

Lorde, A. (2007). *Sister outsider: Essays and speeches*. New York: Crossing Press.

Lupinacci, J. (2013a). Eco-ethical environmental education: Critically and ethically examining our existence as humans. In A. Kulnieks, D. R. Longboat, & K. Young (eds.), *Contemporary studies in environmental and indigenous pedagogies: A curricula of stories and place*. Rotterdam, Netherlands: Sense Publishers.

Lupinacci, J. (2013b). The Southeast Michigan Stewardship Coalition: A deep design of eco-democratic reform that is situational, local, and in support of living systems (Doctoral Dissertation). Retrieved from Eastern Michigan University Digital Commons, Ypsilanti, MI Paper 504.

Lupinacci, J. (2014). K(no)w where to run, K(no)w where to hide: Recognizing human supremacy. Paper presented at the annual meeting of the American Educational Studies Association, Baltimore, MD.

Lupinacci, J., & Happel-Parkins, A. (2015). Recognize, resist, & reconstitute: An eco-critical conceptual framework. *The SoJo Journal: Educational Foundations and Social Justice Education, 1*(1).

Martusewicz, R. (2014, October). Letting our hearts break: On facing the 'hidden wound' of human supremacy. Paper presented at the meeting of the American Educational Studies Association.

Martusewicz, R., & Edmundson, J. (2005). Social foundations as pedagogies of responsibility and eco-ethical commitment. In D. W. Butin (ed.), *Teaching social foundations of education: Contexts, theories, and issues* (pp. 71–92). Mahwah, NJ: Lawrence Erlbaum Associates, Publishers.

Martusewicz, R., Lupinacci, J., & Schnakenberg, G. (2010). EcoJustice education for science educators. In M. Mueller (ed.), *Cultural studies and environmentalism* (pp. 11–27). New York: Springer.

Martusewicz, R., Edmundson, J., & Lupinacci, J. (2011). *EcoJustice education: Toward diverse, democratic, and sustainable communities.* New York: Routledge.

Martusewicz, R., Edmundson, J., & Lupinacci, J. (2015). *EcoJustice education: Toward diverse, democratic, and sustainable communities* (2nd ed.). New York: Routledge.

Mendieta, E. (2011, October 11). Focus on the funk: An interview with Cornel West [Web log post]. Retrieved from http://blogs.ssrc.org/tif/2011/10/06/focus-on-the-funk-an-interview-with-cornel-west/

Merchant, C. (1983). *The death of nature: Women, ecology and the scientific revolution.* San Francisco, CA: Harper & Row.

Merleau-Ponty, M. (2002). *Phenomenology of perception* (2nd ed.). New York: Routledge.

Orr, D. (2004). *Earth in mind: On education, environment, and the human prospect.* Washington, DC: Island Press.

Plumwood, V. (2002). *Environmental culture: The ecological crisis of reason.* New York: Routledge.

Prakash, M. S. (1994). What are people for? Wendell Berry on education, ecology, and culture. *Educational Theory, 44*(2), 135–157.

Shiva, V. (2005). *Earth democracy: Justice, sustainability, and peace.* Cambridge, MA: South End Press.

Smith, G. A., & Sobel, D. (2010). *Place- and community-based education in schools.* New York: Routledge.

Smith, G., & Gruenewald, D. (2007). *Place-based education in the global age: Local diversity.* New York: Routledge.

Sobel, D. (2004). *Place-based education: Connecting classrooms & communities.* Great Barrington, MA: The Orion Society.

Suissa, J. (2010). *Anarchism and education: A philosophical perspective.* Oakland, CA: PM Press.

Weems, L. D. (2013). Guerilla pedagogy: On the importance of surprise and responsibility in education. *Philosophical Studies in Education, 44*, 50–59.

Part IV.
Organizing

"To hell with good intentions."
—Ivan Illich

"It always seems impossible until its done."
—Nelson Mandela

One of the Best Contracts in the Nation? How Part-time Faculty Organized for a Collective Bargaining Agreement

DIANA VALLERA

THE BACKGROUND STORY

It was a typical drive south from Evanston along Lake Shore Drive. Traffic was not too heavy at 9:30 in the morning. The waves of Lake Michigan offered a soothing contrast to the conversation with my grievance chair. She all but screamed, "they cannot do that" to which I replied "I know, but they are." Incensed she stated, "it is a violation of section VII of the contract for Columbia College to assign a course in that manner." Again, I stated emphatically, "I know but the administration does not seem to care so let's talk about our options." I then ask, "can you please write up the facts of this violation, cut and paste the section of the contract violated, reference the College's past practices of course assignments and send it to me?" "Sure" she said in a tired voice, resigned by the situation.

I pull my car in the parking garage at Wabash and Harrison streets, gather my bags, and step out. Within seconds there are two men in black walking about three feet away. At first I feel alarmed and then remember the words of my friend Robert Bruno who reminds me that they only target you because you are an effective president of the part-time faculty union. With this in mind, my feelings shift from concern to amused defiance. I zigzag a nonsensical path toward the classroom where I teach and make a bathroom stop just to be certain that Columbia College security is, in fact, following me and to quiet the little voice in the back of my head that questions whether this is really happening or whether I am simply paranoid.

Upon exiting the bathroom, I see my "companions" are back and off we go toward my classroom.

Each time I think "this cannot be happening," I remind myself of the day that my nanny called to inform me that two people in suits were in a car in front of my house, one of them taking photographs. When I got home that evening, I was concerned and called Evanston police to make a report. As my nanny described the man taking pictures to the police officer, her description sounded very familiar. I pulled up an image of a Columbia College attorney on Facebook and my nanny immediately identified him as the man taking photographs and with whom she spoke. Following these events, I filed a complaint with the college only to be told that I will be terminated for having complained of this intimidation and inappropriate behavior on the part of in-house counsel. But for a mass nationwide petition, demonstrations, and National Labor Relations Board filings, the college relented and assigned me teaching. This was one of the more egregious of countless efforts on the part of the college to retaliate, intimidate, and silence me. Nothing should surprise me anymore.

Tomorrow, however, is a new day. The newly hired president of the college who claims to exercise inclusion, transparency, and cooperation will begin his reign. He comes in bringing an outside specialist in labor management from the Chicago office of the global law firm of DLA Piper LLP who, I am told, will exercise significant authority. We have been negotiating without a new contract for more than three years having gone through three lead negotiators for the administration and two federal mediators with little to show other than two National Labor Relations Board (NLRB) trials and a ruling that the college negotiate in good faith.

It is indeed a new day at Columbia College. We have been engaged in intense and long negotiations and seem to be making progress with the outside labor attorney with whom I share a firm belief in the process of interest-based negotiations, an approach to negotiation that counters positional bargaining by seeking more collaboration and information sharing. Today we agreed to negotiate as long as necessary within the coming days. We have made incredible progress reaching agreement on many of the most contentious sections. Absolute positions and stubborn stances have given way to compromise and collaboration. It is now after 2:00 am and we continue our efforts in the plush law office of the global firm. Champagne is put on ice as documents print at computers. By 3:30 am corks pop and the part-time faculty union celebrate a new collective bargaining agreement with Columbia College Chicago. This agreement will later be posited as one of the best in the country (Flannery, 2013a).

The part-time faculty union (P-Fac) was successful because we had a plan, we had support, and we both endured and fought back. The components of our plan included education, basing our demands on principals valued in higher education and the United States, outreach and alliance building, and a strong legal strategy.

A summary of our successful efforts follows:

1. Education—learn about labor law and higher education;
2. Principals—root your efforts in clearly articulated principals and use them to guide the union and its efforts;
3. Faculty unity—find areas of shared interests to build critical mass;
4. Alliance building—seek out social justice groups, individuals, religious activists and politicians, students organizations, other unions and workers who support your principals;
5. Legal strategy—know what constitutes a violation of labor law and know how to pursue them before the NLRB and at mediation. Make sure area media are aware of charges before the NLRB.

Each of these areas is discussed in some detail in the pages that follow and constituted our response to the environment of academic repression documented by Nocella II, Best, and McLaren (2010).

GETTING EDUCATED BEYOND OUR DISCIPLINES

Despite being affiliated with a national union, we quickly realized that we could not rely exclusively upon the education provided by the National Education Association (NEA). Some of the trainings were valuable but others were questionable and sometimes contrary to information received about labor rights and procedures. Our part-time faculty members are fortunate enough to be located in a major metropolitan area with one of the nation's premier labor education resources in our backyard, though today much is available on line (https://ler.illinois.edu/?page_id=152).

If union members do not know their Weingarten Rights—what constitutes a grievance, how to protect contractual agreements, where to turn when the Collective Bargaining Agreement is violated—then education in the area of labor rights, procedures, and law is needed. Weingarten rights include the right to on-the-spot representation in any situation, like an evaluation, that has the potential to involve disciplinary action. With the interne, these trainings can be accessed around the globe (https://ler.illinois.edu/?page_id=152).

Working with local academic programs can also improve labor education. For us, the University of Illinois Labor Studies Program has been invaluable by offering us training in labor history, bargaining, labor and employment law, steward training, organizing, and strategy trainings. Collective bargaining training covers styles, negotiating skills, and how to achieve a successful contract. Labor and employment law training includes legal rights for union organizing, strikes, and other job actions to defend a contract. Steward training includes learning how to identify and process a grievance and the seven principles of just cause. Internal organizing involves learning how to build collective action. Strategy trainings include how to build a strategic campaign and connect with broader causes. Getting a handle on labor rights and procedure was only one educational challenge. The other was getting educated on the machinations of higher education itself both historically and currently. Here, the American Association of University Professors (AAUP) and the AAUP Red Book was invaluable—all union members need to know how the AAUP came into existence, the climate out of which the U.S. system of tenure emerged, why academic freedom is critical, the fundamental purpose for which institutions of higher education exist, and why the corporate model is not only inappropriate, but also dangerous to the purpose of higher education (Nocella II, Best, & McLaren, 2010). Without it, unions are at a loss at the bargaining table and are presented as self-serving rather than advocating on behalf of the interests of the academy as well as members. Again, we had many local resources to help educate us on AAUP policies and positions but here too, much is available on line (http://www.aaup.org/reports-publications/aaup-policies-reports; http://www.aaup.org/redbook-contents).

The education we received has been absolutely invaluable. Without knowledge of basic labor rights, procedures, and remedies, a union cannot be in the driver's seat. Instead, the local chapter is at the mercy of its affiliate union's legal division or simply flailing in the protection of its members. It is not so surprising to critical thinkers that one's national affiliate union might have interests that differ from the local: like saving money instead of protecting members' interests before the NLRB, for example. Because of these differing interests, the local must be. On the more proactive side, such awareness creates tools in support of policies and procedures that promote fair evaluations and assignments, due process and representation. Without this knowledge, faculty union needs are too often swept beneath administrative claims that seem authoritative and rooted in academic propriety.

Finally, timing is incredibly important. Our education took place over the duration of negotiations—I would not recommend such an approach. The more equipped the union is going into negotiations, the more effective you will be from the start. Our primary source of education in labor rights was the University of Illinois Labor Studies Program and in higher education was the AAUP. Both of these institutions exemplify a principal-based approach to their research and efforts. Perhaps nothing was more important to P-Fac's long journey of contract negotiations than keeping grounded in our principals.

ROOTED IN PRINCIPALS

One of the core tenets of principled negotiation is moving from positions to interests; this strategy served especially helpful for our negotiations (Fisher, Ury, & Patton, 1991). When our leadership team was faced with articulating why we pursued particular positions, we developed the principles that rooted our positions. We did not know it at that moment but as we expressed our rationale to different constituencies, the central principles became clear. These grounded and led us. Through years of negotiations, retaliation, and trials before the NLRB, these principles focused our attention and guided us through uncertain terrain, created by the administration's constant threats to our wellbeing.

Our union membership had faced horrible and worsening working conditions. Instead of valuing our investment in the college and our years of successful student instruction, administration treated part-time faculty as replaceable widgets. Our members faced an administration that would arbitrarily walk into a classroom to conduct an evaluation of a faculty member and the union spent valuable resources challenging and then grieving the evaluation. Through years of contract negotiations, our most experienced faculty were being denied class assignments and those most active in the union faced fewer assignments and opportunities, marginalization, and exclusion. We knew that a dignified work environment was one of our guideposts. We knew that due process and a fair system of assignments and evaluation was fundamental to our cause. The principle of due process also became the basis for having part-time faculty representation on college committees especially those addressing curriculum and helped us to develop our claim to participation in faculty governance.

With each semester that passed, the administration imposed another standardization requirement. These began as shared course goals and objectives, then as shared syllabi, then common texts, and finally prescriptive syllabi. With each policy, academic freedom diminished before our eyes and faculty whether full- or part-time have come to resemble factory line workers. The principle of academic freedom as a cornerstone of the academy became another guidepost. For us, academic freedom went hand in hand with the fundamental purpose of higher education—to pursue truth and advance the common good. Finally, we were guided by the classic union belief that all workers deserve a living wage and the opportunity for advancement.

These principles made their way into most of our outreach communications. They regularly formed the rationale for contract language at the negotiation table. Finally, these principles helped guide decision making when we confronted moral dilemmas or uncertainty in strategy. These principles also helped establish common ground with all faculty whether part time or full time.

ONE FACULTY/ONE WORKER

The central focus of faculty work is threefold including course instruction, research or creative production, and service. While all faculty share interests in each of these areas to varying degrees, it is in the area of instruction that all faculty whether full or part time, share significant interests. These shared interests include academic freedom in instruction, student learning, a healthy learning environment, and quality education. Because what happens in the classroom is influenced and shaped by decisions made on curriculum and other committees, it makes sense that one's status as an instructor should prevail and not whether one is full or part time. Uniting faculty through our common bond as teachers is another of our key strategies.

I learned from studies in history that divide and conquer is as an age-old strategy deployed at first by those in power to keep separate those who would constitute a majority (Allen, 1997; Battalora, 2013). This is no less true in academia. Our part-time faculty union worked hard to unite the faculty at Columbia College including advocating for part-time faculty positions on the newly formed faculty senate. It is unfortunate that among our own college faculty we were the least successful in building unity. We were successful building alliances with full-time faculty at other institutions especially through P-Fac's "Pursuit of Truth Campaign" that brought together full- and part-time faculty from over seventeen colleges and universities in the region (Wilson, 2014).

Our success at the bargaining table involved uniting far more than faculty. Since most workers share the most basic of labor needs—a living wage, health care, safe, and dignified work environment, fair evaluation, and opportunity for advancement—we built alliances with the Occupy Chicago movement and with local and national labor efforts. Major players in the Chicago social justice labor effort supported P-Fac, including faith labor activist Rev. C. J. Hawkins, U.S. Representative Jan Schakowsky, Professor of Labor Studies Robert Bruno of the University of Illinois Labor Education Program, among others. A president of an American Federation of Teachers local in California sent a letter in support of me when Columbia College was threatening to fire me. In addition, some local labor unions for the trades (plumbers, electricians) joined our picket lines.

There was perhaps no more influential alliance than that formed with Columbia College students and outside student groups. P-Fac leadership held open forums on campus and then began to meet with student groups. Together we formed a coalition that held sit-ins, engaged in informational picketing, and letter-writing campaigns. The coalition was forged as much over social justice issues as shared concerns over student learning and the quality of instruction. These alliances are powerful not only because they add volume to the message, but they also help to sustain union efforts especially when retaliation and other harm to members is particularly weighty.

A central piece of our alliance-building strategy was a media campaign that sought to get information out to the wider public. P-Fac organized a media team and drew upon the expertise, resources, and connections that our journalism and media faculty possess. In each message we tried to inform others about what was taking place at Columbia College, to explain the harm to quality instruction and faculty work, and to assert the principals upon which P-Fac based our negotiations effort.

LAW AND JUSTICE

Last but not least, we deployed a strong legal effort to enforce labor law violations. As we learned our union rights, we began to pursue enforcement. P-Fac learned not only about the internal grievance process from trainings, but also about legal options at the NLRB and through mediation. We filed more than a dozen violations at the NLRB during contract negotiations. Our legal team spent countless hours locating supporting documentation, identifying communications, and otherwise preparing for trial at the NLRB. I went to the NLRB office with stacks of four inches binders and spent days and days testifying before any charge was issued and before any trial was set. Outside counsel for Illinois Educational Association/National Education Association, Laurie Burgess, was dedicated, passionate, and worked tirelessly to help P-Fac win almost every charge. We pursued charges that alleged union animus, retaliation, and bad-faith bargaining among others. Our efforts before the NLRB paid off. The rulings were powerful:

> Specifically, the NLRB rulings order Columbia to immediately engage in good faith bargaining—or face federal contempt charges. Stop offering proposals that leave union members with fewer rights than if they didn't have a union at all! Stop changing things, like faculty evaluation systems, without negotiating them first. Because of Columbia's "egregious failure to bargain," NLRB also called on "special remedies" […] Columbia also was ordered to pay thousands of dollars in back wages (Flannery, 2013b).

Legal victories at the NLRB helped bring media attention to the challenges P-Fac faced at the college, to our negotiation platform, and the plight of part-time faculty around the nation (Basu, 2012; Lydersen, 2012; Schmidt, 2012). These victories were also critical to the health of the union. Our members faced retaliation and significant loss of income with little to no abatement until the NLRB victories. Labor rights could be viewed as rights with substance not just verbal claims. The college administration could no longer proceed as a bully with no accountability. An organization of the federal government was watching.

THE UNION TODAY

Without a union, the part-time faculty at Columbia College would have little to none of the voice we have exercised and no place of legal authority to turn to challenge retaliation. In this historic juncture, one all too similar to that which gave rise to tenure and the AAUP, faculty unions are more important than ever. In those states that are so called "Right to Work" which more often means "work without rights" states, unionization is still possible but requires voluntary donations to pay for the work of the union. In other words, the law does not prohibit a union per se but prohibitions the requirement of dues collection. As the list of efforts above indicates, the work of a union is vast and can be costly, but voluntary donations have worked for some unions for decades and long before the antiunion political efforts of Wisconsin Governor Scott Walker and others.

Once P-Fac achieved a strong collective bargaining agreement, our work did not end; it simply switched to contract enactment efforts and enforcement. All of the areas noted above—education, keeping efforts principal based, building unity and alliances, and pursuing legal challenges when warranted—continue today. A significant difference between just more than a year ago and today is that we have a strong contract to enforce.

LESSONS GOING FORWARD

As I reflect upon the challenges, successes, and shortfalls of my years as P-Fac president, I am struck by one approach to challenges that served us so well—turning it positive. No matter what we faced, we spent time and energy exploring how we could both view whatever it was in a positive light and use it in a way to improve as a union and to advance our social justice goals. And, no matter what we faced, we did, after significant reflection and debate, find a positive way to view and use each challenge presented. This practice promoted continuous learning and improvement in terms of how we do and what we do in the service of our members in the context of higher education.

CONCLUSION

There is much that is needed today as unions face significant challenges to their way of doing business and to their mere existence. I would like to share some tactics that I will elaborate on below and that I view as the most critical to the future of labor unions; they include: (1) collecting resources to advance communication;

(2) exploring ways to restructure the union; (3) building alliances; and (4) advancing legislative change.

On a broader scale, a portal for centralized reporting of what is taking place in higher education and how faculty might respond is necessary. We need a place on the internet to report occurrences, to strategize approaches for contesting damaging administrative policies and approaches, to exchange ideas, and to share strategies. It is clear that university presidents and high-ranking administrators share approaches, corporatization goals, and rhetoric through exclusive organizations and publications. Contingent faculty advocate, Joe Berry, has created a newsletter that gathers and spreads news of contingent faculty efforts to support their work and work sites. The AAUP magazine *Academe* is also an important resource for faculty. However, additional resources are needed. We need an informal gathering location that is organized and instructive. Faculty need to be on the front end of strategizing to contest administrative actions that erode academic freedom and tenure, diminish the quality of education, and otherwise move higher education away from its purpose—to pursue truth and serve the public good.

Another area for significant change is in the very structure of the union. In particular, unions that serve part-time faculty must stop utilizing the union model designed for full-time workers. Such unions presume that their members have full-time employment with benefits and health care. Most part-time faculty cannot afford the amount of volunteer time that the full-time labor union expects. Moreover, many have no benefits. What is wrong with having a structure that has both some volunteer time expectations and also paid work when time and job demands exceed the volunteer contribution? In addition, unions need to work across different affiliations to advance shared goals and interests. The future of organizing part-time faculty will depend on this sort of restructuring and rethinking of the union.

Legislative efforts are desperately needed. We have allowed antiunion legislation to roll through state after state and college-to-work policies that are transforming institutions of higher education from centers of learning into the means of production of a low-wage labor force. We need to pool our resources and show the strength of our alliances by changing laws to support the very principals upon which we all hope to labor: a dignified and safe work environment, fair wages, fair system of assignment and evaluation, and opportunity for advancement.

The oppression that we are witnessing in higher education and throughout the labor force can be stopped. And we can stop it. When we build together (i.e., communities, faculty, staff, and students), united in our principals, commit to critical liberatory inclusive affordable education, and adopt activist tactics mentioned previously, we level the playing field of power against administrators and government and corporate investors within higher education.

REFERENCES

Allen, T. (1997). *The invention of the white race: The origin of racial oppression in Anglo-America*, Vol. 2. London: Verso.

Basu, K. (2012). NLRB: Columbia College Chicago violated labor law. Retrieved from http://www.insidehighered.com/quicktakes/2012/07/19/nlrb-columbia-college-chicago-violated-labor-law

Battalora, J. (2013). *Birth of a white nation: The invention of white people and its relevance today*. Houston, TX: Strategic Book Publishing and Rights Co.

Flannery, M. E. (2013a). 365 days later: A different world for part time faculty at Columbia College. *NEA Higher Ed. Advocate, 30*(4), 14.

Flannery, M. E. (2013b). The union that could. *NEA Higher Ed. Advocate, 30*(3), 3–5.

Fisher, R., Ury, W., & Patton, B. (1991). *Getting to yes: Negotiating agreement without giving in*. (2nd ed.). New York: Penguin Books.

Lydersen, K. (2012). NLRB rules in favor of Chicago's Columbia College Professors. Retrieved from http://InTheseTimes.com/working/entry/13596/NLRB_rules_in_favor_of_chicago's_Columbia_college_

Nocella II, A. J., Best, S., & McLaren, P. (eds.). (2010). *Academic repression: Reflections from the academic industrial complex*. Oakland, CA: AK Press.

Schmidt, P. (2012). Columbia College Chicago violated rights of adjuncts' union, labor-relations board says. Retrieved from http://chronicle.com/article/columbia-college-chicago/132979/

Wilson, J. K. (2014). Pursuit of truth campaign. *IL AAUP*. Retrieved from http://www.ilaaup.org/fall201409.asp

CHAPTER ELEVEN

Organizing Adjuncts and Citizenship within the Academy

SEAN DONAGHUE-JOHNSTON AND TANYA LOUGHEAD

"Adjunct Professor Hoping Some Student Leaves Behind Warm Pair of Gloves Today."
— HEADLINE FROM THE ONION, DECEMBER 2, 2015

INTRODUCTION

This essay is cowritten by two philosophers. One is currently an adjunct; the other is a tenured professor. Both have recently been involved in meetings and collective actions on behalf of adjunct rights. Each will look at the role of "citizenship" as it relates to adjunct labor within current higher education in the United States. In this essay, we look at citizenship from two different perspectives: (1) the citizenship of adjuncts within the university and (2) the citizenship of students who are educated by adjuncts.

ADJUNCTS AS NONCITIZENS

Despite the important work that they do as educators, adjunct professors are essentially outsiders and noncitizens of the academy: they teach at many different institutions, yet belong to none. They are the exploited, the marginalized, and the disenfranchised of higher education. They are by far the most highly educated subset of the working poor, and, for this reason, they are among the most easily overlooked. In spring of 2012, Stacey Patton, a reporter for the *Chronicle of Higher Education*, decided to investigate the working conditions of adjuncts:

> For some time, I'd been hearing talk of adjuncts whose wages were such a pittance that they qualified for welfare. These anecdotes got me thinking: Were there really many academics living that close to the margins, or was that mostly hyperbole (2013, para. 8)?

Patton soon discovered that the impoverished PhD was anything but a myth. Her article, which came out in May of that year, told the story of Melissa Bruninga-Matteau, an adjunct professor with a PhD in medieval history who was living on food stamps. "I am not a welfare queen," Bruninga-Matteau explained (Patton, 2012, para. 1).

> The media gives us this image that people who are on public assistance are dropouts, on drugs or alcohol, and are irresponsible. I'm not irresponsible. I'm highly educated [...]. I've never made a lot of money, but I've been able to make enough to live on. Until now (Patton, 2012, para. 7).

Since Bruninga-Matteau's story, many other adjuncts have come forward to share their own experiences. Mary-Faith Cerasoli, for example, known as the "Homeless Prof," is a fifty-five-year old instructor of romance languages who has made headlines for having to live out of her car and crash on friends' couches. She suffers from a life-threatening thyroid condition and, because she receives no health benefits, has added unpaid medical bills to an already-crippling load of debt. "They call us professors," she says, "but they're paying us at poverty levels. I just want to make a living from a skill I've spent thirty years developing" (Kilgannon, 2014, para. 10).

Sadly, stories such as these are by no means uncommon; indeed, they point to a serious and systemic problem in our education system. As universities become more and more corporatized, the substratum of exploited academic labor grows ever larger. Seventy percent of university courses are now taught by adjuncts who make, on average, $2,700 per course, with no health benefits and no job security (Coalition on the Academic Workforce, 2012, p. 2). An adjunct who teaches three three-credit courses per semester over a two-semester academic year (the average course load for a full-time professor) will earn $16,200—putting his or her annual earnings well below the federal poverty line.

Moreover, since most universities enforce a limit on the number of courses that adjuncts may teach—typically two courses per semester—it has become literally impossible for them to earn a living at any single institution. As a result, adjuncts have become the academic equivalent of migrant workers, continually travelling back and forth between two or more different universities and never being certain of employment from one semester to the next. And despite their high level of education, many of them have found themselves underemployed, living in poverty, and relying on public assistance.

For my own part, I scrape out a living working at two universities (one of which involves an hour's commute) and a brewery. I am not represented by any unions, and as a part-time worker, I receive no health benefits. My wife (who works with me at the brewery), my three-year-old son, and I all live with my brother-in-law in his house because rent is too expensive for us anywhere else. Ironically, I teach a philosophy course called "Justice, Ethics, and Poverty," in which students discuss their moral duty to fight poverty and social injustice in the United States and abroad, while I struggle to make ends meet.

On the other hand, I consider myself to be relatively fortunate (emphasis on the word *relatively*). After all, I have had steady employment at two universities (two courses per semester at each for five years, broken only by a brief stint as visiting professor); I have been able to teach a wide variety of courses, many of which have been within my area of specialization; I have been given (shared) office space; and, in general, I have been treated with respect by the faculty and department chairs of both universities. Not all adjuncts are so lucky. Some adjuncts do not know what courses they will be teaching, or whether they will be teaching any at all, until a week before the semester begins. Even at that, classes may be cancelled at the last minute, leaving the instructor suddenly unemployed and with no time to find an alternative source of income. One adjunct in Washington, DC, has tried to safeguard against this problem by aiming for employment at six different universities at a time: "You never know when a class will be cancelled or a full-time professor will bump you at the last minute," he explains. "Sometimes classes just disappear" (Fredrickson, 2015, para. 10).

Given these conditions, it should come as no surprise that the vast majority of adjuncts do not—or at least *did* not—intend to be adjuncts forever. Most are pursuing, are planning to pursue, or have given up on pursuing tenure-track employment (Coalition on the Academic Workforce, 2012, p. 9). Since earning my PhD in Philosophy in 2011, my goal, like that of so many others, has been to land a tenure-track job. Now, five years down the road, this goal is looking more and more like a pipedream. Every year, the field of qualified applicants grows, even as the number of tenure-track jobs shrinks. And the longer I remain on the job market, the less desirable I become as a candidate. (No one wants to hire a professor whom no one else wants to hire: a phenomenon known as "adjunct taint.") Also, I find myself unable to afford the expense of travelling to the American Philosophical Association's annual conference, where most of the philosophy interviews are held, and where candidates are given the opportunity to network with prospective hirers and to attract their attention with presentations of their scholarly work. As the authors of one study observe, "[a]djuncts face systemic obstacles to career growth;" while many universities pay for graduate students and tenured faculty to attend academic conferences, "adjuncts usually must travel to these events, where faculty recruiting often occurs, on their own dime" (House

Committee on Education and the Workforce, 2014, p. 23). And if anyone is short on dimes, it is adjuncts.

One relatively inexpensive way for adjuncts to further their academic careers, of course, is to publish. After all, it *is* "publish or perish" in our profession. Alas! we adjuncts are perishing rapidly. For my own part, between preparing for four courses, grading the essays, exams, and other assignments of up to a hundred and forty students per semester, holding office hours, hustling back and forth between two universities, hauling kegs at the brewery, and spending much-needed time with my family, I find it hard to set time aside for writing. Like most adjuncts, I am caught in a crushing catch-22: If I want time to write, I must find a tenure-track job; if I want a tenure-track job, I must find time to write.

Of course, the argument could be made—though not with a straight face—that competition in the academic labor market, however hard it might be on the "losers," tends to separate the proverbial wheat from the chaff. Only the very *best* adjuncts will rise to the top, overcome their financial difficulties, and escape the catch-22; they will *make* time to write, even if it means giving up valuable time with their families, or sacrificing sleep, or quitting that third, nonacademic job. As a result, tenure-track jobs will only go to the most highly qualified, the most highly motivated, and the hardest working professors. And students, of course, will get the best education that money can buy.

Even if we accept, for the sake of argument, the highly dubious assumption that market principles are appropriate in higher education, it is clear that the market fails in this case. If students are supposed to be getting the best education that money can buy, then why are seventy percent of their courses being taught by those whom the market has ostensibly rejected? Why, in other words, are the majority of their courses being taught by the very "chaff" from which the "wheat" was supposed to be separated?

Needless to say, adjuncts are anything but "chaff." They are, generally speaking, highly qualified and highly dedicated to their students. (Indeed, if they were not, they would not be adjuncts.) When, in November 2013, the House Committee on Education and the Workforce (2014) looked into the working conditions of adjunct faculty, it found (not surprisingly) that, "despite their low pay and lack of benefits, [adjuncts] possess impressive educational backgrounds, often with many years of teaching and industry experience" (p. 25). The House Committee also noted that a "recurring theme" in survey responses was the dedication of adjuncts to their students: "'I believe in what I'm doing,' 'I love my students,' and 'we love teaching and helping our students succeed,' were common refrains from respondents" (p. 4).

Predictably, however, the quality of education suffers when instructors, however dedicated they may be, are underpaid and overworked. According to the study, an overwhelming number of adjuncts feel that they are "missing opportunities to better serve their students because of the demands of their schedule"

(p. 27). Indeed, this is an understatement if ever there was one. Adjunct professors are basically *set up to fail*: they cannot adequately prepare for their courses if they do not know what courses they will be teaching until a week before the semester begins; they cannot hold effective office hours if they have no office space; and they cannot take time to help struggling students if they simply have no time.

If, as the market argument supposes, the academic labor market is supposed to reward the hard work and dedication of instructors, on the one hand, and give students "the best bang for their buck," on the other, then clearly it fails on both counts. *No one benefits from the current adjunct situation.* No one, that is, except the corporate university itself, which profits from the exploitation of a surplus labor force. As Nocella II, Best, and McLaren (2010) put it, universities have been in a "breathless rush [...] to replace tenured professors with adjuncts, contract, part-time instructors, and graduate students" in order to "boost the profits they make off each person enrolled in a class" (p. 32). This dismal state of affairs is disturbingly reminiscent of a passage from Steinbeck's *The Grapes of Wrath* (1969):

> When there was work for a man, ten men fought for it—fought with a low wage. If that fella'll work for thirty cents, I'll work for twenty-five.
>
> If he'll take twenty-five, I'll do it for twenty.
>
> No, me, I'm hungry. I'll work for fifteen. I'll work for food [...].
>
> And this was good, for wages went down and prices stayed up. The great owners were glad and they sent out more handbills to bring more people in. And wages went down and prices stayed up. And pretty soon now we'll have serfs again (p. 312).

Indeed, what are adjuncts if not Tom Joads with PhDs? We make up a vast surplus labor force, not unlike the one described by Steinbeck, the existence of which serves only to keep academic labor costs down even while student tuition continues to soar.

What are students paying for, then, with their outrageous tuitions? The answer: inflated administrative salaries, potentially lucrative (for the university) programs and research projects, sports franchises, expansions of the university (thus making room for more students and thereby bringing in more tuition), and, in the case of for-profit colleges, shareholder profits. As Noam Chomsky (2011) points out, nonprofit universities are "parasitic institutions:" they do not produce commodities for a profit, in the usual sense of the term, and so they rely on public funding; in the absence of public funding, however, they must seek revenue by other means (para. 8). Thus nonprofit institutions have come to behave more like corporate profit centers than providers of a public good. They compete for students' tuition by investing in "student services"—a euphemism for expensive sports programs and nonteaching administrative positions, which in turn *raise* the price of tuition—and reduce their labor costs by hiring adjuncts (see Schoen, 2015). An obvious consequence of this "solution" to the fundraising problem is that students are buried in debt and their instructors are living in poverty. Meanwhile, the corporate university itself continues to expand and profit at their expense.

Yet prospects for adjuncts (and their students) are not entirely bleak. Many adjuncts are organizing and demanding better working conditions. They are realizing, increasingly, that they are not alone and that they are the victims, not of their own failings, but of systematic exploitation; they are seeing that their status as "temporary" faculty is getting to be more and more permanent; and, as a result, they are identifying with each other and developing a class consciousness. Although union representation is still rare and its introduction vehemently opposed by most university administrations, extrainstitutional movements and advocacy groups have been taking shape at both regional and national levels. The New Faculty Majority, for instance, is a national organization that provides support and resources for the organizing efforts of adjuncts. And national labor unions, including the American Association of University Professors (AAUP), the American Federation of Teachers (AFT), the Service Employees International Union (SEIU), and even the United Auto Workers (UAW), have discovered adjuncts to be "an uncommonly unionizable workforce." "There are [unions] who even though they are not in the education space see contingent workers—exploited workers—and want to get into that space," says AFT President Randi Weingarten. "Frankly, there's enough work for everyone in this space because there's lots of exploited adjuncts" (Miller, 2015, para. 32).

Moreover, adjuncts may (in rare cases) be able to find support among tenured faculty and even administrators. A. G. Monaco, for example, a senior human resources official at the University of Akron, considers the treatment of adjuncts to be unconscionable and calls on universities (including his own) to do more toward improving adjunct working conditions. "Wal-Mart is a more honest employer of part-time employees than are most colleges and universities," he says; and yet, ironically, academics are "the ones screaming about how bad Wal-Mart is" (Jaschik, 2008, para. 2).

Ultimately, however, it will be up to students and the general public to call the corporate university to account. They are the ones with the most leverage: they pay the tuitions, and they wield the power of public opinion over those who make education policy. It is our job to educate them, to raise a clamor in their ears, and to show them where their money is going. Students and their parents ought to know how little they are getting in return for their outrageous tuitions; the general public should be made aware of the fact that *they* are the ones who are footing the bill (nearly half a billion dollars every year in public assistance) when universities fail to pay their instructors a living wage (Wessler, 2015, para. 6); and anyone who gives a damn about social justice should realize that universities fail to uphold that value, however much they may vaunt it in their mission statements, so long as they continue to exploit the labor of adjuncts.

UNIVERSITY IS A VERB

Academic freedom: the concept is much expressed in higher education. But what we most often hear when people bring up this concept is a professor worrying about her own academic freedom—being able to teach what she wants or to write about what she wants. Very few in academia worry about the bigger picture of how academic freedom (and lack of it) affects students and—ultimately—our wider culture. When over seventy percent of courses are taught by adjunct faculty, fundamental questions must be posed about this effect. We believe, as Tropea (2010) writes in *Academic Repression*, that the "higher level of apparent allegiance" to academic freedom in the contemporary age is "deceptive" (p. 479).

Academic freedom is also often talked about with regards to what we might call "overt oppression." We would liken this to what philosophers call "negative freedom." But more importantly, and more insidiously, we want to talk about the diminishment of academic freedom that we might liken to "positive freedom." Philosophers generally define "negative freedom" as the absence of obstacles that would block a particular act—it means freedom from restraint. "Positive freedom," however, is when there is genuine possibility of an act or hope being realized—it means full freedom and ability to engage. This first type of block to academic freedom (linked to negative freedom) is what occurs when some administrator tells you what not to teach, when your chair won't let you teach controversial themes in your course, or when the governor bans books. (An example comes to mind: the former governor of Indiana and current president of Purdue University, Mitch Daniels, attempted to ban books by Howard Zinn whilst Daniels was governor. This story was widely published and discussed.) Those things are typically more obvious and thus easier to fight.

In this essay, we want to focus on repression in academia that can be aligned to positive freedom—meaning that a professor does not have the genuine ability and possibility of engaging a class truthfully, critically, and challengingly. This type of repression is internalized within the professor himself (due to systems and structures) when he teaches cautious courses and themes that reflect hegemonic beliefs, teaches them adequately (and maybe even a tad on the *easy* side so that students don't complain), and keeps his job. Most adjuncts are financially struggling, so the impetus to preserve the few crumbs you receive is not to be underestimated. Just as the prevalence of grants in higher education has narrowed the field of what kinds of research gets funded and which types of questions get asked—and *not* funded or asked (see Loughead, *Critical University*); the prevalence of adjunct faculty (appropriately deemed "contingent" and "precarious" increases the likelihood that one will teach safe courses with safe themes in safe ways, and one must wonder which themes and questions within courses are *not taught or asked*). This means that the majority of university education remains within the realm of *status quo* thinking. The *status quo* is—by definition—popular and safe. Students will not be provoked and administrators will not be troubled. No discomfort is produced, and yet many (Hegel included) would claim that learning something new—by definition—includes a certain discomfort. At a time when many define higher education as merely "job preparation," preparing students to unquestioningly take and serve corporations is a trouble-free way to keep your job as a professor.

But those likely to read this book already know how this story goes. In this essay, we argue that the increasing reliance upon adjunct professors simultaneously decreases the amount of positive freedom that academics have. This affects our students and it affects the jobs, fields, and culture into which they flow. Nelson (2010), in *Academic Repression*, writes that "effective governance and job security are interdependent" and that "academic freedom, tenure, and shared governance together" form a three-legged stool that ensures excellence in higher education within the United States (p. 468). If this is true (and we believe that it is), then adjuncts do not—cannot—fully participate in the governance of the university since the other two legs of the stool (academic freedom and tenure) are not available to them. Since (a) the majority of teaching in higher education is now done by adjuncts, and (b) since the numbers of administration has more than doubled in the past twenty-five years (Marcus, 2014), this means that only a minority segment of the professoriate can participate in shared governance or have academic freedom. This means that the power of the faculty has dwindled at the same time that the number and power of administration has grown. This looks more like an oligarchy than a democracy, at institutions who loudly *claim* to be *teaching* democratic values and critical thinking.

Faculty (and administration) make a mistake if they believe that students only learn what we overtly tell them to learn within our classrooms. Just like the old parenting adage that "children learn more from what you *do* than what you *say*," within higher education, our students may learn less from our stated missions, branding, syllabi, and course material than they learn from our behaviors and structures. Since all learning is both conscious and unconscious, much of what our students learn comes from the "how" we teach and "who" we are (not "who" as an essentialist category of identity, but who we can be given our context at that moment)—whether we are excited about the material, whether we openly question *status quo* thinking in our fields, whether we seem secure in our jobs, whether we trust our colleagues on the faculty and in administration, whether we appear to have time to give to them outside of class, whether we are healthy and well-rested, or alienated and anxious. Our fulfillment and courage as human beings can come across in a thousand ways to students. A thousand things can take us away from being fully present to our students. Some of these things are out of our control. But many of them are within our control, *or should be*, in a good university.

To teach the virtue of integrity, we must embody integrity. To teach any virtue—fairness, democracy, respect in dialogue—we must be the kinds of people who are constantly trying to become those things with all of our will. Students are not so gullible and naive as to believe that we have integrity if we put it on a banner or in our mission statements.

Some might say that the university as an organization was never intended to be democratic—that the existence of boards of trustees or regents, presidents, deans, etc., all suggest a vertical rather than a horizontal decision-making structure. But, as AAUP guidelines and Supreme Court documents suggest, power within a university is more dispersed and dependent upon forthright discussion (see Gerber, 2014). The Vice President of Finance cannot tell the Shakespeare professor which plays to teach or how. But the Shakespeare professor—if she has tenure—is a part of the discussion on how major financial decisions are made. When thought about like this, it even suggests that faculty—as a group, not as individuals—do have more power in the university. Faculty are part of the management of the university and they also have autonomy within their courses and fields of specialization. At least, this is the ideal on paper. If faculty have tenure, then they can insist and insist strongly (striking if necessary) upon shared governance. A university cannot function without its faculty since they are the heart of what the university does: educate. Nonetheless, shared governance is not a given but a continually contested right. It is a "use it or lose it" set of practices.

Why is shared governance so important, though? Nelson claims that it "ultimately serves the needs of society because without it, education tends to become more about income generation and job preparation and less about critical participation in democracy" (p. 474). We agree with Nelson. And we believe that many faculty would agree. But how or why is this true and what does it mean in a situation with majority contingent faculty?

A board of trustees' (or regents) task is to ensure that a university has the stability to continue into the foreseeable future. Yet, many interpret the task of "stability" in merely financial terms. That is part of a board's task, surely. Less is said about the role of the board to continue and ensure that the mission of education is being carried out in the best way possible. This stems from a misunderstanding of *what a university is*. A university is not a collection of buildings. It is not a name, a mascot, a mission statement, a strategic plan, or a set of school colors. Simply put, a university is not an "object" for preservation in that way. *A university is more of a verb and less of a noun.*

A university is a process. We take some of our cues here from Hegel, Butler, Kristeva who insist that human identity is in flux: identity is "becoming" and not "being." When we think about preserving the university as if we were preserving an object, we make a category mistake. A university is not a set of buildings; buildings can be bought and sold and take on new meanings. A university is not a brand; brands build image, not reality. A university is not a football team or a mascot; universities can serve their mission well (and better) without them. A university is not a diploma mill that sells degrees as objects; universities can educate without degrees and the receiving of a degree does not guarantee that education has occurred. The necessary and sufficient cause for a university is the process of education, the open and critical search for truth.

A university is what it does. And what it does ought to be protected, preserved, and grown. That is the proper task of boards and administrations: to protect the "verb" of the university. In fact, a university's aspiring sense of *becoming* must be protected by everyone: boards, staff, students, administrators, professors, and even the culture at large. When we believe that this becoming is threatened, we must all be able to engage in dialogue regarding the problems and solutions with creativity, openness, and reasonable safety from reprisal.

It should be clear by now that this integrity and this process cannot be protected and grown with adjunct labor. They do not have the freedom to meaningfully participate in shared governance, to speak "truth." Nor do they have the positive freedom to speak or seek truths alongside their students. There is no integrity where seventy percent of professors are repressed by being restricted to speaking what is palpable, comfortable, and known. This repression is not (in most cases) imposed by the constant firing of adjuncts, but occurs through the self-censorship that happens when people have precarious jobs that they fear they might lose at any moment. The "verb" that education cannot be accomplished within that paddock. As Nussbaum (2010) writes when describing the changes that have led to the contemporary corporate university (that include a significant use of adjunct labor, but is not limited to that):

> Radical changes are occurring in what democratic societies teach the young, and these changes have not been well thought through. Thirsty for national profit, nations, and their systems of education, are heedlessly discarding skills that are needed to keep democracies alive. If this trend continues, nations all over the world will soon be producing *generations of useful machines, rather than complete citizens* who can think for themselves, criticize tradition, and understand the significance of another person's sufferings and achievements (p. 2 [emphasis added]).

Or as I have written elsewhere (2015), "Democracies must be actively sustained by a certain type of citizen: curious, critical, reflective, active, rational, and capable of resisting authority and peer pressure" (p. 22).

Let us assume that you agree with everything so far proposed. Let us be "student centered." A necessary conclusion to what we have so far argued is that students participate in the becoming of education to more or less degrees. Education is not the same "object" no matter what. A bachelor's degree (for instance) does not signify the same process of learning no matter what. Some students will leave their undergraduate education more open-minded and critically thinking than others. The degree of difference in these processes is thanks (in part) to the structures and systems of universities. What is required for this critical and open learning to occur? A teacher. A teacher who is a role model of that very openness and critique, not only in what she says, but in what she does (and what she is allowed to do within the system). A student who experiences teaching that is restricted, safe, impeded will learn consciously and unconsciously that *life is to be lived in that way*, that thinking is to be practiced in that way: closed, fearful, and restricted. Such a student will not become the kind of citizen who can be a critical thinker. Who can whistleblow on a corrupt business or critique the government. Such freethinking must be modeled. A teacher must be a provocateur to openness. A university without such provocateurs is not practicing the verb of education.

Adjuncts cannot model that provocation. We will not say that it is impossible for them to do so. But it is unlikely—a kind of provocation within the paddock of acceptable behavior and accepted truths (as defined by "superiors"). That is, after all, not provocation at all. Adjuncts are not free to best teach our students how to be critical citizens. Because they are themselves not treated as citizens. They live under a regime of fear and popularity. The *verb* and the *becoming* of education will not continue in that setting. And universities will start to become—rather processes of education—mere brands, buildings, mascots. And that's not a university. Call it something else.

LOOKING FORWARD

In order to build academic freedom and justice within higher education, we advocate the following twofold strategy: (a) work toward improved working conditions for existing adjunct professors, and (b) over the long term, build the full-time faculty in terms of numbers and power on university campuses. This strategy can be executed via the following tactics:

1. *Organization:* Form or join an adjunct union; support extrainstitutional adjunct movements.
2. *Education:* Explain to students what adjunct professors are, what they are paid, and how their university uses adjuncts; raise awareness of adjunct working conditions among the general public.
3. *Representation:* Include seats for adjuncts in your faculty senate.

4. *De-adjunctification:* Push for a minimum of eighty percent courses in all departments taught by full-time, tenured, or tenure-track faculty members.
5. *Vigilance:* Keep abreast of how finances at your university are spent (and not spent).
6. *Truth speaking:* If you have tenure, recognize your duty to defend and cultivate shared governance.

REFERENCES

Chomsky, N. (2011, April 6). Academic freedom and the corporatization of universities. *Chomsky. info*. Retrieved from https://chomsky.info/20110406/

Coalition on the Academic Workforce. (2012, June). *A portrait of part-time faculty members: A summary of findings on part-time faculty respondents to the coalition on the academic workforce survey of contingent faculty members and instructors*. Retrieved from http://www.academicworkforce.org/CAW_portrait_2012.pdf

Fredrickson, C. (2015, September 15). There is no excuse for how universities treat adjuncts. *The Atlantic*. Retrieved from http://www.theatlantic.com/ business/ archive /2015/09/ higher-education-college-adjunct-professor-salary/404461/

Gerber, L. (2014). *The rise and decline of faculty governance: Professionalization and the modern American university*. Baltimore, MD: Johns Hopkins University Press.

House Committee on Education and the Workforce. (2014, January). *The just-in-time professor: A staff report summarizing e-forum responses on the working conditions of contingent faculty in higher education*. Retrieved from http://democrats.edworkforce.house.gov/sites/democrats.edworkforce. house.gov/files/documents/1.24.14-AdjunctEforumReport.pdf

Jaschik, S. (2008, October 14). Call to arms for adjuncts [...] from an administrator. *Inside Higher Ed*. Retrieved from https://www.insidehighered.com/news/2008/10/14/adjunct

Kilgannon, C. (2014, March 27). Without tenure or a home. *The New York Times*. Retrieved from http://www.nytimes.com/2014/03/30/nyregion/without-tenure-or-a-home.html.

Loughead, T. (2015). *Critical university: Moving higher education forward*. Lanham, MD: Lexington Press.

Marcus, J. (2014, February 6). New analysis shows problematic boom in higher ed administrators. *New England Center for Investigative Reporting*. Retrieved from http://necir.org/2014/02/06/new-analysis-shows-problematic-boom-in-higher-ed-administrators/

Miller, J. (2015, summer). When adjuncts go union. *The American Prospect*. Retrieved from http://prospect.org/article/when-adjuncts-go-union

Nelson, C. (2010). The three-legged stool: Shared governance, academic freedom, and tenure. In A. Nocella II, S. Best, & P. McLaren (eds.), *Academic repression: Reflections from the academic industrial complex* (pp. 468–490). Oakland, CA: AK Press.

Nocella II, A. J., Best, S., & McLaren P. (2010). Introduction: The rise of the academic-industrial complex and the crisis in free speech. In A. J. Nocella II, S. Best, & P. McLaren (eds.), *Academic repression: Reflections from the academic industrial complex* (pp. 468–490). Oakland, CA: AK Press.

Nussbaum, M. (2010). *Not for profit: Why democracy needs the humanities*. Princeton, NJ: Princeton University Press.

Patton, S. (2012, May 6). From graduate school to welfare. *The Chronicle of Higher Education*. Retrieved from http://chronicle.com/article/From-Graduate-School-to/131795

Patton, S. (2013, October 25). From welfare to the tenure track. *Vitae*. Retrieved from https://chroniclevitae.com/news/97-from-welfare-to-the-tenure-track

Schoen, J. W. (2015, June 16). Why does a college degree cost so much? *CNBC*. Retrieved from http://www.cnbc.com/2015/06/16/why-college-costs-are-so-high-and-rising.html.

Steinbeck, J. (1969). *The Grapes of Wrath*. New York: Bantam Books.

Tropea, G. (2010). Contingent faculty and the problem of structural repression. In A. J. Nocella II, S. Best, & P. McLaren (eds.), *Academic repression: Reflections from the academic industrial complex* (pp. 479–490). Oakland, CA: AK Press.

Wessler, S. F. (2015, April 6). Your college professor could be on public assistance. *NBC News*. Retrieved from http://www.nbcnews.com/feature/in-plain-sight/your-college-professor-could-be-public-assistance-n336596

CHAPTER TWELVE

On Strike in the Ivory Tower: Academic Repression of Labor Organizing

EMIL MARMOL, MARY JEAN HANDE, AND RALUCA BEJAN

INTRODUCTION

As graduate students at the University of Toronto (UofT), we spend much of our time juggling several teaching and research assistantships, taking part in publishing projects, and academic conferences, oftentimes with little time left over to work on our own research. Many of us also struggle to financially survive on funding packages that are far below the poverty line. We are acutely aware of the narrow line of academic freedom we must walk: creative and original enough to stand out from the crowd, but never too critical of the institutions that fund us—"Do not bite the hand that feeds!" as the old saying goes. And certainly, do not engage in any direct action that could undermine the dominant relations of privatization and corporatization of the university. Historically, change has always been effected through direct action. And, although being a graduate student often feels far removed from the experience of direct forms of struggle, we have learned very quickly, through participating in a strike, that to wage a successful action, we needed to do more than simply theorize about forms of oppression or capitalism—we needed to stop our work and directly bite that hand that feeds. Doing so allowed us to see the university in a different light, which revealed concrete and tightly interwoven relations and dimensions of academic repression, surveillance, exploitation, and alienation.

While we were aware that UofT was a highly marketized institution, similar to any elite higher education establishment, and that it heavily exploited graduate student labor, four weeks of being on strike revealed an even darker side of the university. It helped us better understand that the relationship between a highly corporatized, financialized university not only intensifies academic repression and labor exploitation, but that it actually depends on it. We came to develop a more visceral and concrete understanding of how the corporate structure of the university not only made us hyperexploited academic laborers, but also impoverished the quality and critical possibilities intrinsically assumed to be present within higher education institutions. We draw on our experiences as rank-and-file organizers during the 2015 Canadian Union of Public Employees (CUPE), Local 3902, Unit 1 strike to show how academic repression is interrelated with labor exploitation and alienation. We also outline a number of concrete examples of academic repression at UofT in which faculty experienced attacks on their academic freedom, linked to increasingly intensifying corporate partnerships and governance. During a time when graduate student workers were in direct conflict with the university administration, we show how UofT used modes of academic repression to cover up and silence the strike action and fragmented dissenting students, professors, and other workers, with the goal of demobilizing and ending the strike. We will emphasize how much we learned by being on strike in the ivory tower and how solidarity was built across UofT and beyond, in similar ways as those documented in Zaidi's (2010) account of "The Strike at Syracuse."

This analysis of academic repression, explicitly linked to how corporate academia has become a site of labor exploitation and alienation, shows how vaunted notions of academic freedom (Best, Nocella II, & McLaren, 2010; Churchill, 2010) are easily sacrificed during labor actions, and how meaningful and broad labor solidarity is thwarted and prevented through ongoing practices of academic repression within elite and highly corporatized, and surreptitiously privatized institutions such as UofT.

This chapter begins by laying out the ways in which UofT fits the established theories and definitions of corporate and repressive universities. By *corporate* university we understand the manifestation of a so-called corporate culture as "an all-encompassing horizon for producing market identities, values and practices" (Giroux, 2002, p. 429), as particularly reflected in the overall ideological orientation of higher educational institutions and trickled down to the day-to-day activities and practices of running such institutions, which compromise and destroy, in return, the critical aspects of what academic thinking and discourse should be all about.

This repression will be demonstrated by: (1) showing how the governance structure is intimately linked with corporate investors, partners, and relationships; (2) briefly examining how UofT has become financialized through its changing funding structure, also interrelated with neoliberal processes, austerity measures, and privatization schemes; and (3) increased disciplinary measures against academics who did not toe the corporate line. We will then describe the 2015 CUPE 3902 strike, with a particular focus on the increased repression used by the administration during the strike, including the bribing of undergraduates with passing grades in exchange for strikebreaking. We then discuss the relationship between exploitive working conditions and quality of education for both ourselves and the students we teach. We argue that fighting academic repression and waging a successful strike are interrelated processes, requiring actively building broad-based solidarity across faculty, graduate, and undergraduate students as well as other workers outside of academia and social movements more broadly. This requires that CUPE move away from its current "business unionism," to a form of social movement or revolutionary unionism, which we describe in the penultimate section. Finally, we provide specific strategies and tactics that can be used to wage effective strikes against repressive, corporate universities.

UNIVERSITY OF TORONTO AS A CORPORATE AND REPRESSIVE UNIVERSITY

We recognize that there is no idealized past where universities were truly democratically controlled by "the people" or where they did not primarily serve the liberal interests of the ruling classes. Nevertheless, particularly in times of explicit struggle (like a strike), the university is being rapidly wrested away from the public through neoliberal and financial restructuring. In this context, universities like UofT, barely bother to pay lip service to democracy or public interests, making it increasingly difficult for students and academic workers to assert democratic power and direction within these institutions.

Neoliberalism's influence on higher education is most visible through what Giroux (2002) called the "corporate culture of universities." In this culture, politics and democratic citizenship are subordinated to market values, and business is intertwined in every functioning aspect of the university, which, in turn has the effect of compromising any critical and political forms of education as well as commitments to academic freedom. Magnusson (2013) describes how this corporate culture of universities is also linked with the financialization of higher education, where austerity and debt become the norm, and new forms of highly securitized and militarized education, such as military schools, gated universities, Americorp and New Beginnings Education, flourish. According to Magnusson, these neoliberal, corporatized, and securitized sites of education "leave no room to leverage the kind of critical tools and engagement necessary to produce a citizenry that is able to work through and transform the social relations of global financial imperialism" (p. 77).

Measured against this literature (see also Aronowitz, 2000; Bernans, 2001; Marmol, 2015a; Washburn, 2005; Woodhouse, 2009), UofT embodies a range of attributes of a neoliberal, corporate university, and is reflective of the "commercialization, marketization, and corporatization" of higher education (Marmol, 2015a, p. 2). First, like most North American universities, the governance structure at UofT is strongly linked to and invested in the private market. The University's Governing Council, the administrative body overseeing all of its affairs, is comprised of members affiliated with various corporate and commercial companies. The Council is composed of fifty members, twenty-five from within the UofT community, such as administrative staff, teaching staff, and students, with the remaining twenty-five externally affiliated with the University (Governing Council, 2015). Of the twenty-five external affiliations, ninteen appointees have strong ties with the private sector, including finance, asset management, banking, private investment, energy, technology, software development and communications, law, real estate firms, retail companies, media conglomerates, land development, public accounting, and the medical industry (see appendix). Many members of UofT's Governing Council sit on multiple corporate boards simultaneously. For instance, Judy Goldring sits on the board of AGF Management and UofT employs AGF's services through the UofT Asset Management Corporation (Hemmadi & Yan, 2013). Ira Gluskin, who sponsored the Max Gluskin House for the Economics department, is the Chairman of the UofT Asset Management Corporation, responsible for overseeing investable assets on behalf of the University (Bloomberg, 2016). One member was described as having "served as Chair of the Innovations Foundation, the entity then responsible for commercialization of university-based research at University of Toronto" (Governing Council, 2015).

The financialization of UofT is not only visible through the managerial models that have come to dominate the decision-making bodies across and within departments, but also in terms of the University's pro-market orientations, as reflected through investments and management of financial assets. UofT has set up a long-term capital appreciation pool (LTCAP), which includes endowments and trusts managed by UofT Asset Management Corporation (UTAM), in order to maximize the University's profit-making potential (University of Toronto Governing Council, 2007; UTAM Annual Report, 2014). The expendable funds investment pool (EFIP), also managed by UTAM, consists in part of student fees, which are invested, seemingly, to enrich university administrators (UTAM Annual Report, 2014). As of 2014, UTAM was managing $7.4 billion in assets (UTAM Annual Report, 2014). Looking through the UTAM annual reports could leave one with the impression that the university functions primarily as an investment firm, rather than a place of public higher education. A recent report by Valverde and Briggs (2015) also shows how UofT set the trend for Canadian universities to use debentures, a long-term collateral-free bond, to finance a number of non-academic urban development projects, including facilities for the 2015 Toronto Pan/Parapan Am Games. According to Valverde and Briggs, debentures limit the University's ability to adjust tuition levels, set fees and secure government funding.

As will be discussed in further detail below, the pay structure at UofT increasingly mirrors that of a major corporation. Those at the highest administrative levels are paid according to "market value" with decadent six and nearly seven figure salaries and regularly increasing pay raises, while those at the bottom— teaching assistants and course instructors who do the lion's share of the work— earn stagnant poverty-level wages. In an effort to further increase the bottom line, the administration has also engaged in layoffs of support staff, much in the same way that a corporation engages in restructuring (Cribb, 2015). The absence of support staff leaves students without the assistance they require and serves to burden those remaining support staff with higher workloads.

Education more generally is seen as a business, and at the administrative level, students are often referred to as "basic income units." This is the term that UofT's internal documents use to describe its students. Hence, students are now recognized as little more than mere financial instruments. In addition to paying exorbitant tuition fees, these basic income units are targeted for the sale of a variety of goods: computers, cell phone plans, an abundance of university branded items, and food sold on the premises through on-campus retailers, many of which are owned by outside corporations or contractors. This type of piecemeal privatization is a phenomenon occurring across North American universities (Marmol, 2015a, p. 10). Events held on campus must be catered by these firms as outside food is not permitted.

The corporate, financial influence at UofT is also reflected through the financial support provided by corporate entities to entire departments and faculties. Most donations seem to originate from the financial, investment sector, mining, and resource extraction industries:

1. Peter Munk, the founder of Barrick Gold, donated $6.4 million for the Peter Munk Centre for International Studies (Adams, 2002), and $35 million for the formation of the Munk School of Global Affairs in 2009 (Chernos, 2011).

2. Lassonde Institute of Mining at UofT Faculty of Applied Science and Engineering was created with the financial assistance of the Canadian minerals industry and the financial support of Pierre Lassonde, president of Franco-Nevada Mining Company (Canadian Mining Hall of Fame, 2013).

3. Sheldon Inwentash, owner and CEO of Pinetree Capital, which contains a portfolio of junior resource and energy stock spread across several mining

industries, donated $15 million to the Faculty of Social Work (Girard, 2007).

4. The Faculty of Law received a gift of $500,000 (Canadian dollars) to renovate the now-called Fasken Martineau Building (University of Toronto, 2005).

5. The Goldring Centre for High Performance Sport was built with an $11 million gift from the Goldring family (Hall, 2011) via their American Growth Fund (The Canadian Press, 2009).

6. Hal Jackman, the thirty-fifth richest person in Canada and 1638th in the world, largest shareholder in E-L Financial Corporation (Forbes, 2015), donated over $40 million to UofT (Agrba, 2013).

7. Investor Russell Morrison and wife Katherine Morrison, who previously provided funding for Morrison Hall, the Gerstein Science Information Centre, and the Morrison Pavilion, have just committed to support the costs for renovating the Robarts Library, with restorations set to start in the Spring of 2016 (Colero, 2016).

The question arising is not only about the unethicality of exchanging large sums of money to secure the naming rights on university buildings, but also about how academic freedom and critical thought can be fostered within an environment where, in return for funding, departments have to provide their donors with annual progress reports on their programs, activities, and initiatives. How do we expect that any research critical of the mining industry, the financial sectors, or the pharmaceutical industry will ever come from a university when these sectors fund most of its faculties and departments and where these industries steer the direction of research?

The answer is we cannot, especially with UofT's track record. UofT has a history of fiercely protecting its corporate interests through academic repression. As an example, during the 1990s, Dr. Nancy Olivieri, a hematologist and researcher employed by the University and its fully affiliated Hospital for Sick Children, discovered serious potentially life-threatening consequences of a trial drug produced by Apotex. For fulfilling her professional obligation to patients and informing them of these potential risks, she was subjected to harassment, character assassination, and dismissal from the hospital. A special report concluded that the University did not act satisfactorily to protect Dr. Olivieri's academic freedom (Thompson, Downie, Baird, & Canadian Association of University Teachers, 2001). During this time the university president was lobbying the government in order to prevent legislation that would hurt Apotex's profits. Also at stake was the multimillion dollar donation from Apotex that would have been the largest donation ever to UofT. Meanwhile, Dr. Michael Spino, representative of Apotex and a Professor in the Faculty of Pharmacy at UofT, the most prominent figure in violating Dr. Olivieri's academic freedom, was not reprimanded by the university (Thompson, Downie, Baird, & Canadian Association of University Teachers, 2001).

In a similar case, Psychiatrist David Healy was offered the position of Director of the Mood and Anxiety Disorders Program at the Centre for Addiction and Mental Health (CAMH), which is affiliated with U of T. He accepted this position which also included a university professorship. While preparing to take up his new position, he gave a public lecture at a conference that was organized by the Department of Psychiatry and held at CAMH. During his talk he expressed views critical of psychotropic drugs, selective serotonin reuptake inhibitors, and their link to suicide. Shortly thereafter, the offer of employment was rescinded. Media sources claimed his offer was withdrawn due to the fact that about forty percent of the funding for the Mood and Anxiety Disorders Program came from the pharmaceutical industry (Lemmens, 2004). It was also noted that Eli Lilly, makers of the SSRI drug Prozac had very close research ties to CAMH (Lemmens, 2004). David Healy himself suggested alternatively that Dr. Charles Nemeroff, a leading figure in the field of psychiatry with very close ties to the pharmaceutical industry, had used his influence to dissuade university administration from honoring their offer. Whatever may have been the case, administration once again demonstrated that critical research in the public's interest came second to corporate interests.

OUR STRIKE AGAINST THE REPRESSIVE, CORPORATE UNIVERSITY

These corporate, financialized relations set the stage for the largest labor dispute in U of T's history. On February 27, 2015, after facing nearly a year of stalled and ineffective contract negotiations, CUPE Local 3902, Unit 1, took strike action. Local 3902, Unit 1 represents about 6,500 teaching assistants, course instructors, and invigilators/proctors at U of T. Although we were requesting a number of improvements to our contract, the principal demands were an increase to the minimum funding package, and tuition relief for those in the fifth and sixth years of their PhD programs.

Many funded graduate students at U of T earn a minimum funding package of $15,000 a year in exchange for work as researchers, teaching assistants, and course instructors. However, for those with no external funding granted through provincial or federal governmental bodies, this sum is oftentimes insufficient for covering living expenses, placing many of us well under the poverty line, which for 2015 was $23,861 for a single person (www.statcan.gc.ca). During the strike, the administration argued that PhD students receive, on average, $35,109 a year in financial support. This is factually incorrect. While no one without external funding will ever get to $35,000 a year, in some faculties, students might receive a package of more than $15,000 in addition to a tuition waiver. In other departments some receive just $15,000 and no tuition waiver (Wilson, et al., 2015). Yet despite the interdepartmental variances, there has been no increase in the base-funding package level since it was last negotiated in 2008. Of note, graduate students are not typically allowed to take on substantial outside employment to supplement their incomes as doing so puts their funding at risk. Teaching assistants and course instructors provide over sixty percent of undergraduate instruction, yet only 3.5 percent of the University-wide budget is dedicated to their compensation (Peries, 2015). Meanwhile, the salaries of university administrators resemble those of corporate executives, ranging anywhere from $300,000 to over $900,000 (www.thesunshinelist.com). It is not only the amount of the salaries that stands out, but also the yearly increases to these amounts. Administrative pay raises were matched by stagnant amounts for the graduate student funding packages. This relationship is akin to a major corporation's executives relative to its sweatshop workers. Of course, in absolute terms our situation is perhaps not as oppressive, but the exploitative nature of the relationship is very much the same.

The issue of tuition relief was an additional bargaining item brought up during the strike. PhD students in their fifth or sixth years have long since completed their coursework and are typically engaged in their own research. The only university resources they utilize consist of library access, occasional use of space, and sporadic supervisory meetings. Graduate students feel it is unreasonable to be charged tuition fees amounting to tens of thousands of dollars for a library card and occasional meetings with their supervisory committee.

During the strike, the university's administrators made every effort to ensure the *status quo* would be preserved. Similar to a major corporation, they used their influence to sway public opinion and protect their image, disseminating misleading and untruthful information in emails and statements, both on their official website and to major media sources. In official communications coming from the Vice President and Provost Office, the administration presented itself as the neutral player at the table, stating that it was making all reasonable efforts to reach a new collective agreement before the legal strike deadline, and that it respects the decision of CUPE Unit 1 members who continue to work, as well as the decision of those choosing to strike. As the labor dispute continued, messages seemed increasingly reproachful toward the strike and employed more persuasive efforts to encourage strikebreaking. An official communication from March 1, addressed to the University-wide community, stated that the administration had made all efforts to reach a fair agreement and that it was disappointing that Unit 1 members had voted down the settlement. The email included a link for registration through the employee self-service system for those wanting to continue their work. On March 3, a detailed email followed stating that the administration was making an effort to minimize the impact of the strike on undergraduate students (openly disregarding that those on strike were also students) and outlining step-by-step instructions for those willing to work, also including a hyperlink to a "Confirmation of Intention to Work" form. On March 16, the administration made clear that their priority was for students to complete the term based on their purported commitment to students' academic success. After a new tentative agreement was sent out for ratification, the administration sent out communications encouraging CUPE members to learn more about the offer and to vote. After the settlement offer was again rejected by the CUPE membership, the administration communicated that an Academic Continuity Team was set in place to minimize the strike impact and to assist students in completing the term, despite ongoing strike action. Administration framed themselves as the benevolent party and the strikers as greedy and selfish.

University administration were so desperate to crush the strike that they even went so far as to hire undergraduate students to grade the work of their fellow classmates (Brown, 2015a). It stands to reason that hiring undergraduates to assess the work of other undergraduates may compromise academic integrity and may also diminish the likelihood that papers will be evaluated with an adequate level of intellectual rigor and expertise. This is a clear example of how supposed commitments to academic freedom and integrity were easily compromised in the interest of undermining and fighting labor organizing. It also underscored the ways in which satisfactory working conditions correspond with improved learning conditions.

What we consider the most reprehensible and destructive tactic deployed by administrators was the implementation of something they called academic continuity. This was a plan by which undergraduate students who had only completed a portion of their coursework would then be offered a final grade and course credit based on that fraction of work (Brown, 2015b), tantamount to bribing undergraduates with free grades for strikebreaking (Comay, 2015; Hill, 2015). At the time the administration implemented academic continuity, undergraduates had completed roughly twenty percent of their work for the current term. If classes were completed in such a way, then the teaching assistants, course instructors, and invigilators/proctors who were on strike would no longer be necessary for giving lectures, assessing work, or giving exams. This successfully weakened our leverage during the strike. Further highlighting the administration's pecuniary imperatives, undergraduate students were not offered a discount or refund for the semester, despite students' demands to be compensated (Brown, 2015b). In this way, administrators could break our strike while keeping the profits from undergraduate students' inflated tuition fees. This was a brazen public display of greed and total disregard for academic integrity. For the neoliberal administration the goal was, and continues to be, to extract maximum profit and enrich top-level administrators while exploiting academic laborers and undergraduate students. It is clearly of little consequence if graduate students live in poverty and undergraduates are deprived of quality education.

Consistent with the trend toward increased campus policing and surveillance (Nocella II & Gabbard, 2013), administrators hired a private security firm to intimidate strikers and to surveil picket lines to gather information that could later be used against us. There was enhanced security personnel around Simcoe Hall, where the offices of many of the executive administrators are housed. This private security company was present on the picket lines every day during the strike and it is presumed to have come at substantial financial cost, revealing that administrators were much more invested in fighting labor organizing than providing living wages for their workers.

Academic repression (Nocella II, Best, & McLaren, 2010) was especially visible in the form of retaliation during the strike. Teaching assistants and course instructors were prevented from communicating their side of the dispute to undergraduates. Those who used Blackboard, the online platform for course management, to communicate with their students about the strike, had their access terminated—a Kafkian bureaucratic infringement of academic freedom, especially Article 10 of our Collective Agreement, which states that "The University is committed to the pursuit of truth, the advancement of learning, and the dissemination of knowledge. To this end, they agree to abide by the principles of academic freedom with respect to Course Instructors: academic freedom is the freedom to examine, question, teach, and learn, and it involves the right to investigate, speculate, and comment without reference to prescribed doctrine, as well as the right to criticize the University, and society at large" (CUPE 3902 Collective Agreement, 2014, p. 7). Suspending Blackboard communications for the course instructors involved in the strike had purposely infringed on the academic freedom to speak up and to stand against an oppressive institutional *status quo*, by censuring and regulating thought. It is not only about silencing the perspectives that are critical and contrary to the official line presented by the university, but also about the monopoly on the story being told, with no consideration to the fact that students have the right to be informed of alternative perspectives.

Repression also took the form of intimidation toward those heavily involved in the strike. In one case, a graduate student and friend of the authors, whose precarious financial situation forced him to live in the communal graduate office space of his department, and who had been unable to pay for the flight to visit his wife and child overseas, was sent intimidating emails from the chair of his department. These emails impugned his character and accused him of not making wise financial decisions. (Ironically, the department chair was scheduled as the keynote speaker for a symposium on economic inequality that would take place on campus during the strike, thus crossing the picket line by attending.) Academic repression continued after the strike as many of the most active and vocal individuals during the strike were denied teaching assistantships despite being the most experienced applicants. Many of them were eventually offered employment with the University after filing formal grievances. Nevertheless, filing a grievance against the University is a potentially stressful process and is certainly time consuming. In other departments teaching and course instructor job postings were no longer advertised to graduate students and were sent directly to contract instructors, forcing Unit 1 members to take cross-divisional appointments, not necessarily in their field or interest of study.

THE STAKES ARE HIGH

We believe it is necessary to prevent universities from enacting severe anti-student and anti-worker measures such as those mentioned previously. During the strike we all learned more about issues of social (in)justice, labor exploitation, and neoliberalism than we could have from any academic book or conference. We were forced into a situation where we soon discovered that despite our "critical education" at one of the top universities in Canada, there was a lot to learn about how to wage a successful strike action and what was at stake for all of us. We learned in concrete ways how the working conditions of those within the higher education sector have tangible consequences for undergraduate students as well as for those of us who teach them.

"Our working conditions are their learning conditions!" was one of many chants shouted on the picket lines. It is a pithy summary of the reality of how our precarious, below poverty-level living conditions affect our ability to carry out our commitments to students and how the quality of our instruction suffers as a result. Many graduate students at the UofT live in substandard housing, carefully budgeting and stretching their resources to provide for a barebones existence (Yelland, 2015). The stress induced by such precarious living conditions is compounded by our lack of job security, as many of us are forced to reapply for jobs every four months or on a yearly basis. Those of us permitted to take additional employment only delay the completion of our degrees by diluting time and energy that we could be providing to our own research. Research has shown that graduate students who take on additional employment significantly delay their degree completion time, which results in additional years of paying full tuition fees, further enriching the administration while impoverishing themselves (Bost, 2016). This creates an arrangement in which one pays for the opportunity to work for the university, a vicious circle dubbed by some as the feeding of the "debt-monster" (Class Struggle University, 2015). Our stress and time deficits are compounded again when administrators overload courses, which subsequently increases our workload and dilutes our pay. How can we provide the best-quality education to our students, or focus on our own education, under these conditions?

Not fighting for better conditions for those at the bottom of the higher education teaching ladder has a ripple effect on the already high and rising number of low-paid, precariously employed contract or untenured faculty who face living and working conditions similar to our own. In Canada, it is estimated that over half of all undergraduate students are taught by contract faculty (Basen, 2014). These contract faculty live on poverty-level wages, holding teaching positions at several universities with no job security or benefits. They are provided little time to dedicate to their students as they teach overloaded courses and are forced to share an office if they are provided with one at all, having to instead communicate with students via email. In contrast to the administration's goal of profit maximization at the cost of declining quality of education, we are deeply committed educators who want the best for our students. We need to be provided with sufficient time, fair remuneration, adequate resources, and job security to carry out our commitments to students. Our ability to fight for better conditions for all depends upon our collective strength.

On March 25 (twenty-seven days into our strike), UofT President, Meric Gertler, called for binding arbitration as a way to "respectfully and collegially" end the strike, just two days before The Sunshine List (a provincewide listing of public employees earning more than $100,000 a year) was publicly released. It was perhaps not coincidental that the list contained the names of several administrators and other high-level employees at the university who received pay increases in excess of twenty percent (Bejan, 2015b). Vice President and Provost Cheryl Regehr saw a salary increase from $247,355.32 to $311,999.96 (26.13 percent). The salary of Meric Gertler increased from $351,747.72 to $398,737.41 (13.36 percent). William Moriarty, President and Chief Executive Officer of UTAM Corporation, had his salary increased from a whopping $772,547.00 to $937,500.00 (21.35 percent) (www.thesunshinelist.com). During the strike we were repeatedly told that the administration could not increase our funding due to budget shortfalls, an assertion that was proven patently false with the release of these figures. For an institution whose primary role is allegedly educational provision, it is unjustifiable to foster such high administrative salaries, while providing such low rates of funding for their student workers. Yet even more problematic is to continually sustain an increased discrepancy and inequality in the pay levels between those at the top and those at the bottom.

Undergraduate students were directly and negatively impacted by the administration's implementation of academic continuity. One of the authors was approached by a student who was concerned about her performance during final exams. Initially, the student mentioned being thankful for the policy of academic continuity. She said her grade point average did not suffer because she received credit for a class in which she was doing poorly and had only partially completed. However, now in the second year, the very same student shared that she is struggling because she lacks the foundational knowledge in her academic field, which was denied to her through the implementation of academic continuity. This student will never receive a refund and will likely pay additional tuition fees later on to catch up to the level of her peers. The ideological message embedded within the concept of academic continuity also normalizes the idea that the university is not an institution dedicated to learning and critical thinking, but rather a business granting diplomas in exchange for money.

Students and student workers are the lifeblood of any university. However, the forms of academic repression and labor suppression used by U of T during the strike clearly demonstrate that providing high-quality education is a significantly lower priority than serving the university's financial interests, increasing the salaries of top administrators, and successfully suppressing the ability of U of T workers and students to collectively organize and make demands. As the university becomes more financialized and saturated in corporate culture, we should expect these tactics to intensify, making the stakes of resistance higher for academic workers.

MOVING FORWARD

Whether or not the CUPE 3902, Unit 1 strike was successful, or to what degree it was efficacious or not, is a point of contention with a fairly wide range of viewpoints. For critical perspectives and analyses of the strike, please see Bejan (2015a, 2015b), Hande (2015), and Marmol (2015b). Irrespective of our strike's real or perceived gains and/or failures, there is nearly a universal agreement that there are ways of improving the success of future strikes.

As a more general guiding principle, unions should move away from the *business unionism* model, which cannot provide a viable form of collective organizing. Canadian business unionism is described by Camfield as "a unionism that basically accepts existing social relations, has a narrow focus on collective bargaining, usually adopts a cooperative concessionary approach with employers, allows for very little initiative or democratic control by members, and usually supports the political direction taken by the NDP [New Democratic Party] in recent years" (2007, p. 285). Business unionism allows unions to capitulate to and reinforce current neoliberal and capitalist social relations. This model is not designed to fight for significant gains on behalf of workers or society at large. Instead, it advances the interests of those located at the top of the union structure and those who attain office in political parties purporting to fight on the behalf of unions. In order to make gains for workers, unions must assume an antagonistic position in their relationship toward capital and political parties that fight against the interests of the working class.

Two potential alternatives that could replace business unionism are social movement unionism and its more radical sibling revolutionary unionism. Social movement unionism has a broad-based solidaristic orientation, as it works to build community with other justice-seeking groups, community organizations, and unions (Camfield, 2007). It concerns itself broadly with workers' lives, on and off the job, eschewing narrow efforts to simply make gains on wages and benefits, choosing instead to change society for the better. Social movement unionism embraces militancy in the form of direct action, respecting the choice of its adherents to employ a multiplicity of tactics to attain its goals. It recognizes that building a movement is a long-term process of wins and losses. While social movement unionism might strategically call on the support of political parties, it does not depend upon this support, preferring to focus on creating a broad social movement. Democratic control by the membership is considered a central feature for building union power. A strong emphasis is placed on increasing rank-and-file members' knowledge, skills, confidence, participation, and activity. In this way, the bureaucratic, hierarchical, top-down down relationship to union leadership is weakened.

Revolutionary unionism holds similar beliefs and practices to those of social movement unionism, with the exception that it aims to actually bring an end to capitalism, and as such, would be very unlikely to rely on any form of support from any political party (Neal, 2011). Research and, of course, the material history of strike actions, has demonstrated that strategies related to such forms of unionism have been instrumental in winning victories against neoliberal economic reforms and austerity measures (Camfield, 2007). These models of unionism are in stark contrast to the business unionism currently practiced by CUPE at the local, provincial, and national levels.

Of course, there is much to learn from historical and current examples of strike action. Rather than narrowing our focus on U of T and reinforcing the employer and union bureaucratic line, that singularized our labor dispute, we need to explore how it is interlinked with other successful and unsuccessful labor actions (discussed in more detail further). The student strikes in our neighbor province Quebec have been, by far, the most successful strikes waged in academic institutions, and we can only gain from learning from their actions and strategically link our struggles with theirs (see Gross & Swain, 2015, for concrete lessons learned from student labor organizing in Quebec). Viewed in this light, we need to understand that strikes are always political and that a victory for labor depends on outside solidarity and, in turn, bolsters the success of other labor actions.

How do we implement these models and practices? There is much to be done. Most importantly, the rank-and-file need education and awareness of the issues and their potential solutions. Union members should be encouraged to link the restructuring of our economy to social and labor relations and to the ideological imperatives of capitalism and neoliberalism. Experience taught us that these lessons are best learned through a combination of on-the-ground struggles as well as by study and reflection on such struggle. This not only requires that we work with similar groups to analyze the contradictions of the corporate university, but that we also find ways which show students and workers how to claim more power at the university and transform it to serve the public good (see Angus, 2009; Bernans, 2001; Revolutionary Student Movement, 2013, 2015; University for Strategic Optimism, 2011, for examples of how students and student movements have grappled with these issues).

Overall, the strike was aggressively depoliticized—with union bureaucrats frightened to lose control of the action by making larger strike demands and building a broader base of solidarity. It was mainly centered on procedural and logistic elements of the funding package and ways to increase the funding packages across departmental and faculty divisions, but was not collectively seen as part of a greater political opportunity to stamp out the influence of neoliberal ideology on education, to change the corporatization of academia per se, nor to transform the very same structural conditions of financial capitalism that are maintaining the funding packages below the poverty line. Adding a few dollars to the graduate-funding packages will do very little for the generations to come or for other workers who are fighting for better working conditions. If such amounts are not structurally weighted against enrollment rates, inflation, or yearly tuition increases, they will never stop the unequal trends of administrators' salaries substantially growing year after year while graduate student workers' wages remain stagnant.

UofT faculty and professors need to understand that they are also workers engaged in class struggle so that we may bring about a class-consciousness to our labor organizing, as well as to connect in solidarity with other social movements. Rank-and-file militant and radical members should gain access to leadership positions in the union, and if this is not possible, they should continue to subvert and agitate in whatever ways available to them. Leadership should be replaced if they do not accede to the demands and the needs of the rank-and-file members.

STRATEGIES AND TACTICS

Ultimately, better working conditions come about by transforming exploitative capitalist social relations (based on gender, race, and disability) in society as a whole and immediate strike demands should never compromise or obscure these larger goals. In addition to the general and long-term goal of changing the type of unionism described previously, there are specific strategies and tactics that can help to secure demands leading up to and during a strike.

Strategically Initiate the Commencement of the Strike/Work Stoppage

With the possibility that more university administrators may start employing highly problematic tactics such as the euphemistic-sounding "academic continuity," it is important to time the start of the strike carefully so that these methods are less effective. Beginning the strike very early in the academic term can help avoid such administrative intervention. If the strike is well-timed and the term does not get underway, then it is not possible to implement academic continuity as there will be no initial record upon which a final grade can be based. Grades will not be provided for strikebreaking as it would be impossible for administrators to give away grades for a course that never began.

Shut It Down!

The most effective tactic during a strike is to shut down the university's operations as completely as possible. It is likely that nothing else will exert as much pressure on the administration as bringing their operations to a standstill. Work stoppages hurt the administration's image and profit-making potential. Reach out to colleagues and ask them not to scab or strike break in any way, emphasizing that stopping all work means stopping *all* work. If you use an online course managing system to post grades and other resources, make sure you shut that down too. You do not want the university to be able to complete your work (or the course) for you.

Build Solidarity within Your Local

It is imperative that a local and/or union show a unified front. If the local is separated into different units, it is important to foster cross-unit solidarity efforts. For instance, CUPE Local 3902 consists of five units. Before the strike, both units 1 and 3 were bargaining simultaneously. Unit 3 (representing contract academic staff) received an offer from the administration that more or less placated them, and therefore they did not go on strike. This was an obvious "divide and conquer" ploy used by administrators to dilute the strength of the strike, by providing concessions to one group at the expense of the other, and unfortunately it worked. It is important that bargaining units within a local come to an agreement that no unit will accept a new contract unless all units are satisfied with their contracts. CUPE Local 3903 at York University in Toronto, for example, has such an interunit agreement in place, which helped them win improved contracts for all their units.

Enlist the Help of Other Unions on Campus

Reaching out to every other union on campus is also important in building solidarity. That means finding out what unions represent the different employees on campus, including staff members; internal mail delivery; electrical and plumbing workers; heating, ventilation, and air condition workers; sanitation; housekeeping; security; food preparation; delivery services; etc. Some unions have clauses in their collective agreements that they will not cross the picket lines of other unions. Make use of this and ask every union on campus not to cross the picket line. This makes a strike more effective and powerful, providing much-needed leverage by completely halting university operations. If other education workers, at other colleges or universities, are negotiating new contracts, coordinate simultaneous strike action that can help escalate strike demands to a government level—allowing both locals to make higher demands and bigger gains. For example, when both UofT and York University graduate student workers were on strike at the same time, pressure began building on the province of Ontario to increase funding for postsecondary education. This kind of collaboration requires long and close ties to other unions and is not something you can just expect or take for granted. There needs to be continuous relationship building and maintenance of close ties with other unions so that you can call on them or coordinate with them when you need them and vice versa.

Ask for Support/Solidarity from Professors and Faculty

Supportive faculty members can constitute another important source of leverage. If faculty slow down or stop working in support of a strike, this can really tip the scales. The university cannot function if classes are not being taught. Again, such a relationship needs to be built and nurtured over time. In order to bring them onside, faculty must be made aware of the reasons for the strike and the precarious conditions of teaching assistants, research assistants, and course instructors. It might help to gently and carefully remind them that their power at the university is bolstered by the strength of those below them.

Build Solidarity with Undergraduates and Their Student Government

It is important to reach out to undergraduates and inform them of the working conditions of their teaching assistants and course instructors. Many are unaware and might turn against the strike if the messaging coming from the university administration is not countered effectively. During the strike, one of the authors spoke to a group of about ten undergraduates during one of our building-blocking actions. Many students were initially suspicious and blamed us for being greedy and selfish. After they had heard how little money we earn under our funding packages, particularly in relation to the salaries earned by members of the university's administration, they were eager to offer their support. It is very helpful if undergraduate student government holds town halls and question/answer sessions with undergraduates in support of the strike. It is important not be afraid to communicate in whatever way available, including the use of any online and social media resources. Undergraduates talk to the press, their parents and their peers. Solidarity with students can be built by presenting factual information in a respectful manner, by supporting their demands for lower tuition (see as examples, Brown, 2015b; Gardiner, 2013), advocating for their diversity and equity efforts, such as an increasing the number of underrepresented students and academics at the university (i.e., Black On Campus, see Marrelli, 2015), and their campaigning issues: for instance, the fossil fuels divestment movement (see Toronto350.org), or by preserving important accessible programming for marginalized students, such as UofT's Transitional Year Program (Panos, 2013).

Actively Participate in the Strike

Being on the picket line or actively contributing to the strike is a great way to maintain solidarity and morale, allowing one to share stories, strategies, and successful tactics while making new friends. Most importantly it is a show of force, determination, and will to win. A picket consisting of a small percentage of the workforce can send the wrong message. For instance, during our strike, the number of picketers started to wane toward the middle and end of the strike. At meetings, some argued that our strike was weakening based on this observation. Post strike, the administration inadvertently disclosed an email showing that only three out of ten members continued to work during the strike, meaning that about seventy percent of the Unit 1 membership stopped working for the duration of the strike. One could have easily been misled to think that everyone had gone back to work if judging by the numbers on the picket line. Ask your professors and undergraduate students to join the line. Bringing homemade snacks and drinks is always a good way to increase morale, although the union should also provide daily sustenance. Participation also means making sure that people who cannot walk to picket lines (because of disability-related issues or care work responsibilities) are given alternative options for contributing to the strike and compensated accordingly through picket pay.

Get the Message Out through the Media

This can be a difficult task as most corporate media are not friendly to labor and usually disparage the labor movement as a whole. Yet it is effective to write short, factual opinion pieces and submit them to a variety of news outlets. For instance, news pieces critical of the administration written by both graduate and undergraduate students were published by mainstream media, such as the national center-right Globe and Mail (Schwartz, 2015a), by progressive left-leaning national outlets such as rabble.ca (Bejan, 2015; Bejan & German, 2015; Wilson, et al., 2015) or by U of T's own student paper, the *Varsity* (Schwartz, 2015b). One strategy is to reach out to friendly contacts in the press or to send out press releases that can always be drafted in advance, anticipating the university administration's next move. The university's student newspapers are a great starting place for spreading the word as the editorial board would most likely be sympathetic of the cause, and the intended audience will be most effectively reached.

Be Willing to Strike as often as Necessary

The administration needs to understand that exploitation of its employees is unacceptable and that such behavior will be met with a strong response every time. If the administration feels that its employees are pushovers who willingly accept existing social relations then this is how they will be treated. Conversely, if the administration fears that workers will organize effectively and strike, they will be hesitant to undermine worker's health, rights, and pay. Workers can also effectively build on lessons learned from previous strike actions, improving the efficacy of strike action through practice.

Ensure Strikes are Political and that They are Contributing to Larger, Anti-capitalist Organizing and Transformation

This includes building solidarity with important social movements like Black Lives Matter, the Quebec Student Movement, precarious industries and workers, migrant laborers and anti-poverty groups, as well as anti-imperialist international solidarity through groups like Academics for Peace (http://academicsforpeace.ca/about-us/campus-dialogue/). During the strike rank-and-file members at both York University (where CUPE workers were also on strike) and U of T developed a "Joint Strike Committee" that worked not only to build solidarity between both locals and apply pressure on the province of Ontario, but also to show active support with tens of thousands of struck students in Quebec (Bonnar, 2015). Such solidarity work can be built democratically through rank-and-file organizing, effective use of caucuses and solidarity committees, providing donations, and by having union representation at other political events.

ACKNOWLEDGMENTS

The authors would like to acknowledge here that this analysis was developed through collective struggle with our struck comrades at University of Toronto and York University, as well as many other community and union members who joined our picket lines, brought us food, made donations, wrote letters of solidarity and helped us understand that the 2015 CUPE 3902 strike was bigger than us.

APPENDIX: THE CORPORATE AFFILIATIONS OF UOFT GOVERNING COUNCIL

1. Michael Wilson, Chairman of Barclays Capital Canada
2. Judy Goldring, Executive Vice President and Chief Operating Officer at AGF Management
3. Preet Banerjee, Financial Consultant, Editor at MoneySense Magazine and Host of the television show Million Dollar Neighbourhood on the Canadian Oprah Winfrey Network
4. Harvey Botting, former Senior Vice-President of Rogers Communications, Inc.
5. David Bowden, Business Consultant for several major corporations including Sears Canada, CleanTech, Direct Energy
6. Jeff Collins, Senior Portfolio Manager for the RBC Insurance Group
7. Janet L. Ecker, President and CEO of the Toronto Financial Services Alliance
8. Zabeen Hirji, RBC's Chief Human Resources Officer
9. Brian Johnson, the Chief Operating Officer of Mattamy Homes, Canada's largest home builder
10. Claire Kennedy, Tax Partner at Bennett Jones LLP and former Director of Neo Material Technologies Inc.
11. Mark Krembil, former co-owner of Lewiscraft, a national retail company
12. Nykolaj Kuryuluk, Chief Executive Officer at ColdBlock Technologies
13. Brian Lawson, Senior Managing Partner at Brookfield Asset Management
14. Nancy Carolyn Lee, former Chief Operating Officer for the Olympic Broadcasting Services Vancouver
15. Gary P. Mooney, president and CEO of Canadian Lender Solutions Ltd.
16. John Paul Morgan, founder of Morgan Solar
17. Jane Pepino, senior partner at Aird & Berlis LLP
18. Melinda Rogers, SVP of Strategy & Development, Rogers Communication
19. Howard Shearer, President and CEO of Hitachi Canada

20. Keith Thomas, CEO of Vive Nano
21. Bruce Winter, Audit Partner with PricewaterhouseCoopers LLP

REFERENCES

Adams, J. (2002, April 6). Pharmacy school will bear name of donor. *The Globe and Mail.* Retrieved from http://www.theglobeandmail.com/news/national/pharmacy-school-will-bear-name-of-donor/article25294672/

Agrba, L. (2013, October 28). Meet the Honourable Hal Jackman. Former Lieutenant Governor of Ontario has donated over $40 million to UofT. *The Varsity.* Retrieved from http://thevarsity.ca/2013/10/28/meet-the-honourable-hal-jackman/

Angus, I. (2009). *Love the questions: University education and enlightenment.* Winnipeg, MB: Arbeiter Ring Publishing.

Aronowitz, S. (2000). The knowledge factory: Dismantling the corporate university and creating true higher learning. Boston, MA: Beacon Press.

Basen, I. (2014). Most university undergrads now taught by poorly paid part-timers. *CBC News.* Retrieved from http://www.cbc.ca/news/canada/most-university-undergrads-now-taught-by-poorly-paid-part-timers-1.2756024

Bejan, R. (2015a, March 25). Five reasons TAs and education workers rejected UofT's deal. *rabble.ca.* Retrieved from http://rabble.ca/blogs/bloggers/campus-notes/2015/03/five-reasons-tas-and-education-workers-rejected-u-ts-deal

Bejan, R. (2015b, July 21st). Letter to the editor: UofT arbitration result is a slap in the face. *The Varsity.* Retrieved from http://thevarsity.ca/2015/07/21/letter-to-the-editor-u-of-t-arbitration-result-is-a-slap-in-the-face/

Bejan, R., & German, M. (2015, March 18). What does social work have to do with the University of Toronto TA strike? *rabble.ca.* Retrieved from http://rabble.ca/blogs/ bloggers/campus-notes/2015/03/what-does-social-work-have-to-do-university-toronto-ta-strike

Bernans, D. (2001). *Con u inc.: Privatization, marketization and globalization at Concordia University (and beyond).* Montreal, Quebec: Concordia Student Union.

Best, S., Nocella II, A. J., & McLaren, P. (2010). Introduction: The rise of the academic-industrial complex and the crisis in free speech. In A. J. Nocella II, S. Best, & P. McLaren (eds.), *Academic repression: Reflections from the academic industrial complex* (pp. 13–89). Oakland, CA: AK Press.

Bloomberg. (2016). Company Overview of Gluskin Sheff + Associates, Inc. *Bloomberg.* Retrieved from http://www.bloomberg.com/research/stocks/private/snapshot.asp?privcapId=23078039

Bonnar, J. (2015). CUPE 3902 and 3903 members march for better working, living and learning conditions. *rabble.ca.* Retrieved from http://rabble.ca/blogs/bloggers/johnbon /2015/03/cupe-3902-and-3903-members-march-better-working-living-and-learning-c)

Bost, T. (2016). *The quality of quantity: Unevenness and inequity in time-to-completion and graduate student income at the University of Toronto.* Retrieved from https://qualityofquantityuoft.wordpress.com/faq/

Brown, L. (2015a). University of Toronto strike: Weekend mediation yields nothing. *The Toronto Star.* Retrieved from http://www.thestar.com/yourtoronto/education /2015/03/16/university-of-toronto-strike-weekend-mediation-yields-nothing.html

Brown, L. (2015b). UofT students demand tuition refund due to strike. *The Toronto Star*. Retrieved from http://www.thestar.com/yourtoronto/education/2015/04/01/u-of-t-students-demand-tuition-refund-due-to-strike.html

Camfield, D. (2007). Renewal in Canadian public sector unions: Neoliberalism and union praxis. *Relations Industrielles, 62*(2), 282–304. Retrieved from http://search.proquest.com/docview/36875821?accountid=14771

Canadian Mining Hall of Fame. (2013). Pierre Lassonde (b. 1947) inducted in 2013. *Canadian Mining Hall of Fame*. Retrieved from http://mininghalloffame.ca/inductees/j-l/pierre_lassonde

Canadian Academics for Peace. (2009). Campus dialogue. Retrieved from http://academicsforpeace.ca/about-us/campus-dialogue/

Chernos, S. (2011, April 8). Chomsky versus Munk. Keep watch on corporate funding of UofT, Noam Chomsky says. *Now Magazine*. Retrieved from https://nowtoronto.com/news/features/chomsky-versus-munk/

Churchill, W. (2010). The myth of academic freedom: Reflections on the fraudulence of liberal principles in a neoconservative era. In A. J. Nocella II, S. Best, & P. McLaren (eds.), *Academic repression: Reflections from the academic industrial complex* (pp. 179–199). Oakland, CA: AK Press.

Class Struggle University. (2015). Beat back the debt-monster. Retrieved from https://classstruggleuniversity.wordpress.com/2015/03/15/beat-back-the-debt-monster-class-struggle-university/

Colero, E. (2016, January 11). Robarts undergoes first expansion in 42 years. *The Varsity*. Retrieved from http://thevarsity.ca/2016/01/11/robarts-undergoes-first-expansion-in-42-years/

Comay, R. [Rebecca]. (2015, March 25). First, I need to clarify that I am not personally affected by the academic continuity policy: there are no TAs in the undergraduate course I am teaching this semester. However, I like to think I would have the backbone to resist. [Quoted in We Are UofT Facebook status update]. https://www.facebook.com/StudentsForCupe3902/posts/838199806253254:0

Cribb, R. (2015, April 4). OISE faculty call for the removal of dean. *The Toronto Star*. Retrieved from http://www.thestar.com/news/gta/2015/04/04/oise-faculty-call-for-the-removal-of-dean.html

CUPE 3902 Unit 1 (2014). Collective Agreement between the Governing Council of the University of Toronto and the Canadian Union of Public Employees Local 3902, Unit 1. Retrieved from http://www.hrandequity.utoronto.ca/Assets/HR+Digital+Assets/ Policies$!2c+Guidelines+and+Collective+Agreements/Collective+Agreement/CUPE3902-1+CA.pdf

Forbes. (2015). The world's millionaires. *Forbes*. Retrieved from http://www.forbes.com/ billionaires/list/#version:static

Gardiner, H. (2013). UofT students protest planned tuition hikes. *Canadian Lawyer 4 Students*. Retrieved from http://www.canadianlawyermag.com/4514/U-of-T-students-protest-planned-tuition-hikes.html

Girard, D. (2007). $15M gift for social work school. *Toronto Star*. Retrieved from http://www.thestar.com/news/2007/06/16/15m_gift_for_social_work_school.html

Giroux, H. (2002). Neoliberalism, corporate culture, and the promise of higher education: The university as a democratic public sphere. *Harvard Educational Review, 72*(4), 425–464.

Governing Council. (2015). The Governing Council of the University of Toronto. Retrieved from http://www.governingcouncil.utoronto.ca/home.htm

Gross, A., & Swain, M. (2015). Visions of a radical labour movement. *Briarpatch Magazine*. Retrieved from http://briarpatchmagazine.com/articles/view/visions-of-a-radical-labour-movement

Hall, J. (2011, November 11). New UofT centre to be a lab for elite sports. *Toronto Star*. Retrieved from http://www.thestar.com/sports/2011/11/11/ new_u_of_t_centre_to_be_a_lab_for_elite_sports.html

Hande, M. J. (2015). Rank-and-file reflections on the 2015 CUPE 3902 strike. *Action Speaks Louder: OPIRG-Toronto's Field Manual for Those Who've had Enough*, Fall.

Hemmadi, M., & Yan, T. (2013, November 4). Meet Judy Goldring. Family of Governing Council chair has donated over $10 million to UofT. *The Varsity*. Retrieved from http://thevarsity.ca/2013/11/04/meet-judy-goldring/

Hill, D. [Dave]. (2015, March 26). To the Press and the community of the University of Toronto and the academic community globally From Dave Hill Professor of Education Policy at Anglia Ruskin University Visiting Professor at the Universities of Athens Greece and Middlesex, London Trade Unionist and Socialist Coalition [Facebook status update]. Retrieved from https://www.facebook.com/dave.hill.948011/ posts/10206032802715234?pnref=story

Lemmens, T. (2004). Confronting the conflict of interest crisis in medical research. *Monash Bioethics Review, 23*(4), 19–40.

Magnusson, J. (2013). Precarious learning and labour in financialized times. *Brock Journal of Education, Special Issue "The Impact of Globalization on Adult and Higher Education," 22*(2), 69–83.

Marmol, E. (2015a). The corporate university: An e-interview with Dave Hill, Alpesh Maisuria, Anthony Nocella, and Michael Parenti. *Critical Education, 6*(19), 1–25. Retrieved from http://ojs.library.ubc.ca/index.php/criticaled/article/view/185102

Marmol, E. (2015b). CUPE's cooptation and absorption into the capitalist establishment: Observations from the University of Toronto teaching assistants' strike. Manuscript submitted for publication.

Marrelli, M. (2015). Toronto Students Respond to Mizzou with Rallies, Share Experiences of On-Campus Racism. *Torontoist*. Retrieved from http://torontoist.com/2015/11/toronto-students-respond-to-mizzou-with-rallies-share-experiences-of-on-campus-racism/

Neal, D. (2011). Business unionism vs. revolutionary unionism. Industrial Workers of the World. Retrieved from http://www.iww.org

Nocella II, A. J., Best, S., & McLaren, P. (eds.). (2010). *Academic repression: Reflections from the academic industrial complex*. Oakland, CA: AK Press.

Nocella II, A. J., & Gabbard, D. (eds.). (2013). *Policing the campus: Academic repression, surveillance, and the Occupy Movement*. New York: Peter Lang.

Panos, J. (2013). Varsity blues: UofT Provost gets big raise while dismantling program for underprivileged. *Rabble.ca*. Retrieved from http://rabble.ca/blogs/bloggers/campus-notes/2013/04/varsity-blues-u-t-provost-gets-big-raise-while-dismantling-progr

Peries, P. (2015). Striking TA's and part-time staff frozen out of a living wage at University of Toronto. Retrieved from http://therealnews.com/t2/ index.php?option=com_content&task=view&id=31&Itemid=74&jumival=13360

Revolutionary Student Movement. (2013). Limits of the current student movement. Retrieved from http://mer-rsm.ca/limits-of-the-current-student-movement/

Revolutionary Student Movement. (2015). Political Report of the Coordinating Committee of the Revolutionary Student Movement. Retrieved from http://mer-rsm.ca/political-report-of-the-coordinating-committee-of-the-revolutionary-student-movement/

Schwartz, Z. (2015a, March 4). Why UofT, York strikes are more than labour disputes. *The Globe and Mail*. Retrieved from http://www.theglobeandmail.com /opinion/why-u-of-t-york-strikes-are-more-than-labour-disputes/article23279298/

Schwartz, Z. (2015b, February 9). Five myths about the TA strike. The Varsity. Retrieved from http://thevarsity.ca/2015/02/09/five-myths-about-the-ta-strike/

Statistics Canada. Low income cut-offs. Retrieved from http://www.statcan.gc.ca/pub/75f0002m/2012002/lico-sfr-eng.htm

The Canadian Press. (2009, April 15). Warren Goldring, 81: Co-founder of AGF. Toronto Star. Retrieved from http://www.thestar.com/business/2009/04/15/warren_goldring_81_cofounder_of_agf.html

Thompson, J. H., Downie, J. G., Baird, P., & Canadian Association of University Teachers. (2001). The Olivieri report: The complete text of the report of the independent inquiry commissioned by the Canadian Association of University Teachers. Toronto: J. Lorime

Toronto 350.org (n.d.). Divest Uof T. 350.org. Retrieved from http://www.toronto350.org/divest

University for Strategic Optimism. (2011). Undressing the academy or, the student handjob. Brooklyn, N.Y.: Minor Compositions.

University of Toronto Governing Council. (2007). University funds investment policy. Retrieved from http://www.governingcouncil.utoronto.ca/Assets/Governing+Council+Digital+Assets/Policies/PDF/ppjun212007i.pdf

University of Toronto. (2008). UofT's financial model. Towards 2030. Retrieved from http://www.towards2030.utoronto.ca/sec3.html.

University of Toronto. (2005, September 22). Media release: UofT law school and Fasken Martineau unveil new home for downtown legal service. University of Toronto, Toronto, ON.

University of Waterloo. (2013). "Definitions." Institutional Analysis & Planning. Retrieved from https://uwaterloo.ca/institutional-analysis-planning/university-data-and-statistics/glossaries/definitions

UTAM Annual Report. (2014). University of Toronto Asset Management Corporation Annual Report. Retrieved from http://www.utam.utoronto.ca/Assets/UTAM+Digital+Assets/UTAM/UTAM+Digital+Assets/reports/2014annual.pdf

Valverde, M., & Briggs, J. (2015, September). The university as urban developer: A research report. Centre for Criminology & Sociolegal Studies, University of Toronto.

Washburn, J. (2005). University Inc.: The corporate corruption of higher education. New York: Basic Books.

Wilson, R., Bejan, R., Zahrei, S., Carriere, J., Rwigema, M. J., Polack, S., & Gibson, M. (2015, March 10). What the University of Toronto isn't telling you about the TA strike. rabble.ca. Retrieved from http://rabble.ca/blogs/bloggers/campus-notes/2015/03/what-university-toronto-isnt-telling-you-about-ta-strike

Woodhouse, H. R. (2009). Selling out: Academic freedom and the corporate market. Montréal: McGill-Queen's University Press.

Yelland, T. (2015, March 26). Striking grad students on what it's like to live on $15,000 a year. VICE. Retrieved from http://www.vice.com

Zaidi, A. S. (2010). Powerful compassion: The strike at Syracuse. In A. J. Nocella II, S. Best, & P. McLaren (eds.), Academic repression: Reflections from the academic industrial complex (pp. 437–447). Oakland, CA: AK Press.

Part V.
Black Lives Matter In Education

"Only a fool would let his enemy teach his children."

—MALCOLM X

"No one is going to give you the education you need to overthrow them. Nobody is going to teach you your true history, teach you your true heroes, if they know that that knowledge will help set you free."

—ASSATA SHAKUR

Racial Harassment in the "Postracial" Era: A Case of Discipline and Resistance in the Black Female Body

SHANNON GIBNEY

CONTEXT

It's no secret that higher education is in crisis. Numerous news and academic articles point to the failure of our postsecondary institutions to live up to their missions, and successfully matriculate their students (Davidson, 2015; Donahue, 2008). However you measure it, graduation rates are abysmal for the average student—perpetually hovering around fifty percent completion in six years, and even lower for working class, Students of Color, and those at for-profit institutions (National Center for Education Statistics, 2015). Total student loan debt is now up to $1.2 trillion, and rising steadily, with the average borrower accruing $33,000 in debt by the end of their four-year degree (Debt.org, 2015)—a crippling weight to carry as one ostensibly enters the job market. Stories of the negative effects of the corporate takeover of the academy abound (Chomsky, 2014; Schmidlin, 2015), from the ballooning salaries of administrators and endowments to the growing ranks of the contingent, overworked, and horrendously paid professoriate (Jaschik, 2015). As the country's demographics continue to shift, our economy does as well, from industrial to knowledge based, precipitating a huge increase in the sheer number of students entering postsecondary schools, and with them a very different set of cultural, racial, and socioeconomic realities than those that dominated the higher education landscape just one generation before. And yet, the ranks of the professoriate remain stubbornly white, male, and middle class, not at all reflective of these new students entering these institutions, and the experiences and knowledge they bring with them (Jayakumar, Howard, Allen, & Han, 2009). This racial and cultural disconnect between teachers and students has the overall effect of further lowering student achievement (Graham, 2014; Quentin, 2013), while simultaneously alienating Instructors of Color, women, and LGBTQ professors—ironically, those who come from the very historically marginalized communities as their students (Ford, 2011). Indeed, these predominantly white dominant institutional structures cannot support the expression of racial or cultural difference in virtually any location, be it the classroom, the department, or the administrative leadership team. As my case study illustrates, whenever white dominance is challenged in *anyplace* within an institution of higher education, some constellation of its legal, student, administrative, and even academic arms will act swiftly and even violently to repress it. The errant agent will be maligned institutionally, then publicly if necessary, and then finally, silenced via transaction.

TEACHING WHILE BLACK, FEMALE, AND VOCAL

For the past seven years, I have taught writing, journalism, and African diasporic topics classes at a mid-sized, urban community college in Minneapolis. The course load is brutal, at four to five classes a semester, and the student body the most vulnerable in the state. Well over half of our students are women, almost a third are first-generation college students, their average age is twenty-eight, and three-fourths of our students receive some form of financial aid. Moreover, a full fifty-eight percent of our students are People of Color, with thirty-one percent of those being students of African descent (African immigrant or African Americans, the descendants of slaves) (Minneapolis Community and Technical College, 2015).

Like most community colleges across the country, the student completion rate (that is, graduation or transfer rate) remains stubbornly around twenty-five percent for white students, and at our college, it is about half of that, around twelve percent for Black students (Minneapolis Community and Technical College, 2015). The college is also consistent with national trends, in that People of Color make up a very small percentage of the faculty, around ten percent, and are even less represented in administration, which is probably around five percent or lower.

In discussing my case, it is also important to note that there is no acknowledgment or discussion of the different ways that power is enacted through the kinds of racialized bodies that occupy these different social locations at Minneapolis Community and Technical College (MCTC)—be it professor, student, or administrator. This dynamic is problematic on several levels, all of which will be explored through the telling of my own personal story of the collision between the rhetoric of institutional "diversity" in higher education and the reality of racially subjugated bodies in these spaces—*even if these bodies occupy locations that would otherwise be powerful, such as professors.* Indeed, as Gutierrez y Muhs, Flores Niemann, Gonzalez, and Harris write in the introduction of *Presumed Incompetent: The Intersections of Race and Class for Women in Academia:*

> The contributors to this book [contemporary Women of Color academics] find themselves disciplined by colleagues, students, or administrators whenever their assigned and/or claimed identities do not match cultural stereotypes. As the cognitive psychology literature explains, unconscious bias plays a part in the way teachers and students are perceived by others (Chang and Davis, 2010). Given a climate of shared cultural stereotypes and images, it is not surprising that although each of these stories is unique, the authors also describe strikingly similar barriers to their success.
>
> However, just as every unhappy family is unhappy in its own way (as Tolstoy wrote), each workplace structured by caste has unique features. In the academic workplace, judgments of worth tend to be extremely subjective. Reputation is the coin of the realm, and reputations are built not only by objective accomplishments but through images and sometimes outright fantasies—individual or collective—that cling to the nature of the work and the person being evaluated. Academic judgments then are especially susceptible to unconscious bias, although the precise forms this bias takes varies from own institution to the next (p. 4).

For Women of Color faculty who, like me, are extremely vocal advocates for our most vulnerable students (disproportionately first-generation college students, and People of Color), especially in institutions that have historically not served or even taken advantage of these students, our reputations inside the institution may become even more suspect than they might be for those who simply inhabit female and brown bodies, but do not actively challenge the *status quo.* In the market-driven and extremely competitive higher education landscape, in which "diversity" is seen as capital, we are expected to be "grateful" to be even granted entrance into the rarified, predominantly white, older, upper-middle-class world of faculty, administration, and higher education governance. The presence of our bodies themselves are supposed to be "evidence" of the institution's "commitment to diversity." Our bodies are not supposed to act, speak, or god forbid, contradict this narrative of sanitized "progress" in this sphere, and if we do, we are instantly labeled as "unprofessional," "not collegial," "angry," "aggressive," "racist," or any other host of pejorative adjectives routinely used to keep Women of Color in our place.

This was the context in which my story is located, the room which I stepped into on a fateful day in October. My institutional reputation was peppered with the adjectives I just shared with you, and although all institutional players, and the so-called "college and system leadership" knew that our institution was, and I would argue, still is not, a well-functioning one, they saw me and my nonconforming Black female body as a huge part of the problem. I had been disciplined for "not following procedure;" I had been warned that I was "not collegial enough with colleagues." The first Black female head of my department, I had been told in no uncertain terms that I would not be renewed in this position. After challenging the administration's mishandling of concurrent enrollment, I had received a written reprimand in my permanent file, for representing my entire department's viewpoint, on institutional letterhead. I had been issued a warning from my dean after sitting outside the meeting a fellow Black female faculty member was having with administrators about her performance (I was there for support, and because she asked me to).

A few years before, a white male student at the student newspaper had filed a complaint of racial discrimination against me, for asserting the fact that the staff was all white, as well as the fact that a noose had been hung there some years before, might have something to do with their lack of "diversity," and the fact that few people on campus took them seriously. A few years after that, a disgruntled white male adjunct in the department had filed another complaint of racial harassment against me and three other colleagues (the rest of them were white), after we had lobbied hard to include the phrases "knowledge of critical race theory," and "demonstrated connection to communities of color," under "Preferred Qualifications" in the department's call for applicants during a hiring phase. Although I was eventually cleared on both counts, the Legal Affairs Department had slapped my hands by performing lengthy, fairly terrifying top-secret "investigations," and issuing me letters of expectation. In the last case, the administration ultimately pulled the preference for knowledge of critical race theory in the job call, stating that "it would be wrong to favor one theory over another" in our workplace. All of these incidents, as well as many more that it would take far too long to explicate here, are why I became an institutional target for moderating a discussion on structural racism and representation in a Mass Communications class. And also, they are decisively *not* why I became a pariah for such pedagogy. Very simply, the reason why I became an institutional target for moderating a discussion on structural racism and representation in a Mass Communications class was that I was a Black woman faculty member who dared to demand that I be treated the same way as any other (read: white) faculty member.

Two years ago, I came back from maternity leave to a group of mad white men who didn't like the way I approached a discussion on structural racism in a Mass Communications class, and subsequently filed a "Racial Harassment" claim with my school's Legal Affairs Department. My daughter had been forty-one and a half weeks when her heart stopped, for still unknown reasons. The incident in the classroom occurred on my first day back. It was quite a shock to meet the heat of this small group of students who became angry during a discussion initiated after another student's presentation on People of Color in newsrooms nationally. What they said was, "Why do we always have to talk about this?" *This* meaning the legacy of ongoing racism in American life? *This* meaning something that they did not want to talk about? *This* meaning topics in Mass Communications? I blinked at them in confusion, and at the general energy of the class, which was not downright hostile, but could not be described as welcoming by any stretch of the imagination. The students had had a substitute—a very capable and kind white woman—for the first five weeks of the course, while I had been away. They were understandably a bit off-kilter, wondering how the course would proceed, with this whole new person at the helm. But there was something more to it, something that could be seen as intangible, but which was to me, all too familiar in its ease of location: animosity at this Black female body in front of them. Leading the class with authority. Determining the terms of the discussion and course content, deciding whether each of them passed or failed. That was the "this" they objected to. "This" was not the class, the world, they had signed up for.

My body was tipsy with loss, my heart still far from healed, but I tried my best—what was my best in that moment, on that day, anyway—to moderate. I mentioned the ongoing history of white domination in newsrooms, as well as in every other aspect of American life. I said that I was definitely not talking about individuals, as in, "You! White person over there!," but rather, about whiteness as system that privileges certain groups of people while it penalizes others. When mentioning the long tradition of newsrooms dominated by white, middle-class men, I was conscious that my voice was not as solid as it could have been. I could see in their eyes that they weren't convinced. No, they were angry. And feeling dangerous. While I was tired, and feeling broken. Later, I learned that two of these students had filed their "Racial Harassment" complaint with Legal Affairs right after class. Legal Affairs notified me of the complaint and carried out their subsequent "investigation" soon afterwards. Almost a month later I received notification that I had, in fact, been found guilty of "Racial Harassment" against two white male students, and that MCTC was issuing me a formal letter of reprimand, which would remain in my permanent file.

> I can remember holding the letter of reprimand in my dining room, reading it incredulously, my hand shaking. My faculty union grievance rep, who had represented many, many faculty during institutional "investigations" like this, had assured me after our interview with the head of Legal Affairs, that, "they have nothing. This is completely ridiculous. It will come to nothing." And yet, out of around 172 student complaints of faculty that year, mine was the only one that had been ruled in violation of policy, and the only one that had been disciplined. As tenured faculty in what was arguably the most powerful department on campus, I could not be fired out of hand. But what I could be was disciplined for not conforming to the *status quo* on another issue. And the irony that I was being attacked through the very civil rights legislation meant to *protect* Women of Color and other minorities in white dominant spaces was particularly discomfiting.

STRATEGIES USED

I appealed the policy-violation determination, as well as the discipline, through my institution and the system's approved structures. Via breathtaking feats of illogical logic, misreading and misapplication of policy, and extreme structural violence, the appeal was denied. In a state system that is healthy, unlike the Minnesota State College and University's (or Minnesota State, as it is popularly referred to), working within might have produced an acceptable outcome. However, neither my school nor the system it operates in are healthy, so I wasn't really surprised by this outcome. And any serious student of social change knows that most systems exist merely to reproduce themselves, so appealing to them via reason, ethos, or ethics is not often successful once you are identified as "a problem."

The next form my resistance took was through my faculty union. I appealed everything via their formal grievance process. Although the union fast-tracked my case, it still took seven months for it to reach the final step of the grievance process, arbitration, in which each side presents their case to an impartial adjudicator, who assesses all the evidence, and later comes to a final and binding decision. Arbitration decisions and materials become part of the public record once a decision is reached, so my union grievance reps and legal counsel were not exactly surprised when the president of my college wrote me a letter stating that he was removing the letter of reprimand from my file, right before arbitration was scheduled to begin. The whole process took seven months, quite possibly the longest seven months of my life, even with fast tracking. And although my state union reps, leadership, and legal counsel presented a public face of support, they knew that politically, there would be payback for going after Minnesota State in this way, and they were not eager to pay the price. Generally speaking, the faculty union is weak and Minnesota State is strong, in no small part because of the incestuous relationship state-union officers have with the system, in which they are often awarded jobs in the system following their union service.

I was surprised—flabbergasted, shaken to the core, more like—when, right before arbitration was scheduled, I was offered "a blank check" to leave my institution altogether. I just blinked at my union rep when she told me this, and asked her to say that again. There was no actual "offer," ever made, nothing on paper, nothing that could in any way prove that such transaction was ever suggested. The Minnesota State Legal Affairs Office had simply called my union rep, and asked her to make me the verbal offer and judge my response. After she did, and answered negatively, she told me that I could never tell anyone about it. I just stared back at her in further disbelief, thinking, "By now, doesn't she know who she's talking to?" And the sheer shock of this pay-off strategy has really never gone away. Never, in all my years as a writer, teacher, and scholar, had I entertained the notion that it might be possible to get paid—just for being me. We were facing around a $44 million system deficit, and the "leadership's" biggest priority was getting rid of a noncon-forming Black female faculty member, who wasn't afraid of talking to tell her story? The whole thing was just profoundly demoralizing. As someone who has suffered from three bouts of clinical depression in my life, I am either less free or more free not to make decisions that could ultimately jeopardize my spiritual and psychological health. Taking hush money to go away, and essentially embrace others' perception of me as *a problem*, and also turning my back on my community and deeply held values would definitely qualify as a bad-health decision, in this context. Therefore, accepting the money and just going away was never an option for me.

Bad leadership is like a cancer—it spreads everywhere and weakens and can even kill its host. So, the college president at the time had targeted, set up, and even fired many other college employees who stood up for our students and/or were just trying to do their jobs to the best of their abilities. Many of these people were, like me, from historically marginalized communities, and therefore did not "fit in" with the upper-middle-class, white, heterosexual, male culture of MCTC, Minnesota State, and higher education in general. One colleague, who was very high in the bureaucratic hierarchy, determined that she had to leave the institution after less than a year of service, because the climate was so bad it was starting to negatively and seriously affect her health and well-being. She was an extremely qualified Queer Woman of Color, who had grown up in a working-class community, and was passionate about helping our students find a path to educational empowerment and achievement. She felt that her institutional treatment had everything to do with her inability to conform to the white-dominant culture of the college and system, and therefore, filed an Equal Employment Opportunity Commission complaint of "Racial Harassment." Soon after my case ramped up, I decided to do the same, and filed against both MCTC and Minnesota State. Three other Employees of Color, two faculty members, and one administrative employee, did the same. Eventually, one of the faculty members and I also filed a claim of "Racial Harassment" against the state-faculty union, for not doing everything in their power to protect their protected class members against the shocking white dominant violence of the school and system. This same colleague and I also met with a lawyer independently, to see what our options were for suing the institutions in district court (we ultimately determined that they were not good, and would require our silence and also thousands of dollars that we didn't have, so we abandoned this strategy).

Understanding the history and culture of the American legal system, and that it was not designed for women, People of Color, or anyone in a nondominant category, I had little faith that these complaints would go anywhere. Three years later, I finally heard back from the EEOC. Via voicemail, they said that they were dismissing my case. This was after they had dismissed my colleagues' cases long ago. MCTC administrators and employees who were part of the regime that so blatantly targeted, surveilled, and disciplined us and other Employees of Color with impunity have been slowly leaving the school, under the leadership an interim and new permanent president. I will probably never know if this is due to our collective EEOC complaints, this new leader's pressure, or other factors. However, organizing with my fellow targeted workers was energizing, and allowed us to imagine other possibilities of resistance.

One of these emergent strategies was forming a community group with friends and allies, called Higher Education Justice Minnesota, or HJEM. When people in my community, especially Organizers of Color, started hearing about my case, their response was quick and energetic: rage and incredulity. They knew me, knew my work, and some had even been my students, or had friends or family members who were. We rallied the troops as it were, and had several meetings where people listened, shared stories, and strategized. They wrote letters to the Minnesota State board, attended a board meeting, created a wiki, Facebook page and public HEJM website to get the word out about my case and issues of institutional racism at MCTC and throughout the system. They wrote articles. They even created a website asking former and current MCTC students to post messages detailing how the institution had created barriers for their matriculation and academic achievement. Although the group has not been very active since my case died down, I believe that it showed the college and system that communities can successfully organize around issues of equity in higher education, and that they will stand up for those they feel are "their own." Perhaps more importantly, the group also created new and powerful connections between individuals and communities that had previously had little to no interaction before, and allowed them to dialogue and organize around a social issue that deeply affects them.

But I have to say, the most successful strategy of resistance that I employed by far was going public with my story, and telling it on my own terms, in my own words. Ironically, this is exactly what most of my friends, peers, and colleagues in academia told me *not* to do, because it would ostensibly ruin my career. However, for better or worse, I have always made the most important decisions of my life with my gut, and in this case my gut was telling me to resist through storytelling, and to do so publicly and respectfully, but unapologetically. What I mean when I say "respectfully" is that in the telling of your story, you approach all parties—even those that maligned you—as evenhandedly as possible. Powerful institutions and people want to paint you as "crazy," especially if you come from a community that is routinely demonized in the mainstream. Your job is to not give them the opportunity to do so, by remaining as professional as possible while revealing their gross ineptitude and unethical behavior to the rest of the world, via your story. First-person storytelling by People of Color is such a potent site of resistance because, as Critical Race Theory (CRT) pedagogues Ladson-Billings and Delgado have stated elsewhere, it forces listeners to "analyze the myths, presuppositions, and received wisdoms that make up the common culture about race and that invariably render Blacks and other minorities one-down" (Delgado, 1995, p. xiv). In embracing storytelling as a strategy of resistance in my case, I was embracing a CRT central tenant—that "Critical race theorists [...] integrate their experiential knowledge, drawn from a shared history of 'other,' with their ongoing struggles to transform a world deteriorating under the albatross of racial hegemony" (Barnes, 1990, p. 1864).

The MCTC student newspaper broke the story, assembling a video interview of me telling my side of the story that went viral in a week. Soon, *The Chronicle, Inside Higher Ed, Al Jazeera,* local news outlets, and even *CNN* were contacting me for interviews. I have to underscore the fact that I was terrified during all of this. The college president at the time had issued a moratorium on all employees speaking to the press, for obvious reasons, and although the union and others thought that this would not hold up in court, no one wanted to be the "test case," and risk losing their job. As the person in my house who holds down the stable job, my family could have been plunged into economic chaos if I had it. I, however, felt that I really had no other choice at this point, and that in the end, going public would protect me. But again, nothing was sure at this point, and I had many sleepless nights. This is why I have to underscore the fact that one has to do what's right because it's what's right, not because you are expecting or counting on any just or equitable outcome. You have to be smart and strategic, honestly and soberly assessing the microlevel and macrolevel politics at your site, making alliances and seeking out information as appropriate. Your actions must be governed by your heart, but your mind must carry them out. Take nothing on its appearance and understand that everything, *everything* is about power—who has it, who wants it, who doesn't have it. Know where you stand in relation to your institutional and community power, and then act accordingly. Each of us will come to different conclusions based on their personal experiences, politics, and resources. This was mine.

I kept waiting by the mailbox for the letter of dismissal that never came. And I kept on talking to *select* individuals, from *select* media outlets. I didn't respond to requests from conservative publications, because I didn't trust them to be fair and balanced. Nor did I respond to many mainstream news media requests, because I felt that they would not be able to understand the complicated, instersectional identity of a Black female professor. For this reason, I did not respond to *CNN* or *The Chronicle,* but instead decided to do an interview for *The Melissa Harris-Perry Show,* a progressive current affairs newscast that airs on MSNBC for two hours every Saturday and Sunday morning. As a fellow Black feminist academic, I had confidence that Harris-Perry would do the story justice, and place it within the larger context of white dominant institutions and their concurrent neoliberal push. Harris-Perry did just that, and the story went viral again. Following this story, a friend and editor at *Gawker* asked me to write something about what was going on. MCTC and Minnesota State administrations had warned me that if I continued talking about the incident, I could be violating the students' privacy rights, since the public might deduce their identities, so I had to be careful to discuss what happened in very general terms, and place it within the larger context of ongoing institutional racism. I did just that, and wrote about another time I had been the victim of white male violence at MCTC. The story went everywhere, and put even more pressure on the college and Minnesota State to account for their actions. They tried to put a public relations spin on the whole thing, and put out a general message that the public did not know all the facts of the case, that they couldn't release them because of privacy laws, that I was simply a disgruntled employee, etc. I believe this tactic, which had probably worked for them in other cases, didn't work for them this time for two reasons: (1) I had already gotten out in front of the story and "framed" it, by establishing what the issues were and—just as importantly—what they weren't—through writing my story and establishing parameters/context for reporters who I chose to talk to. This caused my employer to be reactive and on the defensive, not the other way around. (2) Their own racism did not allow them to see that I was not just "another angry Black woman," but that I was actually a well-respected, known entity in the larger local community, and that many people who knew me would be further insulted by their implications.

The court of public opinion is, in many ways, the most powerful one of all, and they decisively lost in it. If I could have prevailed without ever entering it, I would have in order to save myself from professional embarrassment and ostracism, but the college and the system forced my hand. I truly believed, and still believe that I had no other option. And now that everything is said and done, I am glad that I took this tactic. It has shown a light on the unsavory management and organizational practices of an institution and system whose mission is supposedly to serve and educate the students of this state—*all* of the students of this state, and challenged them to actually live up to it. It has forced the institution, and some of its key stakeholders to grapple with the fact that institutional racism will not be tolerated when it is exposed for what it is in the public eye, that integrity and honesty will be rewarded, and that in telling our stories, we make ourselves and our communities free.

CONCLUSION

As my case illustrates, the landscape of higher education in this country is one that is under siege in a variety of contexts—from student completion to public defunding, to increasing corporatization. And we haven't even begun to touch on the student loan or contingent labor crises. All of these factors converge on our collective and individual campuses, in a moment in which the majority of white-dominant students and administrators believe is "postracial," to create an environment in which multiple sites not only uphold white supremacist values and policies, but actually create and perpetuate them. In this environment, capital is aligned with whiteness, and those who challenge its dominance will be subject to the largely impersonal surveillance and discipline of the institutional machine. Using a CRT lens, we can see that, as Sutherland (1990) states, "structural arrangements and sociopsychological conditions create disharmonious relationships between professors of color and the White academic institution" (p. 17). Given the fact that so many of these "structural arrangements" are economic, it is perhaps inevitable that there would be such a clash between the corporate university and the Bodies of Color that make it run. Again, as Gutierrez y Muhs, Flores Niemann, Gonzalez, and Harris write in the introduction of *Presumed Incompetent: The Intersections of Race and Class for Women in Academia:*

> While many of the formal barriers have been lifted, academic institutions remain, at their core, profoundly inhospitable to the experiences and points of view of those formerly excluded. The Third World Feminist movement of the 1970s on college campuses around the country succeeded in planting women's studies and ethnic studies departments where there had been none (Hu-DeHart, 1993; Sandoval, 2000). Yet, in the end, the values that animated the founding of these departments were at least partially eclipsed by the larger culture of the university.
>
> Regrettably, the culture of academia overall remains not only remarkably blind to its own flaws, but deeply invested in a thoroughgoing denial [...]. The culture of academia, ultimately, is impervious to change because its power structure is designed to reproduce itself (p. 7).

Given this grim reality, many of us who have been targeted by this apparatus have found that the only real way to fight back is by:

1. Going outside our institutions, and telling our stories in local and national media, community groups, and organizing.
2. Pursuing legal avenues of defense, but not surprisingly, that domain is very closely aligned with the powerful, of which higher education institutions are part, and does not often or always lead to justice.
3. Interrogating, through CRT, the race and racism of our American institution and advocating resisting these insidious "traditions" by telling our stories and engaging in intersectional analysis.

There is no place to start like the horse's mouth.

REFERENCES

Barnes, R. (1990). Race consciousness: The thematic content of racial distinctiveness in critical race consciousness. *Harvard Law Review, 103*, 1864–1871.

Chomsky, N. (2014). The death of American universities. *Jacobin Magazine*. Retrieved from https://www.jacobinmag.com/2014/03/the-death-of-american-universities/

Davidson, A. (2015). Is college tuition really too high? *The New York Times Magazine*. Retrieved from http://www.nytimes.com/2015/09/13/magazine/is-college-tuition-too-high.html?_r=0

Debt.org. (2015). *Students and debt*. Retrieved from https://www.debt.org/students/

Delgado, R. (ed.). (1995). *Critical race theory: The cutting edge*. Philadelphia, PA: Temple University Press.

Donahue, F. (2008). *The last professors: The corporate university and the fate of the humanities*. New York: Fordham University Press.

Ford, K. (2011). Race, gender, and bodily (mis)recognitions: Women of color faculty experiences with white students in the college classroom. *The Journal of Higher Education, 82*(4), 444–478.

Graham, E. (2014). NEA report: Lack of teacher diversity jeopardizes student achievement. *NEA Today*. Retrieved from http://neatoday.org/2014/05/16/nea-report-lack-of-teacher-diversity-jeopardizes-student-achievement-2/

Gutierrez y Muhs, G., Gonzalez, C., Harris, A., & Niemann, Y. (eds.) (2012). *Presumed incompetent: The intersections of race and class for women in academia*. Logan, UT: Utah State University Press.

Jayakumar, U., Howard, T., Allen, W., & Han, J. (2009). Racial privilege of the professoriate: An exploration of campus climate, retention, and satisfaction. *The Journal of Higher Education, 80*(5), 588–563.

Jaschik, S. (2015). Administrator pay up 2.4%. *Inside Higher Ed*. Retrieved from https://www.inside-highered.com/news/2015/03/02/study-finds-gains-college-administrators-salaries

Ladson-Billings, G. (1998). Just what is critical race theory and what's it doing in a nice field like education? *International Journal of Qualitative Studies in International Education, 11*(1), 7–24.

Minneapolis Community and Technical College. (2015). *Campus fact sheet*. Retrieved from http://www.minneapolis.edu/About-Us/Fact-Sheet

National Center for Education Statistics. (2015). *Fast facts: Graduation rates*. Retrieved from https://nces.ed.gov/fastfacts/display.asp?id=40

Quentin, S. (2013). Good teachers embrace their students' cultural backgrounds. *The Atlantic*. Retrieved from: http://www.theatlantic.com/education/archive/2013/11/good-teachers-embrace-their-students-cultural-backgrounds/281337/

Schmidlin, K. (2015). The corporatization of higher education: With a system that caters to the 1 percent, students and faculty get screwed. *Salon*. Retrieved from http://www.salon.com/2015/10/10/the_corporatization_of_higher_education_with_a_system_that_caters_to_the_1_percent_students_and_faculty_get_screwed/

Sutherland, M. E. (1990). Black faculty in white academia: The fit is an uneasy one. *The Western Journal of Black Studies, 14*(1), 17–21.

CHAPTER FOURTEEN

On Academic Repression, Blackness, and Storytelling as Resistance

KELLY LIMES-TAYLOR HENDERSON

INTRODUCTION: WHAT WE SEE AND DON'T SEE IN SCHOOL

There is something about a student's sitting in a classroom and seeing all of her classmates' experiences and histories reflected in both text and visual media, but never seeing her own culture and knowledge reflected there. It's possible to take this even further: how would a student feel if he shared skin tone, vernacular, socioeconomic status, or any other social identifier with an entire school population, but was still subjected to curriculum and pedagogical practices that labeled him as "other," "minority," and "deficient," despite even the best of intentions?

This problem does not disappear once these students reach the university level: course catalogs, while perhaps in a more specific manner than what is found in secondary schools, feature nonwhiteness as a classification or defining feature in a way that whiteness is not. This framing of whites' histories, cultures, and experiences as "normal" within educational institutions has its foundation in white supremacy and makes nonwhites the perpetual "other." This framing means that anything related to nonwhiteness, rather ever being perceived as normal or valuable in its own right, will only be understood from the perspective of and in relation to whiteness (Dwyer & Jones, 2000; Welcome, 2004). Such othering is devastating when it occurs within the academy, our knowledge-making and -perpetuating institutions. As it normalizes a white-supremacist frame for seeing and understanding the world in research and teaching, it allows researchers and educators to disseminate this practice to other institutions, including elementary and secondary schools.

Othering and other issues within academia are not new information to many, of course. In their introduction to *Academic Repression: Reflections from the Academic Industrial Complex*, editors Best, Nocella II, and McLaren (2010) note that since

> the academy is a microcosm of social life in the United States, and this nation—as a hierar-
> chical, exploitative capitalist society—has never been free or democratic in any meaningful
> way, we should not be surprised to find higher education to be a place of hierarchical
> domination, bureaucratic control, hostility to radical research and teaching, and anathema
> to free thinking (p. 13).

Extending upon teaching practice and course availability, then, these editors point to structural problems within the academy. They also highlight the "ideological smokescreen" that obfuscates the inequality, the hierarchical organization, and the capitalist and exploitative practices inherent to the academy (p. 14).

The same editors go on, however, to note the academy's positioning within the nation's "perilous decline into a militarist, soulless tyranny of a surveillance society" (p. 29), while Parenti (2010) avers that academic connections with the marketplace make the nation's colleges and universities not unlike "other social institutions such as the media, the arts, the church, schools, and various professions" (p. 113). Fontan (2010) expresses her chagrin that the "land of the civil rights movements, of Dr. Marin Luther King Jr." has become, during this era of the "War on Terror," "the land of racial profiling, the USA PATRIOT Act, false imprisonment, torture, and extraordinary renditions," and the land that so quickly and unabashedly per-secuted her for her truth in academic research and reporting (p. 289).

Fontan's reference to King here is important. The work of King and his myriad named and unnamed cofighters throughout the Black freedom struggles of the 1940s, 1950s, and 1960s occurred precisely because the United States has never been a land of racial profiling, false imprisonment, torture, and rendition for the Black body. It has never not persecuted Black people for telling our truths. Black people have been denied entry to the university and the schoolhouse, the museum and the church, and have also watched these institutions dehumanize us. There has always been tyranny over the Black mind in the United States. There has always been surveillance of Black spaces, both by state police forces and citizens that take policing upon themselves.

I speak of Blacks particularly here because these intrusions, both within aca-demia and in the wider social context, may seem like correctable injustices when they happen to non-Black progressive, leftist, and radical academicians. However, for many Blacks—including those of us within academia—these smaller injus-tices are part of the wider, unjust system in which we find ourselves, one that is predicated upon the enslavement, subjugation, and fungibility of the Black body, and the negation of Black personhood (Hartman & Wilderson, 2003). In other words, repressive instances within academia, while undoubtedly emotionally and psychologically shocking when experienced by any of us, simply reflect the repressive nature of a larger system of which academia is a part. As the group whose subjugation is part of the national foundation, Blacks' experiences in the United States are telling in that they show that repression is a rule in our society, rather than an aberration to be corrected, or about which we should even be surprised. As part of the wider repressive structure, this rule has held true within the academy and continues to hold true today.

As a starting point, I agree with Best, Nocella II, and McLaren (2010) that if "*academic freedom* involves the right of professors (and students) to research, publish, teach, speak, and lead political lives as they choose, then *academic repression* is the manifold denial and negation of this right" (p. 27, authors' emphasis). I also understand academic repression as something more extensive; however, in addition to silencing individual voices and preventing individual acts within the academy, academic repression also privileges certain ways of knowing and being—and certain ways of understanding knowing and being—over others. This privileging is not accidental, but is rooted in the history of Western colonialism that promotes white heteronormative Christian able-bodied patriarchal supremacy, domination, and oppression. This chapter is dedicated to challenging this dominant false narrative, while giving space to storytelling and autoethnography.

THE PROBLEM: THE ACADEMIC EFFECT OF COLONIZATION

In the European Medieval era, when most of the populace was illiterate, European clergy hand-copied, translated, and stored texts. As the printing press was invented and literacy became more widespread, the monasteries still remained warehouses of available knowledge, but a new class of intellectuals, not as intimately tied to the Church, began to grow. In Europe, the university—or, as Sium and Ritskes (2013) call it, the "Euroversity" (p. i)—soon began to emerge around well-read men who tried to infuse the concept of reason into the religion-based dominant thought. While not necessarily negating the existence of God, man assumed a place in the European narrative of the learned that he had not previously occupied (Wynter, 2003).

At the same time, outside the halls of learning, Europe was embarking on another adventure: imperialism. As European nations began to compete for trade routes, precious metal, and territory abroad, they looked for ways to justify their abuse of the indigenous people that occupied these lands and with whom they had previously had friendlier relationships (Diop, 1981/1991). Wynter (2003) asserts that while the new lay intelligentsia of the Enlightenment period tried to usurp the position of the historically formidable Church as the constructor and perpet-uator of knowledge, it assumed the dichotomous ontological structure that the Church had already established.

This "rupture" of the Church's control over knowledge and its dissemination had two effects. First and perhaps surprisingly, it created an almost seamless meld-ing between certain religious ideas and certain scientific ones; second, this melding was quite convenient for the European imperialists travelling the globe. While other ontologies (and the epistemologies that came from them) undoubtedly existed in Europe during the Medieval and Enlightenment periods, the Church and the academy, respectively, were the dominant knowledge-creating, -perpetuat-ing, and -legitimizing institutions. Wynter's assertion, then, leads to an important conclusion: rather than a violent, unjust anomaly, imperialism and colonization have been justified by a church-based system of knowledge that allowed for the existence of groups of people that were inherently sinful, irrational, expendable, and exploitable. Unfortunately, rather than using its position to fundamentally trouble such a system, the academy has perpetuated it. Smith (1999) directly speaks to this perpetuation, noting that "the term 'research' is inextricably linked to European imperialism and colonialism," and that the "ways in which scien-tific research is implicated in the worst excesses of colonialism remains a powerful remembered history for many of the world's colonized peoples" (p. 1).

James (2010) extends this idea by also concluding that the academy has histor-ically privileged Western epistemology and theory making, decided that Western epistemological and theory-making practices are "universal" rather than Western, and marginalized any opposing thought. This "'white solipsism' masquerades as philosophy within the myth of European 'racial,' therefore intellectual, superior-ity" (James, 2010, p. 339). Both James' and Smith's discussions show how the academy has simultaneously supported and been supported by Western interests, at the same time that it provided itself the intellectual justification for atrocities committed by European imperialists and colonialists as it was researching a world increasingly cowed under Western domination. While "the West," then, is typi-cally understood as the group of regions where European-descended people are in the majority, it more accurately represents the group whose members—albeit at varying levels—simultaneously perpetuate and profit from the past five centuries of European colonialism and imperialism. It is important to note that the West-ern researcher is not necessarily white, but must only be trained in and adhere to the ideas of white European-descended normalcy and dominance—even if that adherence is not a conscious one (Fanon, 1961/2004; James, 2010; Sullivan & Tuana, 2007; wa Thiong'o, 1986/2008; Welcome, 2004; Yankah, 2006).

These Western-based traditions have continued with the rise of the acad-emy within the United States. The development of the United States as a settler colony—where a conquering group grows to represent the controlling majority of a region (Smith, 2010; Tuck & Yang, 2012)—requires that the aforementioned practices of normalizing, othering, and repressing occur within its borders and continue throughout its existence. Our institutions, including educational institutions, both undergird and are undergirded by our settler colonial society, and the "colonized peoples" that Smith (1999) discusses exist within the United States' own borders rather than in some distant land.

Naming indigenous genocide and Black slaveability/anti-Black racism as the foundations of a white supremacist, capitalist and settler colonial society, Smith (2010) elucidates the bloody foundation upon which this country was built. This history of erasure and oppression makes itself evident in our educational institutions in a variety of ways, from the oft-mentioned achievement gap and less-discussed achievement debt, to the school-to-prison pipeline, to growing school segregation and the for-profit charter school movement (Alexander, 2010; Ahlquist, Gorski, & Moñtano, 2011; Anderson, 2004; Ford, 2012; Ladson-Billings, 2006; Lipman, 2011; Payne & Knowles, 2009; Ravitch, 2010; Saltman, 2007; Swartz, 2007; Wynter, 2000).

While it is out of the scope of this chapter to extensively discuss these and the many other examples of settler colonial oppression and eradication within our educational institutions, there is a way that we may begin. As academics interested in decolonizing practice collect and explore the histories and literature of those most oppressed in the settler colonial context, we may find in these very stories the keys to resisting these wider repressions, as well as the academic repressions that they include, as well as learning ways of knowing and being outside of that of the West.

Pérez (2010) indicates this when she notes that "we have all inherited a history of colonialism" and that, because of this, "we have been blinded by the nation's patriotic discourse, which functions as an alibi to justify colonization throughout US history" (pp. 364–365). Related to the obscuring discourse that Best, Nocella II, and McLaren discuss, Pérez argues that the "lies, injustices, and naked power dynamics" that are the foundation for the colonial narrative must be supplanted by what she calls the "decolonial imaginary" (p. 365). This imaginary highlights those marginalized by this country's settler colonial past and present, allows us to "rethink history," and, ultimately, "construct new stories, identities, values, and, ultimately, societies" (p. 365). Constructing new stories may seem quite removed from creating new societies, but they are, in fact, inextricably linked.

RESISTANCE: TELLING A NEW STORY

Resistance to colonial repression is not simply a theoretical enterprise; indeed, presenting and learning different ways of knowing and being are quite possible. This new knowing will occur over time and in a variety of ways; however, it will begin with new language. Said in another way, it will begin with a new word. The word represents a concept that is more specific than language in general, in that it indicates the moment that the human first created verbal and/or visual representations of abstract thought. Wynter (as quoted in Gagne, 2007) asserts that an important part of thinking outside the Western paradigm involves our rejection of the Western idea of the human beings as the result of strictly biological and evolutionary processes, as other animals are. Rather, humans are humans because of the word. She asserts that humans' nascent ability to think in abstraction pushed them out of "subordination to the genetic programs which prescribe the behaviors of purely organic life" (Wynter, as quoted in Gagne, 2007, p. 259). While our lives are still greatly influenced by these genetic programs, Wynter asserts that, since its creation, humans have been subordinate to "the Word/Myth" (Gagne, 2007, p. 259).

Human subordination to word/myth has come to be a valuable tool in the era of Western imperialism and colonialism, as one of its most vital areas of control is the "mental universe of the colonized, the control, through culture, of how people perceiv[e] themselves and their relationship to the world" (wa Thiong'o, 1986/2008). The metropole's control of the mental universe of the colonized comes in the form of linguistic domination, as our languages are not only a means of communication in the present, but also the banks that hold the evolution of a culture, including what is known and what can be known. A conquering group's insistence that economic and educational transactions occur in its own language rather than the language of the dominated, coupled with the conquering group's privileging of its own history and literary traditions, effectively recreate the world of the colonized to fit the image of the colonizer. Not only does the physical world become the property of the colonizer; the world of the past and a group's entire imaginary has transferred hands as well. This domination, in essence, rewrites the colonized groups' stories about their own existence.

Pérez (2010) notes that the "colonial mindset," which "establishes the naming of things," will automatically "leave something out, leave something unsaid, and leave silences and gaps that must be uncovered" (p. 365). Thus, a very early step in resisting Western colonialism in the form of academic repression is to use research to explore those gaps and silences, to see the holes within the West's story of itself and us, and to then understand this naming as something that is not ubiquitous or permanent. We can then understand ourselves as something outside of the Western definition of human and humanity that requires the eliminations and enslavement of Indigenous and Black life—namely, as our being human because we have the ability to name ourselves and the world around us, and discuss (and, thus, decide) what and who we will be. It requires us to use research to tell new stories about ourselves, our histories, and our universe.

While wa Thiong'o (1986/2008) argues for the use of indigenous language as resistance to colonial domination, for many, the language of origin is the language of the Western colonializing nations. Here, the academy becomes an important location for resistance to Western colonization and its effects. As the academy has historically written and disseminated the colonizer's stories about marginalized people, decolonizing researchers may use the colonizer's own language to listen to and disseminate the stories marginalized people tell about themselves through the same academic channels, thus troubling and providing a nondominant narrative to the narratives that the colonizer's language tells. This resistance can happen in two ways: the collection of stories and storytelling acts that defy the colonial narrative, and a reconfiguration of the colonizer's language, which will simultaneously generate and summon, from long rejected and repressed histories and stories, new worlds for the ones embedded within each word of the language. This creating and recalling presents counters the narratives housed and perpetuated in the Western academy, and could also become a resistance guidebook from those who have survived attempts of Western colonial eradication, as well as from the resilient and adaptive traditions of those that have been designated as nonhuman, yet manage to affirm their humanity, even if only to themselves.

ONE FAMILY'S STORY

To contribute to the decolonizing effort of self-naming and telling counterdominant stories, I collected nine family members' oral histories about the educational life history of my grandmother, then melded these stories' elements into a four-part novella. Featuring my own family was an intentional act: as land and kinship have been primary sites of white domination over Indigenous and Black life since the beginnings of the Western colonial era, I believe that the Black researcher's study of self and kin adds to the body of knowledge that troubles a Western ontology that requires Black enslavement and Indigenous erasure, and whose goal is decolonization. In addition to this, I wanted my work to add both primary and secondary historical sources to the increasing body of historical texts that resist and exist outside of the dominant deficit narrative about Blacks and Blackness that currently influence schools and the schooled, as well as add to the growing body of literary works of resistance as well. This historical and literary work gives credence to King's and Justice's assertion that all we are is stories: the narrative is the way that we understand ourselves and the world around us, whether we name that narrative history or fiction (Ginzburg, 1980; Justice, 2008, p. 150; King, 2008, p. 14; White, 1978).

One example of the way a Black activist-scholar interested in decolonizing practices can listen to and explore narratives outside of the dominant one may be found in my work of gathering data for and writing *One Hundred and Sixteenth*, the historical fiction novella based on the life of my maternal grandmother and her family. What follows is a discussion of how I engaged in this process of data collecting and writing, both as a Black researcher within academia and as a Black woman situated within the wider settler colonial social context.

COLLECTING AND CREATING *ONE HUNDRED AND SIXTEENTH*

The first methodology employed in my study was oral history. While a methodology that has long-gained acceptance within the Western colonial academic paradigm, the methodology itself is still influenced by the aforementioned standard of white normalcy. While there has been a discussion of the four paradigmatic shifts in the field of oral history—implying long-standing academic methodology—the presence of oral history courses and documents within the history department has not sufficiently troubled the academic privileging of writing over orality, thus potentially excluding people from nonliterate and/or orality-dominant groups, whose testimonies may be understood as folklore or mythology, rather than history (Thomson, 2007, p. 50; Whiteduck, 2013, p. 73). Thus, while oral historian Paul Thompson notes that oral history collection can make the academic field of history "more democratic," the methodology's ability to present points of view and stories that previously received little attention in the academy may still privilege some points of view and stories over others (Thompson, 1998, p. 29). Further, in the case of groups whose storytelling and historical traditions are primarily oral, collection of these groups' narratives within the oral history canon may reflect Western academic traditions of taking from oppressed or marginalized groups in order to benefit Western interests. An example of this is the collection and publication of the Uncle Remus tales (Harris, 1974). Though based on Black oral historical collection, the stories were not published (or, later, turned into a Disney movie) in the interest of resisting Black oppression or dehumanization,

While it is a methodology accepted by the academy, then, researchers that wish to resist academic repression through oral history collection from marginalized groups, particularly those that have extensive oral traditions, must be willing to trouble dominant Western standards of fact and fiction, of what counts as historical evidence as opposed to a nonfactual story. The collection of Black oral histories is an important example of this. Citing historian Clark-Lewis, Nunes (2011) notes that, for "historians of a predominantly oral culture," storytelling is "a fundamental source for the writing of African American history," and scholars should "listen and record the testimonies that will constitute the cultural heritage of the coming generations" (Nunes, 2011, p. 2). While the orality of Black American culture has multiple reasons—for example, the oral African cultures that were introduced to the Americans through enslavement, as well as prohibitions against teaching enslaved people to read and write, and the subsequent, century-long resistance to Black schooling after emancipation—acknowledgement of its prominence is important here, in that it recognizes that a primary way that historians can learn about this history of Black American survival and resistance within the white supremacist context is through asking Black Americans themselves, as written histories of Black from their own perspective have only recently become part of the Western historical canon.

Writers interested Black history, then, will have to explore "sources often dismissed by traditional approaches to history" (Nunes, 2011, p. 3). Nunes further asserts that the writing of fiction based on historical data is the Black writer's way to "recreate the 'historical records' that were destroyed, or never existed," to write for and about "those who remained outside the pages of history" (2011, p. 4). The writing of historical fiction based on Black oral histories, combined with the collection of Black oral histories themselves, represent not only a potential for a new canon of historical documents within the academy, but, and perhaps more significantly, the potential for a new historical imaginary that contradicts that of the dominant paradigm.

Throughout the oral history collection process, I employed what I have termed the Black-Indigenist paradigm. Black-Indigenism recognizes the aims of Indigenist methodologies as the primary vehicle for decolonization within (and outside of) the academy, while recognizing Blackness as an integral factor in the argument for Indigenism. The Black-Indigenist paradigm, like other Indigenist paradigms, focuses on kinship and the story within research; like Indigenist practice, it also understands that wider decolonial goals of Indigenous self-determination and the end of settler colonialism should inform research practice. However, unlike other practices, Black-Indigenism attends to the observation and analytical practices of American Blacks as those who have experienced the attempted erasure of their indigeneity and whose continued understanding of their own humanity can provide the examples we need to re-Word our world. Moreover, this paradigm challenges traditional Western colonial white supremacist schooling systems, and while many white scholars would like to locate this under qualitative methodology, autoethnography participatory activist research, or activist ethnography, this is not the roots of this method as it challenges the white intellectual capital information and challenges the notion that all must locate with or under white research and white thinking. This chapter specifically addresses the ways Black-Indigenism can inform oral history collection and fiction writing, and articulates methodological requirements that include:

1. a foundational investigation (personal or within literature review) of the histories of Indigenous genocide and Black enslavement and anti-Black racism within the United States and within its academy.
2. the inclusion of decolonization/Indigenous sovereignty and eradication of anti-Black racism within long-term research goals and implications.

3. researcher self-questioning regarding the ways that research will benefit marginalized groups, particularly Black and Indigenous groups.
4. the inclusion of community input regarding all aspects of the research process, from the necessity and feasibility of a particular study, to an investigation of potential harms due to publication of study results.
5. the willingness to trouble existing academic research historically conducted on Black and Indigenous groups, as well as academic practice that excludes and/or devalues Black and Indigenous linguistic, cultural, and philosophical practice.
6. the willingness to both use and create decolonial, Indigenist sources and resources that resist anti-Blackness.

When adhering to the Black-Indigenist paradigm, the use of the oral historical account in research provides a way for the researcher to not only include the voice and perspective of kin/community, but can also allow that voice and perspective to be the primary focus of the research, potentially privileging the experiences of kin/community in addition to (or instead of) the researcher's.

In my research project, the focus of the oral history interviews was to be the life of the participants' mother, my maternal grandmother, giving particular attention to what they knew about her experiences in her early twenties and later, specifically as they applied to education and schooling. In talking to the participants, however, I did not believe that the flow of the interview lent itself to such a strict focus. Reading from and constantly redirecting my participants' conversations toward a list of questions that I created would have formed an interview process primarily based on my priorities but not necessarily those of my participants, which would have been at odds with a kin/community-centered Black-Indigenist paradigm. The interviews generally consisted of my first making the introductory request "Tell me who I'm talking to and where we/you are," a tip from Studs Terkel (Terkel & Parker, 2006, p. 123). After asking an opening open-ended question about the participant's childhood or memory of his/her mother, the interview became more of a conversation, with my participants speaking generally dominating the interview session, while I asked clarifying questions as the participant spoke. Because of this open-endedness, some participants spent large parts of their interview discussing their own lives, the life of their father, or the community in which they were raised. Except for three of the participants that discussed school and schooling rather extensively, most of the participants' discussions of school were relatively brief and were diversions from the main points of their conversation—community and family.

The interviews with my participants were eye-opening and sometimes challenging, in that I learned things about my family that I did not know, both positive and negative. In this work, I was a researcher and daughter and niece, all at the same time. I closed each interview with a heart and mind that was simultaneously heavy with stories about the circumstances my family had to endure in South Carolina and New York, and light from the stories of humor, love, and triumph.

An example of this is one of my participants' discussions about living in the ghettos of Harlem. Whether encountering teachers that do not believe in their students' mental abilities, the disrepair of their buildings and streets, or the prevalence of contraband (of which other communities partake but do not claim), the child and adult of the ghetto are told that they are worth very little as far as their city, state, and country are concerned. They are ignorable, silenced, and disposable. Even more so for the Black ghetto child and adult: in a country where Black bodies are disposable and Black minds superfluous, a community of poor Black people renders an entire geographical area disposable and superfluous. One of my participants briefly discussed this idea:

P: Harlem was the ghetto […].

It was the ghetto. It, you know, it was, it was, um [pause] an isolated area and not, not just […] you had Harlem and, I mean, you had Harlem and you had Spanish Harlem, um, but it was, uh, predominately Black, and Spanish Harlem was Puerto Rican, or, you know, immigrants from somewhere, and then a little further down on the same street—we lived on a Hundred Sixteenth Street—further down on the eastside was Little Italy, you know, where it was mostly, uh, predominantly an Italian, um, community, but if you, if you lived in Little Italy, you was just Italian […]

[…] but if you lived five or six blocks over, you were poor [pause] and you were probably poor, uneducated and, and livin' in […] and, and such was obviously not the case, um, but, a lot of times, when most people migrated from the south to New York, as Dad and Mom did, that's where you wound up, in Harlem, because you're usually coming to a relative that lives there. And, and, um [pause] Dad and Mom came to my father's sister, a sister who lived there, so that was home. So, um, and it was an infestation of, um, people living from paycheck-to-paycheck, uh, some much worse off than we were […].

[S]o, um, we had this, um [pause] very [pause] festering, um, drug academy […] epidemic, which was heroin, and so, um […]. And then there was robberies and, and then there was, uh, people who didn't attend to their kids and, you know, all of that. So it was a stereotype.

The participant went on to discuss white flight from Harlem, as well as all of the cultural richness of the area of which she took advantage as a child and young adult—exposure to various cultures and ethnicities, the ability to visit museum and attend concerts, the proximity of famous venues like the Apollo Theatre as well as a few blocks' walk to Central and Mt. Morris Parks. She asserted that these things, immediately surrounding her ghetto community, provided a wealth that money could not buy. Still, the settler colonial structure in which she lived told her something different:

P: Um [pause] the subway told me that, um [pause] the television told me that, um, it, it, it told me that, um [pause] I lived in a cesspool. And, and that's, that's when I said where that embarrassment came from is because that's what society said [...]. "Where you are, where those people are, is, is the gutter," you know [...].

As the participant explained the messages she received from broader society about her community, she was also able to detail how those messages made her feel: confused about her love for a place that she was supposed to despise and fear; displacement because she, as a product of that community, was not supposed to have the abilities that she indeed possessed. Purported to be a negligible someone within a negligible somewhere, my participant found herself instead to be someone who mattered, somewhere that mattered. Based on this and my other participants' stories like them, I wanted to create a single narrative that, while inspired by past events, primarily addressed themes that I detected from their narrations, themes that were not aligned with the dominant narrative that understands Blackness as something inferior or deprived. In this creation of Black-authored historical fiction that resists the dominant anti-Black narrative, I hoped to follow in the footsteps of Haley (1976), Dash (1999), Walker (1967), and Morrison (1987/2004). While these stories happened to be the stories of my family members, I believed that stories like them—stories of humanity in the face of dehumanizing circumstances—could be found in myriad members of marginalized groups in the settler colonial context. To combine these stories, I turned to historical fiction as a way to extend the decolonizing historical imaginary while extending the accessibility of the oral historical accounts to an audience that may not as readily access interview transcriptions.

Hirsch and Dixon (2008) assert that the writing process is "a combination of our dynamic oral tradition and a finite structure, a guide we impose on half of the story" (p. 188). When writing fiction in particular, Leavy (2013) says that researchers must tap into their "creativity, attention to craft or aesthetics, reflexivity, and openness (or adaptability)" (p. 53). The researcher writing fiction must be prepared to constantly critique and revise her own work and be intentional about "the process of layering and weaving meanings together" in writing projects that will be complicated, multifaceted representations of the world (Leavy, 2013, p. 53). This process of layering and weaving can become even more intricate for the writers of historical fiction.

Kaye (1920) long ago noted that the historical fiction writer "does not talk about the characters or report their deeds," but instead her characters "live, talk, and act for themselves in his representations." In addition, historical fiction writers, as opposed to writers of other types of fiction, "deal with the audiences of the past in the events and affairs of the world" (Kaye, 1920, forward). However, contrary to what Kaye averred, a writer of historical fiction can indeed be a historian as well. Manzoni (1984) notes that some writers not only organize and present these past events, but also craft a narrative that is enjoyable to read. And while historical fiction writing may indeed be inspired by the writer's "lofty purpose" to represent historical events "as they ought to have been," Manzoni (1984) took for granted that the past can always be known, (p. 84). Though there are undoubtedly extant documents that can attest to the past existence of particular people or events, there are people and events for whom documentation did not exist, as the questions of the previous section indicate.

When historical work is primarily understood as pulling together narratives and evidence of past events in order to piece together a broader narrative that bears some similarity to what has passed, it takes for granted that the causes and effects of events are intrinsically observable, and that surviving evidence and narration of the past—or the lack thereof—is indicative of what is worth knowing and what can be known. While researchers and writers of fiction working under these assumptions may indeed produce historical works, those researchers interested in questions of Blackness, indigeneity, and resisting the dominant settler colonial system must look beyond them to what has been erased, ignored, and devalued in the past, and evaluate how we understand both that past and our present. When that erasure and devaluing are further understood as tools and imperatives of settler colonialism, rather than accidental forgetting, the decolonial researcher may also come to understand concepts as truth, fact, and, of course, history as potential tools of the settler colonial project as well. I tried to resist such an erasure and devaluing in my own work.

As I reviewed my family's interview transcriptions and my interview notes, and contacted my participants with follow-up questions, I tried to insert myself into the past, as much as is possible for any historian, and with the knowledge that a complete insertion—or a clear picture of the way it "really" was and why—would never be possible. Indeed, it is not truly possible even for the people who lived it: interviewing nine people about the same woman, neighborhood, and era produced nine accounts that bore as many differences as they did similarities. The aim of the historical fictional account, the novella called *One Hundred and Sixteenth*, was to evoke a sense of the people, places, and times addressed in my participants' oral historical accounts, using both the accounts themselves and my inferences from them. What follows are two excerpts from the novella based on my participants' accounts of living in their Harlem neighborhood:

> As Andy strolled back up 116th Street, Harlem was just starting its day. School kids raced down the wide sidewalk toward Madison Avenue to Cooper and P.S. 79, which were just a few blocks north, on 119th and 120th. Women in the worn shoes of the domestic and women in the smart skirts and hose of the Financial District walked past him toward the 116th Station and Downtown. A brother from the Nation—no one else would be wearing a bowtie that early in the morning—was passing out flyers for the next time Malcolm

would be at the temple. On the ground floor of his building, Sal was propping open the door to his bodega while box trucks rumbled down the street.

Andy loved Harlem. He loved his place and these people. The streets were alive. There was never a dull moment, and it was never still. Like the high school hallways, cafeteria and gym, there was always someone to see, some drama to be part of, some new thing to do. But the classroom was boring. Andy did well in the classroom, especially when it came to science and math, but the classroom wasn't alive like the streets were. Both his parents expressed the importance of education, but textbooks, papers, and chalkboards held nothing for Andy. As he got older in school, what he heard and read in the classroom seemed less and less relevant to what he saw going on his block. Guys his age were getting rich before his very eyes, and families were losing sons and brothers, wives and sisters to the streets, to Vietnam. What did Shakespeare or the Pythagorean Theorem have to do with that?

****

"They aren't here at the moment." A voice behind Rochelle scared her out of her thoughts. She turned to see a tall woman filling an apartment door. "Didn't mean to frighten you, baby. But Mrs. Emile isn't there, and the kids are downstairs. May I help you?"

Rochelle sputtered for a moment. She was used to folks' keeping their doors closed and minding their business in a way that belied the City's crowdedness. It was like Harlem was full of people yet completely empty. The fact that a neighbor would know one's whereabouts and, what's more, tell them to a stranger, momentarily confused the young teacher.

"I—I wanted to talk to Mrs. Emile about her son," Rochelle finally said.

The tall woman smiled. "Which one? She's got a lot."

Rochelle didn't know how to respond to that one. "Um, Phillip."

"Oh! That one." The tall woman smiled and shook her head as if there were many stories to tell about the child and it was a shame that Rochelle didn't have the time to hear them. "Too smart for his own good, that one. Just a minute."

Rochelle watched the woman leave her front door and head to the window directly behind her. She opened it, stuck out her head and yelled, "Berta Mae! Someone's here to see your mother about Phillip!" The woman then shut the window and walked back to her front door.

Again, Rochelle didn't know what to say. "Um, thank you."

"You want some tea biscuits while you wait?"

Rochelle was trying to find the words to politely decline when she heard a rumbling downstairs.

"You have to take a bath anyway, so there's no reason to fuss." An older girl's voice.

"I don't want to take a bath! It's the middle of the day! And I smell just fine!" Rochelle knew that was Phillip.

"You smell like the great outdoors," said the older girl again.

"I'm going second." Now a small girl.

"Third," an even smaller voice piped up.

"Hey! I didn't even hear Doreen start!" Now a boy, but not Phillip.

"Vickie doesn't get to pick. She's too little," Phillip said.

There was a moment of small child babbling, and the girl—not the older one, but not the small one—said, "Lena said she's going fourth," followed by general laughter.

Rochelle looked back at the neighbor, whose dancing eyes were on the landing. She smiled warmly at the voices. When the neighbor caught Rochelle's eye, her smile broadened from one of love and admiration to one of amusement. Rochelle could only guess at her own facial expression, but she wanted to know: How many of these children were there?

In the above excerpts, which were based on my nine participants' discussions of growing up in Harlem, as well as throughout the novella, I tried not only to use storytelling to relay a consolidated version of past events, but, and more importantly, also to illuminate interview themes that countered the dominant narrative about impoverished Black families. While the novella dealt with the typical issues that are often addressed in deficit-based discussions of Blackness—impoverishment, drug use, crime, academic disparity, and colorism—it was important to me to also show other themes, such as familial unity and neighborhood pride, that my family members strongly indicated in their interviews but that are often not heard in mainstream discussions about the Black family and community.

CONCLUSION: NEXT STEPS

Gagne (2006) notes that Blacks are uniquely positioned to resist and reverse the Western narrative of binary and separation: as permanent outsiders, people of African descent are fully cognizant of the failings of being/aspiring toward what Wynter (as quoted in King, 2005a) has termed the "bourgeois/Western mode of Human" and, after having survived it for hundreds of years, have proven themselves adept at "dismantling" it (Gagne, 2006, p. 261). Although many of us are unable to return to the indigenous languages of our ancestors, it behooves decolonial researchers and writers to take as examples the oppressed's naming of *themselves*, telling their own stories, constructing narratives that turn white-supremacist discourse on its head is the first step in the dismantling process. Gagne (2006) notes that Wynter (1976) called this defining, this self-naming/self-creation "autopoiesis" (p. 206).

1. This **self-naming** is no trivial task: in the same way that the oppressive institutions came to be through language, through the word, our liberation from this pernicious system must, too, be based in the word, words that describe—and, thus, create—a new world. Gagne (2007) discusses the revolutionary potential of autopoiesis through the example of Black people in the Americas: we can trace a historical pattern of autopoiesis in the transplanted African cultures in the Americas, for, as Gagne (2006) notes when she cites Wynter (1976), "it was in this culture that the blacks reinvented themselves as a we that needed no other" (p. 259).

2. I could recognize this pattern within my own participants' stories: while they freely discussed the challenges that they experienced in life, they also emphasized aspects of Black life in the United States that *resist dominant narratives* about it: the importance of marriage and fatherhood within the Black family; the suspicion of and resistance to narratives that presuppose links between education, schooling, and progress; the Black understanding of self apart from whiteness and the white gaze; and tropes normally negatively associated with Blackness in the dominant narrative—the ghetto/impoverished neighborhood, the drug dealer/user, the dropout, the single mother, the abusive/absent father—as multifaceted in their own right.

3. These stories are important and are necessary presences in the work of the *decolonizing* researcher trying to push back against academic repression. They are stories that those of us in schools need to present and discuss with students who move through institutions that otherize them, that tell them they are what they know they are not. As the keepers and disseminators of knowledge, those of us in the academy and in schools interested in resisting their colonial legacies and underpinning should begin by developing new stories, new connotations for *Black* and *white*, for *rich* and *poor*, for *ghetto* and *urban*, even for *oppressed*.

4. Taking my own work as a point of departure, I argue that we in the academy and schools can find clues for *resisting repression* from the settler colonial structure and its institutions in the very communities we understand to be most oppressed and marginalized. What are people in those communities doing to remind themselves of their own humanity that others are not? How do they teach their children that they exist when their world tells them they do not? How do they resist the slaveability that has been assigned to them? Then, most importantly: what can we learn from these practices in order to resist the dominant structure that requires slaveability, negation, and erasure in order to survive? How can we use our understandings of these practices to work together with these

communities to dismantle a system that oppresses all of us? How can we incorporate these understandings to affirm the humanity of all students, regardless of race and class, and how can we incorporate these understandings to better serve Black, impoverished, urban students in particular?

I want to end here where I began, with the student sitting in the classroom, wondering what the short story or history chapter in class has to do with her. That wondering is not random, but is the result of hundreds of years of colonization and institution building that selectively benefits and harms based primarily on one's class status and race or ethnicity. That wondering is the result of academic repression, repression that mirrors the wider repressions of its settler colonial society, repression that has historically silenced and ignored Black and Indigenous voices in the name of nation building. Resisting that repression will take, among other things, highlighting these voices in the academy as they remind us about ways of knowing and being outside of the Western context, and presenting these voices to young people who need to know where their stories are in the history books and novels that they read.

REFERENCES

Alexander, M. (2010). *The new Jim Crow: Mass incarceration in the age of colorblindness*. New York: The New Press.

Ahlquist, R., Gorski, P., & Moñtano, T. (2011). (eds.). *Assault on kids: How hyper-accountability, corporatization, deficit ideologies, and Ruby Payne are destroying our schools*. New York: Peter Lang.

Anderson, J. (2004). The historical context for understanding the test score gap. *National Journal of Urban Education and Practice, 1*(1), 1–21.

Best, S., Nocella II, A. J., & McLaren, P. (2010). Introduction. In A. J. Nocella II, S. Best, & P. McLaren (eds.), *Academic repression: Reflections from the academic industrial complex* (pp. 13–89). Oakland, CA: AK Press.

Dash, J. (1999). *Daughters of the dust*. New York: Plume.

Dwyer, O. J., & Jones, III, J. P. (2000). White socio-spatial epistemology. *Social & Cultural Geography, 1*, 209–221.

Fanon, F. (1961/2004). *The wretched of the Earth*. R. Philcox (Trans.). New York: Grove Press.

Fontan, V. (2010). From Colgate to Costa Rica: Critical reflections on US academia. In A. J. Nocella II, S. Best, & P. McLaren (eds.), *Academic repression: Reflections from the academic industrial complex* (pp. 280–291). Oakland, CA: AK Press.

Ford, G. (2012, May 9). *Corporate assault on public education*. Retrieved from http://www.blackeducationnow.org/id22.html

Gagne, K. (2006). Fighting amnesia as a guerilla activity: Poetics for a new mode of being human. *Human Architecture: Journal of the Sociology of Self-Knowledge, 4*(3), 249–264.

Gagne, K. (2007). On the obsolescence of the disciplines: Frantz Fanon and Sylvia Wynter propose a new mode of being human. *Human Architecture: Journal of the Sociology of Self-Knowledge, 5*, 251–264.

Ginzburg, C. (1980). Morelli, Freud, and Sherlock Holmes: Clues and scientific method. *History Workshop, 9*, 5–36.

Haley, A. (1976). *Roots: The saga of an American family*. New York: Doubleday.

Harris, J. C. (1974). *Uncle Remus: Tales*. Savannah, GA: Beehive Press.

Hartman, S., & Wilderson III, F. B. (2003). The position of the unthought. *Qui Parle, 13*(2), 183–201.

Hirsch, A., & Dixon, C. (2008). Katrina narratives: What creative writers can teach us about oral history. *The Oral History Review, 35*(2), 187–195.

James, J. (2010). Teaching theory, talking community. In A. J. Nocella II, S. Best, & P. McLaren (eds.), *Academic repression: Reflections from the academic industrial complex* (pp. 337–346). Oakland, CA: AK Press.

Justice, D. (2008). "Go away, water!": Kinship criticism and the decolonization imperative. In C. Womack, D. Justice, & C. Teuton (eds.), *Reasoning together: The native critics collective* (pp. 147–168). Norman, OK: University of Oklahoma Press.

Kaye, J. R. (1920). *Historical fiction*. Chicago, IL: Snowdon Publishing Company.

King, J. (2005a). Race and our biocentric belief system: An interview with Sylvia Wynter. In J. King (ed.), *Black education: A transformative research and action agenda for the new century* (pp. 361–366). Mahwah, N.J.: Lawrence Erlbaum.

King, T. (2008). The art of Indigenous knowledge: A million porcupines crying in the dark. In J. G. Knowles & A. Cole (eds.), *Handbook of the arts in qualitative research* (pp. 13–25). Los Angeles, CA: Sage.

Ladson-Billings, G. (2006). From the achievement gap to the education debt: Understanding achievement in U.S. schools. *Educational Researcher, 35*, 3–12.

Leavy, P. (2013). *Fiction as research practice: Short stories, novellas, and novels*. Walnut Creek, CA: Left Coast Press.

Lipman, P. (2011). *The new political economy of urban education: Neoliberalism, race, and the right to the city*. New York: Routledge.

Manzoni, A. (1984). *On the historical novel*. (Sandra Bermann, Trans.). Lincoln, NE: University of Nebraska Press.

Morrison, T. (1987/2004). *Beloved*. New York: Vintage.

Nunes, A. (2011). *African American women writers' historical fiction*. New York: Palgrave Macmillan.

Parenti, M. (2010). Academic repression: Past and present. In A. J. Nocella II, S. Best, & P. McLaren (eds.), *Academic repression: Reflections from the academic industrial complex* (pp. 112–121). Oakland, CA: AK Press.

Payne, C., & Knowles, T. (2009). Promise and peril: Charter schools, urban school reform, and the Obama administration. *Harvard Educational Review, 79*, 227–239.

Pérez, E. (2010). Decolonial critics for academic freedom. In A. J. Nocella II, S. Best, & P. McLaren (eds.), *Academic repression: Reflections from the academic industrial complex* (pp. 364–373). Oakland, CA: AK Press.

Ravitch, D. (2010). *The death and life of the great American school system: How testing and choice are undermining education*. New York: Basic Books.

Saltman, K. J. (2007). Schooling in disaster capitalism: How the political right is using disaster to privatize public schooling. *Teacher Education Quarterly, 34*(2), 131–156.

Sium, A., & Ritskes, E. (2013). Speaking truth to power: Indigenous storytelling as an act of living resistance. *Decolonization: Indigeneity, Education and Society, 2*(1), i–x.

Smith, A. (2010). Indigeneity, settler colonialism, white supremacy. *Global Dialogue, 12*(2), 66–90. Retrieved from http://www.worlddialogue.org/content.php?id=488

Smith, L. T. (1999). *Decolonizing methodologies: Research and Indigenous peoples.* London: Zed Books.

Sullivan, S., & Tuana, N. (eds.). (2007). *Race and epistemologies of ignorance.* Albany, NY: State University of New York Press.

Swartz, E. (2007). Stepping outside the master script: Re-connecting the history of American education. *The Journal of Negro Education, 76,* 173–186.

Thompson, P. (1998). The voice of the past: Oral history. In R. Perks & A. Thomson (eds.), *The oral history reader* (pp. 25–31). London: Routledge.

Thomson, A. (2007). Four paradigm transformations in oral history. *The Oral History Review, 34*(1), 49–70.

Tuck, E., & Yang, K. W. (2012). Decolonization is not a metaphor. *Decolonization: Indigeneity, education and society, 1*(1), 1–40.

wa Thiong'o, N. (1986/2008). *Decolonising the mind: The politics of language in African literature.* Portsmouth, NH: Heinemann.

Walker, M. (1967). *Jubilee.* New York: Bantam Books.

Welcome, H. A. (2004). "White is right": The utilization of an improper ontological perspective in analyses of Black experiences." *Journal of African American Studies, 8,* 60–73.

White, H. (1978). *Tropics of discourse: Essays in cultural criticism.* Baltimore, MD: Johns Hopkins University Press.

Wynter, S. (1976). Ethno or socio poetics. *Alcheringa: Ethnopoetics, 2*(2), 78–94.

Wynter, S. (2000). Rethinking origins/knowledges/the achievement gap: Black education after 'Man.' *Commission on research in Black education: Working colloquium.* Retrieved from http://www.coribe.org/pages/IManifesto.html

Wynter, S. (2003). Unsettling the coloniality of being/power/truth/freedom: Towards the human, after man, its overrepresentation—An argument. *The New Centennial Review, 3*(3), 257–337.

Yankah, K. (2006). *Education: Scholarly authority and the quest for a new world academic order, inaugural lecture.* Accra, Ghana: Black Mask, Ltd.

CHAPTER FIFTEEN

Black Student Unions and Identity: Navigating Oppression in Higher Education

Z. B. HURST

INTRODUCTION

The Black Students Union (BSU) at Luther College in Decorah, Iowa, whose reformation was official after lots of paperwork and an encouraging Diversity Center Executive Director gave a gentle push, gasps its first rattling breaths. By no means is our room packed every Thursday evening, but those who are there expel some strange demons—loosening some sly and barelythere fingers from around their throats. We have a group message on Facebook for emergencies, and our emergencies happen every eight hours. VonDerrit Myers Jr. is killed with a sandwich in his hand while wearing a Global Positioning System anklet and no charges are filed against the officer who thought he was holding a gun (Byers, 2015). We have run out of things to satirize; we are out of outlandish impossibilities. We discuss our goals: what will we do with the atrocities we inherit? Who do we ask to exact justice when justice is the one who errs? Will we never know again what it feels like to trust a flag, a uniform, that ever lunges for the throat? What kind of dystopia have they replaced our boundless world with while we slept?

Marissa Alexander's sentence is overturned (Carmon, 2015) and Jordan Davis's murderer is convicted (Pantazi, 2014). We cannot be thankful. Months passed wherein a Black woman who fired a warning shot to deter the abuser who threatened her languished in a cell, after a conviction that took only twelve minutes of deliberation. Jordan's mother spent two years seeking justice for her son—a young man murdered for playing loud music in a car with his friends. Justice has shown us that it is a crime to defend our Black bodies, to be Black and a teenager—to be Black and unwilling to take up less space. Yes, community members reconstruct Michael's memorial each time it is destroyed (Wooten & David, 2015), and GoFundMe catches serious flack for having been a fundraising mechanism that paid his murderer (Zara, 2014), but just because the hands cleaning the wound are gentle doesn't make the loss of blood less fatal. I write a paper on the prevalence of food deserts in the modern amerikkkan city and encounter antiwelfare rhetoric that criminalizes the body that dares to be Black while poor. All the tenderness in the whole white world will not bring back the children they call "lost"—ignored even as their mothers rapped at the window for years at a time. BSU sets up a table at the club fair with a flag bearing the Black Power fist and we are gawked at like we have set fire to the redwhiteandblue. Red from the blood of the Black and Indigenous people that were enslaved, raped, objectified, and murdered. Blue for all the racist, sexist, homophobic, and ableist police. And white for the racist educators, politicians, and aristocrats; for the "not-racist" bystanders who stayed silent as we were ground to a pulp; for the moderates MLK warned us would be our biggest obstacle to justice. *Eric Garner couldn't breathe.*

I am writing this, this unapologetic, ugly, hate/love letter, to everybody with a body like mine. This is something only for us: the—unpretty, poor, Black, and perverse—unwanted yet eternally desired. I am putting the pen to paper because this was burned out of me and I would rather be wrung dry a thousand times than hear you wail again during a long, moonless night. This is because we hurt. Because they ask that we be joyful for the opportunity to be oppressed, repressed, and suppressed. Because we will finally learn to keep our minds, bodies, and souls in check—lovingly guided by the dry, white hand that could close the curtain on our so-called higher learning whenever it so chooses. *The higher the learning the more easily that hand can strangle.*

Academic repression, while a new term to some, is a lived truth for those who are oppressed and marginalized. Our parents and grandparents witnessed racially segregated education, mental hospitals, and a Child Protective Service protocol that was less about protecting and more about paranoia. They watched the classroom's composition changing, while the overseer-educator sent us home, suspended, and expelled us for having the same disobedient black bodies that were spat on in Little Rock. The people who taught us cursive taught us to curse ourselves and enjoy it. A different way to kill—boys in blue wield a nightstick, firearms, thick-soled shoes, but teachers humiliated us. Each time we were told to sit facing the corner we burned with rage, learning our "discipline" was for someone's entertainment. We hated our dark faces in yearbooks. We learned to cry while walking home from school. Malcolm X brilliantly stated "Only a fool would let his enemy teach his children." My story is a story that is common, standing at the crossroads of systems of oppression such as racism, sexism, ableism, homonormativity, and classism.

You know how it is: Occupying space as a poor, queer, Black, trans, femme, nonbinary person with severe mental illness is to occupy a liminal space. I am (and We are) able to relate to the *majority* in every sense of the word without receiving that same empathy, equipped with the tools necessary to respect the pain of others and given none of the systemic power to prevent the pain in the first place, perhaps innately able to conceptualize the Other's place in the divine, while pushed further and further from mainstream theology's godhead figures.

It is difficult and treacherous for us to continue carving out a space for ourselves in a world that would love more than anything to purge us from it. This lesson is stark for all Black students whose postsecondary academic careers begin at non-Black historical colleges/Primarily White Institutions (PWI), expected again to revere Dead white Men (DwM) who thought we were animals. The first three semesters I spent at my own illustrious PWI complete with picturesque scenery, natureloving community, and eerie similarity to the generic liberal arts school portrayed in *Dear White People* (Brown, et al., 2014) were no different. We are in tense times and the importance of community that reflects us (not just a distortion, or a clumsily empty frame) cannot be overemphasized. Neither can the resistance we face when we ask (politely at first, like Booker T. Washington would have wanted, and then unwavering like Marcus Garvey) to be heard.

BE THEY FRESHBREATHED OR FETID, OUR DREAMS WILL NOT EXPIRE

Behind the veil, last children of the seventh son, we are continually beckoned to release the cloth binding us to each other, and to the ancestors before, back and back into the red morning. They don't see that the fabric is sewn to us—one and the same with our flesh—even as we are a living holdfast between worlds, between wisdoms.

The lessons we learn aren't included on the syllabus; no one assigns reading on the white guilt tripping behind asking for Black forgiveness (Ericksen, 2015) or what to do when allies are patting themselves on the back for doing nothing (Mckenzie, 2015). The questions we constantly ponder aren't on study guides: How are we supposed to react when the people we trust are in positions purposely left bereft of power, or when those in power continuously silence and violate us while having the nerve to say they are hurt to know they don't have our trust? Career centers don't include weekend sessions on "how to respond to a tenured, beloved professor who calls you 'radical' and doesn't mean it as a compliment."

Mock interviews don't give us tips on what to say when our nationality is questioned because of the color of our skin. It is a passive violence masquerading at peacekeeping—to play host and offer a seat at the table *coincidentally* next to the guest with hands that strangle.

I am writing this, a truthtelling kind of letter, because without a record that exists outside of my own breathing this is a story that feels too unique, too foreign, too fantastic to be believed. I am writing this because (as well all know) it is none of those things.

FOR THE FAMILIES OF BROWN KIDS THINKING THEIR NOT QUITE GROWN CHILDREN ARE FINALLY HAPPY

It's not anxiety, the ten days leading up to class at a PWI for a Black body, and a queer one at that. It's dread. I spent the first year at my institution grappling with culture shock 200 miles north of my hometown, tucked between the prairie and the bluffs of Northern Iowa. I was unofficially designated the "weird, fat, Black kid" as if it was 2004 in Johnson County (Keene, Padilla, & Geronimus, 2010) and I was yet again assumed to be from the innercity, despite my decidedly unfashionable kicks and inability to navigate any and all buses. No one sat next to me in my classes. A girl wrote about "Negroes" in a paper I had to workshop in class and I was expected to hold my tongue because she'd "probably never interacted with Black people" at home. A taxi driver asked me my nationality and confessed he'd only inquired because of the color of my skin. He laughed. At no point was I encouraged to pose these same questions at my peers or my faculty. Responsibility to continue business as usual rested on my shoulders—not theirs.

Two days after Christmas in 2013 I shaved my head in my auntie's kitchen, pricking my fingers on my newly shorn curls. The day after Valentine's Day I found myself coerced into an inpatient psychiatric ward by a medical professional who didn't trust that the emergency plan my counselor and I had come up with (in case of my major recurrent depressive disorder and suicidal ideation coming to bear strange, desperate fruit) would work. I spent my spring semester feeling as raw and naked as I'd been in the showers there—faced with the same cold, disinterested eyes. I took a class about Black Women's history in the United States and left class to vomit after hearing about Fannie Lou Hamer's forced sterilization (Sebring, 2007) during a "routine" appendectomy. I was learning the validity of ancestral anxiety while my peers checked off all college requirements. I wrote about the course like one does with great literature—present tense, ever unfolding. The heavy-handed script had been revised, yes, but passed down for centuries—giving the Black body and the whiteness surrounding it roles that could not be reversed. Researching the gentrification of Jazz in the United States (Adelt, 2007) had me coming to the edge of (but not crossing into) naming the specter that lurked in the air—the same specter that had my peers sagging their pants and blasting Kendrick while never going further south in Chicago than downtown, never daring to sit next to anyone brown in class, especially if they weren't foreign born. I never told my family any of this—not until the year was almost over, and my body grew used to being a furled, purpleraw thing. When you are Black and trying to become the greater Blackness (injected with spheres of fire, marred by confounding, worldshredding emptiness) you are trying to find a home that doesn't always smell of scorched wood or saltwater. You are not ungrateful, just fresh to the cloying stillness of being hunted. The shame comes at realizing that you are hope turned rancid. The world was supposed to be better for you, they thought. That was the promise made in iron, red as Louisiana dirt. When someone who held you before you could speak cries at hearing how you tried to fling the sacred water of your shared blood over the packed earth, something in them splinters while another thing in you hardens forever. We are born into lying hands, lest we fall into the great Hurt of Truth.

FOR ASHYKNEED HELLIONS WITH SCRAPED PALMS AND SWOLLEN EYES

The end of July 2014 is a fuzzy, supersaturated, VHS tape. Resplendent in its bluegold light, we look grainy and vibrant—something we swapped for disturbing clarity in the new millennium. It's a summer that feels like it'll never end; we'll keep marveling at how bright it is all hours of the day, keep driving to the lake after work, keep freezing fruit in ice cubes for weekend sweet tea until the end of time. Everything smells like briquettes and bug spray. My skin is always hot to the touch: I am dark and getting darker.

On the ninth day of August, Lesley McSpadden's son is left in the street for hours (Bosman & Goldstein, 2014), and I am at work. The interviews taken by news crews wobble with heat, but the shadows don't falter at all. Multiple bathroom breaks leave raw indents of incisors in the meat of my palm. Links in news stories lead me to John Crawford III, guilty of carrying a lopsided smile, goes into Wal-Mart while talking on his cellphone and doesn't walk out (Izadi, 2014). *Michael Brown woke up this morning, but he won't tomorrow.*

People won't stop asking about cigarillos (King, 2014) and I heave into porcelain, trying fruitlessly to ease the sensation of frayed rope tickling the back of my throat. The sacred space of our bodies, our Blackness has never been more apparent. The tape steadies, only to sway again. While making signs to hold up as we march across the Pentacrest, old songs from my mom's days in praise band swell in my ears.

I scan textbooks for endless waves of white, middleclass college kids and only think of Michael; had he already done his backtoschool shopping on tax-free weekend? Did they have tax-free weekends in Ferguson? Canisters of tear gas launched at the longpalmed mourners of Ferguson turn into advancing tanks (Rankin, 2015) and they are already salting the field, not even waiting for the ashes to cool. After two weeks of conflicting stories and unarmed protests, after unsettling, strange absence of surprise when my aunties discuss what is bubbling in Missouri (and everywhere) something is released from its place in the beyond where it was held for me. For us. There is new tenderness, deeper rage, and the darkness of us is roiling. Despite never having been to the mountains, I can tell the air is getting thin.

I revisit texts from my last semester and consult the thinkers I never thought I'd relate to: Kwame Turé, W.E.B. DuBois, James Cone. Prose fills the small legal pad I keep in my backpack, interspersed with freewrites that circle back to anxiety about returning to school, my desperation to be understood, my ongoing flirtation with genetic destiny. Convocation is in three days and maybe five people from my PWI have posted about *anything* related to racial profiling or police brutality. I tell myself I am being melodramatic, and remind myself to buy coconut oil before I leave town.

The last days before I pack the car and drive north for classes, I learn my first chants outside of the Center for Worker Justice of Eastern Iowa. My mother's pastor drives past us and I can tell she is praying for our divisive, rebellious spirits. I decide, chanting on a corner in downtown Iowa City with an old friend, that if God doesn't want me to be angry, then God must not want me to feel anything at all. I decide God can kiss my ass. We hit refresh on our Tumblr dashboards and find new martyrs. We know something holy has left us, but if we kneel we will lose ground. "Start wearing only boots," we murmur to each other. "They keep your ankles strong. Never know when you'll need to crush the adder underfoot." Our hands are always shaking. They are praying.

FOR STUDENTS WHO FOUND FALL SEMESTER 2014 TO BE A LONG HELL, AND EVERY DRIVE HOME TO BE A PILGRIMAGE

Hours after moving into the house where I'll spend my sophomore year, I wake and wring a cold washcloth out in the sink. With coolness on my forehead that recedes in my sleep, I fantasize that the past two months have been a fever dream. The body I live in has begun to keep secrets from me. Maybe compartmentalizing my distress at having found a campus whose professors and administration refuse to acknowledge that anything has boiled over, despite the activism of a select few who leave for Ferguson, it has ceased maintaining anything resembling a regular sleep schedule. Unfortunately, I have no one to talk to about these proceedings, as school policy was already stretched thin at having let me maintain appointments with the same counselor for an entire academic year. I try a new therapist, but quit after she asks me to define *bisexuality* for her. Four hours a night isn't bad until it turns into two—but the extra hours give me time to assemble a new, unshattered face to plaster on at dawn.

I try out for a play and land the role of a Black wet nurse whose rage at sustaining the life of a middleclass white couple's infant comes only after she loses Henry, her youngest son, to fever. When I read Elizabeth's monologue, that old collective Wound opens and smallwristed ghosts with big eyes (playing in the church basement, shooting hoops before school, sitting between the knees of mamas with brushes and hair oil) crowd close. In that moment, I begin to understand the violence of a Black parent's love. Milk-sweet breath and shallow heartbeats are fragile enough without the weight of hue adding to a new life's tenuous hold to this world. This is my Black history. This, without the ruse of goatskin or the offering of spicy stew, was my birthright.

We watch the interviews and surreptitious recordings until the videos feel voyeuristic, until we read about Tamir Rice and his sister and the minutes that a little boy spent bleeding and alone (Shaffer, 2014). Powerful positions in every office are silent and we vibrate with tension. We buck against the label of "paranoid" as a squadron of *maybe* thirty Black-amerikkkan bodies on a campus that boasts us as its brightest blights. Not all of us are willing to stand in the corner of the room together, acting like the glares we get are provoked for our own amusement instead of garnered by our boisterous existence. We laugh louder, until the tears in our eyes make it impossible to see anything but each other: BSU is teaching us how to save each other's lives because it gets old, knowing that because the bruises take longer to bloom, we are tended to last, if at all.

November 4, 2014 limited me—I'd finished watching *Snowpiercer* during the first serious snowfall of winter when the world learned that Michael's killer would never be faced with charges (Bennett & Berman, 2014). Some folks I knew spiraled into depressive states; some reassembled their shards of hope; some turned completely to stone, refusing to react altogether. For me, it was the first night I felt murderous rage—my first time comprehending that to walk around in this skin is to be made deserving of violence done to it and to be expected to apologize for fighting back. The news broke the day before Thanksgenocide break.

A family friend brought her new baby, Amir, to our family dinner. We gathered around him (his tiny fingernails, his cheeks, his belly) and sent our own private wishes to whatever powers there were at our disposal: *may we never have to chant his name/may every person on his path know his toes were once pearls/may he*

never be likened to something conjured/may the only secret name for him be Sweet Love.
He murmurs something—contemplating this new way of being—and we exhale,
shuddering. We are in love again.

FOR THAT UNEASY THING KEEPING YOU FROM SINGING AND THE UNLEARNABLE, DIVINE MOURNING

December sees Claudia Lacey's son lynched (Blackwell, 2014), Antonio Martin
murdered (Smith & Davey, 2014), and Leelah's parents unable to mourn
their daughter properly (Fantz, 2015). In North Carolina, a family wonders if
seventeen-year-old Lennon was hung from a swing set because he was dating
an older white woman. Two days before Christmas, Antonio is shot outside of a
gas station, and five days later a trans girl takes her life after her parents' Penta-
costal beliefs allows them to justify depriving their daughter of social interaction.
They intentionally misgender her during every interview. They regret nothing. My
stomach has taken to heaving its contents multiple times a day without my permission—like the body that purges me from it, though I call it home. My eyes hurt.
Danez Smith delivers his notelegy (Button Poetry, 2014) and my aunties reminisce
about their childhood, about Christmases past, about narrow hands. This is the
world once removed: wrapping paper on the doors, hot chocolate on the stove. If
I ever fall asleep, I will wake with a mouth full of battery acid. Remember how
I used to ask Santa for blue eyes? I am learning how it feels to be a problem, WEB,
and it burns.

FOR THE OTHER SIDE OF THE COIN AND THE BLACK KIDS WHOSE GRANDPARENTS WERE STRUGGLED INTO BEING DURING TUMULTUOUS RECONSTRUCTION DAYS

Social cataracts, like the ones that make your favorite uncle unable to drive, are
easy to deny until they aren't. Eventually, the tires thudthudthudding against the
shoulder wake up everyone in the backseat. That thudthudthud was my amerikkkan Political Thought class, and I was carsick. This wouldn't have been an issue
had I not been raised to perform my own particular brand of assholery—clever,
never disrespectful, coded with academic frippery—but it was; I had been. A
word to those with similarly poor self-preservation instincts: save moral analysis
of amerikkka's secular religion until after the Federalist papers have been beaten
to death. Again. If you don't, you run the risk of being called a radical in class,
and again during office hours. The thing about performing the narrative is that

the stage directions are never said aloud; they just scroll along the bottom of the frame:

AGING WHITE PATRIARCH turns to BLACK ZEALOT, stands like a military man at ease. PATRIARCH is tall and broad, backlit by white morning light. ZEALOT is charmless, foul-faced. Shadow of PATRIARCH's shoulder cuts across that pointed chin.

"Read ahead if you want," the spectre in my dreams murmurs incessantly. "It won't change a thing. They'll throw you on top of the kindling at the end of the scene whether you expect it or not."

FOR RELUCTANT NONBELIEVERS WHOSE FAITH HAS BECOME SYNONYMOUS WITH SHAME WHO CAN'T MANAGE TO SHAKE ITS DUST FROM THEIR SOULS

I grew up in a church that asked me to abandon my body (marred/black/limp-wristed) for a better one: whole, male, violently heterosexual. A splinter of this notquiteme still writhes with want at the feet of a white Christ. This prostrate thing is what recoils at meeting Dr. Jacob, the Bible 101 instructor. The first time I saw her was a month after leaving Mason City's psychiatric ward, serving as a panelist during campus conversation about immigration policy. Two days into Bible 101, she asks us to consider if Abraham's great sin (the reason YHWH never speaks directly to him again after Isaac is bound on Mount Moriah) is that he never gave voice to his doubt, never dared to disobey. Couldn't it be possible, she posits, that spineless obedience is reviled by the divine? Couldn't it be possible that the most grave sin is *not* talking back?

The image won't leave me alone: Abraham has liver spots but is still a strong man, strong enough to wrestle Isaac (of the patchy beard, of the girlthin hips) to the altar. Why is holiness so often hogtied by hands that once cradled it? Yes, the ram is caught in the thicket before the end, but they will both have bruises before the moon sets. Maybe some bruises are a father's knee on the chest of his son. Maybe Isaac's shoulder never set correctly and pained him in a strong wind. Maybe he never spoke to his father after that.

Dr. Jacob teaches me to reclaim my allegedly errant body, the first trench surrendered to an ambivalent Overseer. She opens a door into the cellar of the thing, where the purpleraw pit continues to shudder. Feels like the two days before my menses—tender and strong in its aching. There is a fresh wind in the house. Does it count as a Messianic Complex to find the ties between Yeshua's body and mine? I stop caring about blasphemy and find the thread that can't be cut. Performing his mother's tradition with active conviction, a Brown boy wants to know who he'd be without occupying forces looming at the edges. He's not that charismatic. He's sullen, cryptic, paranoid. Maybe he has a stutter, writes melodramatic prose about figs and boys and the Galilee tasting different after falling in love. Burying his cousin flips a switch and he is so *human*, this Yeshua. Occupied Palestine births a revolutionary whose entourage draws blood when militarized police come to lay claim to his body, and Empire still manages to make him a poster boy for forced assimilation. Super Divine Magic Jesus is white and athletic—not a "barbarian" anymore. Not real, either.

Because we are in the wrong bodies, Dr. Jacob and I, we must be careful. Illustrated as either the whore or the genderless martyr, we are to open our legs or our palms—never our mouths. Do you know how to confuse the establishment and ignite the lust of its peons? Take joy in all three. The silences written around bodies like ours speak that most ancient tongue: dissidence. We are dark skinned *and* holy, background characters for no one. She will not hear excuses because she knows that when flame licks at our soles we only have so much callous to burn through. She teaches me that bravery is when actual movement becomes more important than possible loneliness. She teaches me to stop fearing flight.

FOR THOSE WHOSE PAIN IS TURNED INTO A COLD AND STERILE CLASSROOM DISCUSSION WHILE THEY ARE EXPECTED TO BE GRATEFUL FOR THE OPPORTUNITY TO CRY HUMILIATED, TERRIFIED TEARS

The last month of my sophomore year falls apart spectacularly. Two weeks after the #BlackSpringtime love letter is published (Moore & Green, 2015), my institution protects a student who used blackface in his senior project from critique. His triptych asked for a lighteyed white woman to be handpainted the color of dirt, and for her face to be looking at the viewer from that same earth—like a cadaver, like we are robbing another black grave.

It is an old kind of terror to see it: there is an active KKK chapter within thirty miles of campus and one of my close friends is followed by blue and red lights as he walks on foot. Will whiteness break our noses off again, before it is over? April saw a coalition of students, professors, and clergy keeping vigil for victims of police violence, but this image has us keeping watch for another kind of passage. Like a surefooted man with a quick blade, it comes.

I try my hand at diplomacy and find myself the target of many barbs, none that rattle me as much as the way my hackles raise when I walk alone on campus at night. People I thought were my friends point fingers and call me "race-baiting" while a 400 year-old specter stares silently. My mettle is not shaken until my friends and I are followed by flashlightwielding shadows. We cover half a mile of cutback prairie and cut across into a parking lot where we make dry jokes about *Cold Case*, the police melodrama series on CBS. Somehow the laughter doesn't reach our eyes. From where we sit on the curb, we can see the flashlights across the soccer field.

What do you do when eggs are thrown at you from a slowmoving red pickup the night before you are to attend a glorified mediation? What do you when your feet slap against stillhot asphalt just to read that a classmate of yours—an anonymous moderator of a vitriolic "confessions" page you were banned from months ago for calling out a sorority's Dreamcatcherthemed party equates attempts to stand up for yourself to hate speech? What do you do when the administrator whose office you sob in confirms that yes, the school has been tipped off about this student before? What do you do when they then ask you to email Facebook if the comments are really getting to you, if they don't want to hear about the eroding of your esophagus lining even as you sprint from the office to spasm bile out of your throat?

My aunties call to ask me not to be involved with protests, lest an unnamed bullet finds its way to me. They are comforted to know there's nothing of that nature going on at my school—no rallying forth in Norwegian-amerikkkan farm country—so I don't spoil their peace with the tang of my fear. I held a megaphone to speak about Darrien Hunt and three weeks later realized Decorah could turn into Saratoga Springs (Swaine, 2014) in a heartbeat. The oozing pus of white supremacy spills over the long, swaying grasses, floods even the rolling prairie. I don't go back to class until it's time for finals.

FOR THE SAKE OF SAYING IT

The heart is a disobedient, courageous thing. Even when all signs point to complete desolation, it can coax a bud to bloom in utter darkness. And no, Kendrick, I wouldn't trust it (Duckworth, et al., 2013). Poetic justice has no place in the rationale of a heartsick black not-boy I occasionally call *me*, especially when the only irony is that the vase her hands made still hold the best orchid of an admittedly mediocre collection.

Maybe Judas dreamed about kissing a honeyeyed man's cheek too, tortured himself imagining the sharp taste of his neck. Maybe he tried to pursue a shepherdess, or a fruit vendor: someone with a sweet face and hands that didn't look like *those* hands. Maybe this went on for nine months. Maybe he spent nights on the stoop burning clove cigarettes, hearing Yeshua cry about his sometimes lover. Maybe he wrote bad poetry and let the orchid die before summer's end.

My story is intense and visceral, as I stated, but my story—while it (and others like it) needs to be heard—must end; therefore, we must act up. Without disrupting the *status quo*, these accounts of marginalization will grow in volume until they swallow us whole. So we must not give up, give in, or give way to systems of oppression, but must begin to organize through student clubs, such as BSU. We must support BSUs and press our administrators to foster positive environments in the following ways:

1. *Share knowledge of Black culture.*
   Attending a PWI is not an excuse to extend the shelf life of compliant oppression. When we are not actively celebrating each other, we are tearing each other down. Expect growth outside of the classroom, and not at the expense of Black students.

2. *Share practices of Black culture.*
   The diasporic Black experience is not homogenous—we can never dictate to our peers that their experiences are false simply because they do not match up with our assumption. Encourage students to live authentically and be thankful for their presence.

3. *Share history of Black culture.*
   This shouldn't be confined to an all-college requirement that could equally be fulfilled by Beginner's Calligraphy. To receive an education in amerikkka that doesn't explore the nuances of Blackness is to receive an education in a white vacuum. Blackness stars and supports its own multiple roles in amerikkkan society and deserves to be recognized for its own merits.

4. *Organize against white supremacy and other systems of oppression.*
   All members of an educational institution should be made aware of the space they occupy—whether or not it is intentional. If students that are traditionally ignored (after having been almost obsessively recruited) ask for spaces that lessen their isolation, we should ask ourselves how we can establish those spaces. Not how we can appease them only to move on.

5. *Organize for alternative nonoppressive educational practices, pedagogies, and procedures.*
   Again, the safety and dignity of Black students should never come at their expense. The same can be said for all students negatively affected by institutionalized violence. It is irresponsible and negligent to place the burden of revision on students when they pay their dues in expectation of a welcoming, affirming environment. No student should fight to be seen as legitimate.

6. *Organize for Black staff, faculty, students, programs, and departments.*
As stated earlier, if we are not actively celebrating each other, we are passively permitting our hypervisible community members to be singled out. When we form a united front and dedicate ourselves to pushing our own limits and understanding while dismantling rhetoric we have perpetuated unthinkingly, we can only grow stronger. We must ask each other to talk back (and protect each other in the aftermath), or accept stagnation. We must bring Blackness from the corners of the room to center stage. We must honor each other.

The burden is not solely on us, however. Administrators must also recognize the role they play as climate controllers; they need to create comfortable conditions where students and faculty do not feel repressed and do not have to constantly struggle for their freedoms. It cannot continue to be accepted that we ask marginalized people to share their lives with us at our institutions and then demand that they fight every second to prove they deserve to remain in them. Every student should be able to trust that the first pit stop in their self-made education will feel like home.

LONG LIVE Malcolm X, Fred Hampton, Eric Garner, Mike Brown, Oscar Grant, Freddie Gray, Tamir Rice, Emmett Till, Sandra Bland, Trayvon Martin, Ezell Ford, Renisha McBride, Kimani Gray, Sheron Jackson, Angelo Clark, Rekia Boyd, Ousmane Zongo, Aiyana Stanley-Jones, Sean Bell, and the millions of others who have lost their lives to white supremacy.

"It is our duty to fight for our freedom. It is our duty to win. We must love each other and support each other. We have nothing to lose but our chains." – Assata Shakur

"We must be very strong and love each other to go on living." – Audre Lorde (from *Equinox)*

REFERENCES

Adelt, U. (2007). Black, white and blue: Racial politics of blues music in the 1960s (Doctoral Dissertation). Retrieved from http://ir.uiowa.edu/etd/128

Bennett, D., & Berman, R. (2014, November 25). No indictment. *The Atlantic.* Retrieved from http://www.theatlantic.com/national/archive/2014/11/ferguson-verdict-grand-jury/383130/

Blackwell, V. (2014, December 15). N.C. teen's hanging death ruled a suicide; mother says it was a lynching. *CNN.* Retrieved from http://edition.cnn.com/2014/12/15/justice/north-carolina-lennon-lacy/

Bosman, J., & Goldstein, J. (2014, August 23). Timeline for a body: 4 hours in the middle of a Ferguson street. *The New York Times.* Retrieved from http://www.nytimes.com/2014/08/24/us/michael-brown-a-bodys-timeline-4-hours-on-a-ferguson-street.html?_r=0

Brown, E., Le, A., Lebedev, J., Lopez, A., Simien, J., Waithe, L. (Producers), & Simien, J. (Director). (2014). *Dear White People* (Motion picture). United States of America: Lionsgate, Roadside Attractions.

Button Poetry. (2014, November 17). *Danez Smith—"Not an Elegy for Mike Brown"* [Video file]. Retrieved from https://www.youtube.com/watch?v=ujxShArG7Ks

Byers, C. (2015, May 18). No charges against St. Louis officer who killed VonDerrit Myers. *St. Louis Post-Dispatch*. Retrieved from http://www.stltoday.com/news/local/crime-and-courts/no-charges-against-st-louis-officer-who-killed-vonderrit-myers/article_5641ecfd-4b37-54c1-b717-1a7d84500892.html

Carmon, I. (2015, January 27). Marissa Alexander released from jail. *MSNBC*. Retrieved from http://www.msnbc.com/msnbc/marissa-alexander-may-be-released

Duckworth, K., Graham, A., Molina, E., Harris, J., Jackson, J., & Lewis, T. (2013). Poetic Justice. On *Good Kid m.A.A.d City* [CD]. Santa Monica, CA: Aftermath/Interscope Records.

Ericksen, A. (2015, July 9). Black forgiveness, the hypocrisy of white America, and atonement. *Patheos*. Retrieved from http://www.patheos.com/blogs/teachingnonviolentatonement/2015/07/black-forgiveness-the-hypocrisy-of-white-america-and-atonement/

Fantz, A. (2015, January 4). An Ohio transgender teen's suicide, a mother's anguish. *CNN*. Retrieved from http://edition.cnn.com/2014/12/31/us/ohio-transgender-teen-suicide/

Izadi, E. (2014, September 25). Ohio Wal-Mart surveillance video shows police shooting and killing John Crawford III. *The Washington Post*. Retrieved from https://www.washingtonpost.com/news/post-nation/wp/2014/09/25/ohio-wal-mart-surveillance-video-shows-police-shooting-and-killing-john-crawford-iii/

Keene, D. E., Padilla, M. B., & Geronimus, A. T. (2010). Leaving Chicago for Iowa's "fields of opportunity": Community dispossession, rootlessness, and the quest for somewhere to "be OK." *Human Organization, 69*(3), 275–284.

King, S. (2014, October 28). What Mike Brown did and did not do inside of the Ferguson convenience store. Retrieved from http://www.dailykos.com/story/2014/10/28/1339820/-What-Mike-Brown-did-and-did-not-do-inside-of-the-Ferguson-convenience-store

Mckenzie, M. (2015, November 4). How to tell the difference between real solidarity and 'ally theater'. *Black Girl Dangerous*. Retrieved from http://www.blackgirldangerous.org/2015/11/the-difference-between-real-solidarity-and-ally-theatre/

Moore, D. L., & Green, K. M. (2015, May 2). A love letter to our people in #BlackSpringtime. *The Feminist Wire*. Retrieved from http://www.thefeministwire.com/2015/05/a-love-letter-to-our-people-in-blackspring-time/

Pantazi, A. (2014, October 17). Michael Dunn gets life, plus 90 years for Jordan Davis killing. *The Florida Times-Union*. Retrieved from http://jacksonville.com/news/crime/2014-10-17/story/michael-dunn-gets-life-plus-90-years-jordan-davis-killing

Rankin, K. (2015, July 1). Report: From tear gas to snipers, dogs to tanks, Ferguson police violated Mike Brown Protestors. *Colorlines*. Retrieved from http://www.colorlines.com/articles/report-tear-gas-snipers-dogs-tanks-ferguson-police-violated-mike-brown-protestors

Sebring, S. (2007, December 6). *Fannie Lou Hamer*. Retrieved from https://mississippiappendectomy.wordpress.com/2007/12/06/fannie-lou-hamer/

Shaffer, C. (2014, December 12). Tamir Rice autopsy shows he was shot once, suffered hemorrhaging before death. *Cleveland.com*. Retrieved from http://www.cleveland.com/metro/index.ssf/2014/12/tamir_rice_autopsy_shows_he_wa.html

Smith, M., & Davey, M. (2014, December 24). Cautions against Ferguson comparisons after officer kills black teenager. *The New York Times*. Retrieved from http://www.nytimes.com/2014/12/25/us/berkeley-missouri-police-shooting.html

Swaine, J. (2014, September 16). Utah authorities alter account of Darrien Hunt shooting by police. *The Guardian*. Retrieved from http://www.theguardian.com/world/2014/sep/16/darrien-hunt-shot-in-the-back-by-utah-police-says-family-attorney

Wooten, S., & David, M. (2015, April 23). Police brutality supporters destroy Mike Brown 'memorial tree' just a day after it was planted. *Counter Current News*. Retrieved from http://countercurrentnews.com/2015/04/mike-brown-memorial-tree/

Zara, C. (2014, September 2). Officer Darren Wilson GoFundMe donations halted as organizers sort out legal questions. *International Business Times*. Retrieved from http://www.ibtimes.com/officer-darren-wilson-gofundme-donations-halted-organizers-sort-out-legal-questions-1676430

Afterword

Southwest Colorado Sociology Collective[1]

THE IMPORTANCE OF *FIGHTING ACADEMIC REPRESSION*

Fighting Academic Repression is a much needed praxis handbook to complement the current theoretical literature documenting the ideological assault on public higher education by the neoliberal academic industrial complex and its concomitant followers. We are surprised that there is not more outrage and resistance from the masses of students, staffs, and faculties in the United States whose work experience and dignity have been severely compromised by the actions of the neoliberal academic industrial complex. Other countries have shown much more outrage and resistance at the neoliberal assaults on students, staffs, and faculties with much less repression. This book separates itself from the existing literature on academic repression by serving as a practical manual for resistance to academic repression and the neoliberal academic industrial complex. From the manuscript's Introduction to the Afterword, it offers a foundation from which to resist repression, fight tyranny, and create change.

What makes this book unique is its handbook style for responding to various manifestations of academic repression. This book is replete with cases studies, specific situations, and events in which agitated students, staffs, and faculties resisted administrative overreach and repression. As demonstrated throughout this book, there are a diversity of voices which capture student, staff, and faculty struggles as well as specific struggles linked to People of Color, women, and international students and faculty. Especially notable is the last section of the book focusing on why Black Lives Matter in education, an inquiry sorely lacking in academic circles. When it comes to specifically addressing strategies for resistance in the iron cage of the industrial academic complex, no other book in the current literature on neoliberalism in higher education is organized this way. The subject matter, the content, and the well-organized structure of this book make it an invaluable contribution.

What follows in this Afterword, are some pragmatic strategies for addressing how to maintain an academic department which resists both the ideology and machinations of the neoliberal academic industrial complex. How does a small academic department such as the Department of Sociology at Fort Lewis College (FLC), a public liberal arts school in Durango, Colorado maintain the values of honesty, loyalty, trust, interdependency, community, and friendship in a toxic environment of corporate-styled, bureaucracy? How can an academic department prevent the submission of human beings and their knowledge into roles of service to power and wealth? Here are some suggestions for resisting this type of structural tyranny in the pursuit of maintaining dignity, integrity, and community.

RESISTING COLONIZED SCHOOLING: THE INSIDIOUS REPRESSION OF NATIVE AMERICAN LIVES

Fort Lewis College, with a little less than four thousand students, started as an Indian boarding school. The U.S. abducted Navajo, Pueblo, Ute, and Apache students by military force for the purpose of assimilation, a crusade-derived notion of conversion. The State of Colorado, coveting the lands upon which the boarding school sat, negotiated to acquire the lands and took over the school planning to make a college. A significant tuition waiver for Natives was part of the deal. Now, FLC is operating as a twenty-first century boarding school where the force used to get Indians here is dire poverty and disempowerment, and the curriculum is still assimilation, perniciously disguised as a college degree.

To further manifest the assimilation, the FLC administration is currently seeking federal legislation to reimburse the State for its charitable troubles. There are over seven hundred Native students here, yet without those students the College would likely financially fail. Each department of the college, if it succeeds at all, does so with help from the funds that Native students bring to their departments. It seems the college owes a moral debt for this ineluctable truth. Indeed, the United States has made a mess of the "Trust' concept, allowing condescension, neglect, and abuse to be tolerated within its Supreme Court interpretations; however, this College owes a duty of trust to its Native students. How it defines that trust, it can take lessons from those who have tried and failed.

Mohandas Gandhi once implored a confessed Hindu murderer, in penance, to raise a Muslim child as a Muslim. The recently adopted *Declaration on the Rights of Indigenous Peoples* sets the preservation of Native cultures as a primary global objective. The moral contours of an American education for Indians ought to educate Indians as "Indians."

George Orwell in *1984* warned against the burning of books, but Aldous Huxley, in *Brave New World* foresaw that people would ignore books altogether. This college gets away with its insidious repression of Native lives because it can ignore them—those powerless, voiceless, Native seekers of knowledge. It offers a technocratic education to Natives, certain in its narrow bureaucratic calculations that it is doing them a great favor. Pope Francis, in his encyclical, *Laudato Si'*, warns of the globalization of the technocratic paradigm. Indigenous people make up over seven hundred million of the world's populations and they are not necessarily upon a trajectory to be absorbed into the expansive capitalist, popular cultural regime of globalization. Native students deserve to be raised as the Natives they can become as part of the cultures into which they were born.

As a human being entitled to basic human rights and freedoms, a Native person has a right to know how his or her people have become dispossessed by the colonial machine. Each has a right to know that the nation state within which he/she resides ought to serve in a remedial role to that dispossession and prominently so through its educational structure. There are issues in academia regarding the consultation required with these dispossessed peoples, questions about the dimensions of scholarship, the necessity of a comprehensive program of acquisitions of scholarly materials on Native peoples, questions about the permissible contours of research on Native concerns.

But even if academic institutions see the wisdom of such changes, they must recognize that these goals can only be accomplished with real money. Native students need support beyond tuition: they need to cover student fees, books, lab fees, room, and board (and, in some cases, child care). Institutions must be proactive in hiring Native faculty and employees, even if legislation is needed to do so. Native studies programs must have prioritized funding so as to achieve a diverse staffing—this incipient field is best benefited by a constellation of vantage points. Yet, nothing can be accomplished without the delicate and rare quantum of political will to do what is right. Such "will" requires an American conscience.

RESISTING THE MONOPOLIZING PEDAGOGY

With the neoliberal turn in higher education, faculty are increasingly tasked "assignments" from administrators. Many of these tasks often creep into greater administrative control of curriculum. Becky (Rebecca Clausen) became Chair of our department just as a new collective of high-level administrators were recrafting our college. Everything was changing, especially shared governance and faculty control over the curriculum. Under this new regime, departments were regularly tasked with a variety of curricular assignments regarding things like assessment, alignment with state mandates, credit hours, and standardization policies. The assignments came in a flurry, one on top of the other, most often with rushed deadlines.

For the Department of Sociology, our resistance to this assault on our curriculum comes through reflexivity and strategy. At times we push back outright, and sometimes we are successful in our aims, but more often we need to complete assigned tasks for the various offices of the administration. As a collective we pause despite hurried deadlines and ask, how can we continue to teach and be involved with our students in a way that authentically reflects our values? Though this may sound intuitive, it requires an inversion of priorities set out by the administration. Neoliberal thinking assumes that the authority and the values of "the office" come first. Thus designing curriculum and teaching become more about the needs of the office, which consist of forms, policies, procedures, proposals, and assessment, with little discussion about the actual education of our students.

In the neoliberal academic industrial complex, it is easy to fall prey to this Weberian obsession with the means while giving little attention to the ends. We are continually reflexive about who we are as a department and who our students are to resist the monopolizing forces of bureaucratic exercises and policies. Reflexivity allows us to develop a strategy about how to navigate new curricular policies and procedures without compromising our pedagogical values. As an example, departments were told to rewrite their learning outcomes (based on "new" standards) guided by a newly created "office of learning and assessment." With this came the requirement to attend multiple workshops where there was a strong push to have the "Bloom's Taxonomy," a continuum of learning with the assumption that learning is linear from the simple to the complex, by a guiding force in how we craft our learning outcomes and thus our curriculum. These workshops created a climate of fear and anxiety among faculty who were now under the surveillance of so-called learning and assessment experts. Because of the intense pressure related to assessment, it was easy to let the goals of "the office" be the driver of our learning outcomes. Reflection and strategy enabled us hold tight to our pedagogical beliefs, resist principles of standardized learning, and craft "new" learning outcomes that authentically reflected our long-held values.

In the Department of Sociology, talking formally and informally about pedagogy is a constant. We ask what kinds of learning are valuable, how do students learn best, how can we offer a diversity of teaching styles and contexts, and what do they need to know to face an ever-changing world? Equally important we ask, who are our students and what do these specific students need to be compassionate, engaged, whole citizens of their communities. Who we are, who our students are, and what we value is always our starting point. This indeed is resistance to the top-down pressures to control and standardize curriculum.

DEFENDING RADICAL PEDAGOGY AND TEACHING

The Department of Sociology's radical social justice inclusive pedagogy is unique and rare in higher education because it seeks to prioritize the experiences of students in conjunction with a scholarly disciplinary content. We focus on the experiences of those students who have been taught how to be illiterate and disengaged by K-12 education because of their race, class, gender orientation, or different physical or mental abilities. Giving voice to experience empowers all students, even those who have benefitted from a mainstream pedagogy. Education is seen as a tool to empower rather than to bully. We embrace education to disrupt the bell-shaped curve that benefits the proverbial one percent. Students, who have not been bullied by the K-12 tracking system, also find new and surprising levels of authenticity and integrity in their work.

Using Brazilian educator Paulo Freire's idea of *generative themes*, we work to facilitate an interface between field experience, student biography, and disciplinary content as the basis of our pedagogy. As we bring the experiences of *students* to the center, we work to turn notions of assessment, evaluation, accountability, and bell-shaped curves that are traditionally used to divide and conquer to promote more important pedagogical purposes: reflection, such as building honest and genuine friendships with one another and with students; understanding, such as defending one another against repressed or oppressed no matter what; and empowerment, such as organizing vigils, protests, and poetry open mics with students and the community.

This work goes beyond standard education to engage the student as a whole person. Most students come to college with deep traumas and insecurities from historical, educational, and structural inequities. It is the role of the professors (who must also wrestle with their own insecurities and egos) to validate and empower students. Fundamental to this notion is to reject as much as possible the demands of the disciplinary cannon and the bureaucracy. Instead, we are focused on *praxis*—a word that is overused and yet still essential—to explore the dialectical relationship between lived experience and theory. Students tend to prioritize the experiential portion of praxis over book learning. However, if book learning is introduced as fundamental to understanding their life experiences, their outlook changes.

Everything about the standardization of the academy makes this kind of education more difficult and therefore more critical. Higher education seeks to deal with backlash against obscene tuition costs by pushing students to finish in four years or standardizing class periods. This process neither reduces tuition costs nor improves education. Higher education also continues to engage in costly mechanisms that include hiring more administrators, maintaining offensive salaries for administrators and coaches, developing expensive tools for evaluation and assessment, and promoting technologies that further alienate students from each other and their professors.

Meanwhile students live in a world of stress, shame, and guilt as they juggle loans, expectations of parents, weak job markets, and political, economic, and environmental problems. It is imperative that we fight to maintain space for deep thinking, critical analysis, and social/self-reflection in order to better ourselves, our society, and our world.

BUILDING A COMMUNITY, NOT A DEPARTMENT

Fighting academic repression requires external resistance as well as internal solidarity. The internal solidarity can occur among faculty if we strive to cultivate community rather than competition within our departments. When we treat our colleagues with distrust and disrespect, we invite administrators to do the same. This competitive behavior among faculty furthers the repression from above, as it lends itself to divide and conquer strategies. Creating community can not only be a defense to academic repression, but also a source of renewed inspiration to hold to what we value and put into practice the potential for liberatory education.

Most faculty can relate to the personal and emotional toll of a highly competitive academic culture. The shaming and exclusionary behaviors of graduate school are fresh in our minds as we enter a new department, expecting the same climate of competition. The first step of a department is to recognize the "grad school hangover" that any new colleague will bring with them, stemming from the experiences of anxiety and constant scrutiny through a hierarchical system of rank. The department can create a compassionate stance toward new faculty, expecting that they will have a lingering sense of constant self-evaluation, questioning "am I good enough?" A group of faculty within a department can encourage new faculty to shed this individualist mentality by modeling basic tenets of community building rather than community-breaking behaviors. We now offer six strategies to create a community based on honest and genuine friendships rather than simply reinforce a bureaucratic department:

1. Build trust: Trust within an academic community means adopting a position of assumed competence of our colleagues, rather than constant surveillance. We may not immediately understand a colleague's position or pedagogy, but we begin by assuming they are competent and worthy, rather than in need

of immediate correction and/or redirection. This is especially important to hold on to in the current climate of hyperassessment and evaluation.

2. Build respect: This does not mean respect as a scholar alone, but rather respect of a department member as a whole person. Build a community by marking life events, celebrating maternity/paternity leaves, asking for and accepting help when difficult life situations arise.

3. Build honesty: Creating an academic community through honesty comes at moments of difficult decisions, particularly when new hires are being made. Being able to speak your truth, hearing the truth of others, and prioritizing the collective good of the whole are key elements in building honest and authentic relationships.

4. Build interdependency: The interdependency of a department can be structured by flattening out a hierarchical model of rank. Our department has done this by (1) adopting a rotating Chair model, rather than one chosen by seniority, prestige, or vote (2) prioritizing collective achievements of the group rather than individual achievements, (3) talk through decisions through a consensus model rather than majority vote, (4) seek out collaborative research projects wherever possible, and (5) call and talk to one another about personal needs and ask for help and advice from one another on personal-life issues.

5. Build communication: Faculty meetings, Roberts Rules, and set agendas have their place for reasons of efficiency, but they can also break down the capacity for authentic communication. Our department has found that conversations in small groups over time, preferably while walking around campus, going to one another's home, eating together at a café or restaurant, organizing pot lucks, and hanging out socially create places for real communication to take place.

6. Build friendship: Becky's "new faculty orientation" into the Department of Sociology at FLC consisted of the current Chair inviting her to work in her garden with her once a week over the summer. Through this experience, they built the foundations of a friendship that could weather any storm of corporatization, standardization, neoliberalization, and academic repression.

These examples show how a department can move in the direction of community building rather than community breaking. As demonstrated in this book, it is the strength of community that provides the best defense against the current trends of academic repression that attempt to demoralize and narrow the work that we do.

This book is not supposed to examine academic repression—that was the purpose of *Academic Repression: Reflections from the Academic Industrial Complex* (Nocella, Best, & Mclaren, 2010)—its goal is to provide readers tactics and strategies to fight back against academic repression by challenging and dismantling the academic industrial complex. This book seeks to further develop a growing community of concerned students, staffs, and faculties who are currently fighting academic repression for the sake of what they believe in most—that education matters more than wealth and that the time for change is now. We are not in a state of academic freedom but a state of differing levels of academic repression. We need to fight academic repression and dismantle the current school system as we know it, because it is grounded on Christian, ableist, heterosexual, white, patriarchal, elitist ideals, and supremacy. We are simply educating and being taught in a twenty-first century boarding school.

Now that you have read this book, we encourage you to talk to others, organize groups, build strategies, and take our schools, colleges, and universities back from the hands of corporations and administrative bureaucrats. There is no time to waste, act up and act now!

NOTE

1. The Southwest Colorado Sociology Collective are the professors of the Department of Sociology at FLC, which include Keri Brandt, Becky Clausen, Janine Fitzgerald, Mark Seis, and Carey Vicenti (minus Anthony J. Nocella II who did not participate in writing in this chapter). Writing in academia has become a highly competitive act, where people are measured on who the first author is, where the publication was published, the topic of the publication, and if the publication was single-authored or coauthored. We want to resist this hierarchy and elitism, wherever and whenever we can.

Contributors' Biographies

Camila Bassi's Ph.D. research in Birmingham and Shanghai focuses on the interplay of "race" and sexuality within and through urban political economy. Her more general project is to demonstrate the benefit of a reinvigoration of Marxism (as an alternative to the seeming necessity to reconfigure Marxianisms via poststructuralism), in order to think through subtle accounts of capitalism and resistance. For example, Camila's critique of the revolutionary left vanguard of England's antiwar movement is steered by the task of building a third camp of independent and internationalist working class politics, and an excavation of early Marxist work on the Jewish question guides her writing of a book on the Palestinian-Israeli conflict.

Raluca Bejan is a Ph.D. student in social work at the University of Toronto. Her proposed doctoral study, funded by SSHRC's Joseph-Armand Bombardier Canada Graduate Scholarship, aims to explore how political discourses of newcomers' labor market integration are conceptually produced and epistemologically positioned within the knowledge production field. Raluca is a Research Assistant for a University of Toronto-Oxford University study comparatively assessing labor migration in the construction trades in Toronto, Canada, and London, UK, and a Book Review Editor for *Transnational Social Review*, a social work journal based in Germany and published by Routledge.

Geoff Boyce is a Ph.D. candidate in the School of Geography and Development at the University of Arizona. He researches and writes on immigration, surveillance, and Homeland Security-related issues, has published in a variety of popular and scholarly fora, and is a regular contributor to *NACLA Report on the Americas*.

Keri Brandt, Ph.D., is Associate Professor of Sociology and Gender and Women's Studies at Fort Lewis College in Durango, Colorado. She is passionate about teaching as a creative endeavor to inspire and create social justice. As a qualitative ethnographer, her research explores the complex worlds humans and animals share together. She focuses, in particular, on human-horse relationships and human-animal dynamics in the context of agriculture. She is endlessly fascinated with the ways in which humans and animals cocreate meaning systems and gendered construction of human-animal bonds. She can be reached at brandt_k@fortlewis.edu.

Peter Burdon is Senior Lecturer at the Adelaide University Law School and Deputy Chair of the International Union for the Conservation of Nature Ethics Specialist Group. Since 2005 Peter has worked with Friends of the Earth Adelaide in the Clean Futures Collective. Peter was a founding member of the Global Alliance for the Rights of Nature and he currently sits on the management committee of the Australian Earth Law Alliance.

Conor Cash is a Ph.D. candidate in the School of Geography and Development at the University of Arizona. He has published in a variety of fora, including *Affinities: A Journal of Radical Theory, Culture, and Action*, and he believes that the police are the greatest social problem in the world.

Ward Churchill is a former professor of American Indian Studies and Chair of the Ethnic Studies Department at the University of Colorado/Boulder, now retired. A veteran activist and prolific author, his more than twenty books include the award-winning *Agents of Repression* (with Jim Vander Wall). Beginning in early 2005, due to his expression of political views regarding the September 11, 2001 attacks on the World Trade Center and Pentagon, he was targeted by ACTA, Fox Noise, and Colorado's then-governor, Bill Owens, to be purged from the academy. In November 2011, the Colorado Council of the AAUP concluding that Churchill had committed *none* of the scholarly offenses of which he'd been "convicted" by the university, and that both administrators and collaborating faculty members had systematically "distorted and ultimately created a false public perception of his academic record."

Nick Clare is a Ph.D. student from the University of Sheffield who works in Latin America and the United Kingdom. His research focuses on the political subjectivity of migrants and draws on anarchist and autonomist theory, in particular the ideas of class composition and radical approaches to territory.

A member of the IWW, he is involved with a range of struggles within and beyond the academy. Nick can be contacted at n.clare@sheffield.ac.uk.

Becky Clausen is an Associate Professor of Sociology. She is also an affiliate faculty member in the Environmental Studies Program. Clausen is an environmental sociologist whose research interests include the social drivers of environmental change, the political economy of global food systems, and marine sociology. In 2015, Clausen coauthored and published *The Tragedy of the Commodity: Oceans, Fisheries, and Aquaculture*. She thinks the best part of her job is working side-by-side with students on farms and homesteads around the Southwest.

Sue Doe teaches courses in composition, autoethnographic theory and method, reading and writing connections, research methods, and GTA preparation for writing instruction. She does research in three distinct areas—academic labor and the faculty career, writing across the curriculum, and student-veteran transition in the post-9/11 era. Coauthor of the faculty development book *Concepts and Choices: Meeting the Challenges in Higher Education*, she has published articles in *College English* and *Writing Program Administration* as well as in several book-length collections.

Sean Donaghue-Johnston is an adjunct professor at Canisius College and Niagara University. He earned his Ph.D. in philosophy from Binghamton University, State University of New York, in 2011. In his doctoral dissertation, "The Ethical Work of Character: Reading *On Liberty* as an Aesthetic Manual," he examines the liberal philosophy of John Stuart Mill through the lens of Foucauldian genealogy. He has published articles on Mill and Foucault and is now engaged in the struggle for adjunct justice, as both scholar and activist.

Laura L. Finley earned her Ph.D. in sociology from Western Michigan University in 2002. She is currently Assistant Professor of Sociology and Criminology at Barry University. Dr. Finley is the author or coauthor of thirteen books and numerous book chapters and journal articles. Additionally, she is actively involved in a number of local, state, and national human rights and social justice efforts. Dr. Finley serves on the Boards of No More Tears (which assists victims of domestic violence), the Humanity Project (a bullying prevention program), Floridians for Alternatives to the Death Penalty, and the Peace and Justice Studies Association.

Janine Fitzgerald lives in Southwest Colorado, where she has lived most of her life. She farms with draft horses, writes poetry, throws balls for her border collies, and grows heart-shaped tomatoes. She has traveled extensively in Latin America and has engaged in activism against the drug war, intervention in

Central America, welfare reform, oil and gas development, and environmental racism. She holds a Ph.D. in sociology from the University of New Mexico and a Masters in Latin American studies. She teaches sociology and environmental studies at Fort Lewis College.

Shannon Gibney is a writer, teacher, and activist in Minneapolis. Her critical and creative work have appeared in a variety of publications, including *Gawker*, *Gazillion Voices*, and *The Crisis*. Her young adult novel *Hank Aaron's Daughter* is currently available from Land of a Gazillion Adoptees and CQT Press. She teaches English, journalism, creative writing, politics and community organizing, and African diasporic topics at Minneapolis Community & Technical College and lives in the Powderhorn neighborhood with her son and husband.

Mary Jean Hande is a rank-and-file member of CUPE 3902 and 3907 and a doctoral candidate in the Adult Education and Community Development Program at the Ontario Institute for Studies in Education, University of Toronto. Her research examines both informal and formal disability care provisions and organizing within the context of a rapidly financializing global economy and class struggle. She is committed to revolutionary antipoverty, labor, and disability organizing.

Mary Heath is Associate Professor in the Law School at Flinders University, South Australia. Her research interests have included rape law, the regulation of protest, and the wellbeing of queer women. She is a consensus decision making and nonviolent direct action trainer and is currently the coconvenor of a First Year Law Teachers' Community of Practice.

Z. B. Hurst is a young Black intellectual studying economics and French. Focusing on the intersectional effects of religiosocial and economic policy in diasporic communities, Z.B. also served as Vice President of the BSU at Luther College for two years. Z.B.'s research interests include migrant integration into the labor markets of former colonizers, heterodox economics, and the feminized liminal state of Christian martyrs. Z.B. is currently looking for an institution whose arms feel like home.

Erik Juergensmeyer is Associate Professor of Composition and Rhetoric in Durango, Colorado where he also coordinates the Peace and Conflict Studies Program. His research interests include community-based action research, argumentation, and conflict transformation, and he is especially interested in ways inquiry can assist community activism. His work has been published in *Rhetoric Review, Community Literacy Journal, Peace Studies Journal,* and *The Public Work of Rhetoric.*

Kelly Limes-Taylor Henderson is a doctoral candidate at Georgia State University's College of Education. With a concentration in the social foundations of education, Kelly's research focuses on settler colonialism, and the ontologies and epistemologies that undergird it and that can resist it. Her current work incorporates oral history and fictional accounts in order to examine the roles of the narrative, of kinship networks, and of land/place connection in learning and navigating the settler colonial context.

Tanya Loughead is Professor of Philosophy at Canisius College in Buffalo, New York. She specializes in the fields of phenomenology, feminism, critical theory, and continental philosophy. She has published articles on the works of Maurice Blanchot, Jacques Derrida, Julia Kristeva, Emmanuel Levinas, Herbert Marcuse, and Simone Weil, amongst others. Themes on which she has published include the relationship between justice and education, the ties between psychoanalysis and education, friendship and love, and critical theory. She is Co-Coordinator of the international Radical Philosophy Association. Loughead is the author of *Critical University* (Lexington Press, 2015).

John Lupinacci is Assistant Professor at Washington State University. His ecocritical work in education is interdisciplinary and draws heavily from critical social theory through anarchist philosophy, critical animal studies, poststructuralism, and queer-ecofeminist philosophy. His experiences as a high school teacher, an outdoor environmental educator, and a community activist all contribute to his research, teaching, and organizing direct actions aimed at examining the relationships between schools and the reproduction of the cultural roots of social suffering and environmental degradation.

Emil Marmol is a Ph.D. student at the University of Toronto on the minimum funding package of $15,000. He became active in the labor movement after being denied his paid parental leave by a University of Toronto manager who earns in excess of $150,000 yearly. He has served as Grievance Officer for CUPE, Local 3902 and Chief Steward for CUPE, Local 3907. His website www.comparenews.org helps to promote critical media literacy by allowing users to compare and contrast the differences in content and form between commercial and noncommercial news websites. He can be reached at emilmarmol@gmail.com.

Anthony J. Nocella II, Ph.D., long-time anarchist activist, is Assistant Professor of Sociology, Criminology, Peace and Conflict Studies, and Gender and Women's Studies at Fort Lewis College and has published over fifty scholarly articles or book chapters. He is the editor of *Peace Studies Journal*, cofounder and Executive Director of the Institute for Critical Animal Studies, Director of the Academy for Peace Education, Editor of the Radical Animal Studies and Total Liberation book series, and National Co-Coordinator of Save the Kids. He has published more than twenty books, most recently including *Policing the Campus: Academic Repression, Surveillance, and the Occupy Movement.* His website is www.anthonynocella.org.

Emma Pérez earned a Ph.D. in history from UCLA and has been a professor of ethnic studies at the University of Colorado, Boulder since 2003. Pérez has published fiction, essays, and the academic book, *The Decolonial Imaginary: Writing Chicanas into History.* She has also published three novels: *Gulf Dreams* (1996), *Forgetting the Alamo, Or, Blood Memory* (2009), and *Electra's Complex* (2015). She continues to research and write about queer Chican@s/Mexican@s in the borderlands as well as theorize decolonial methods across genres.

Mark Seis is Associate Professor of Sociology at Fort Lewis College in Durango, Colorado. He has published on a variety of topics ranging from the juvenile death penalty, to environmental topics including the Clean Air Act, global warming, ozone depletion, and acid rain, to various types of environmental crime, to globalization and the environment, to issues concerning radical environmentalism. His primary research interests include sustainable communities, all things environment, anarchist studies, and radical pedagogy.

Ryan Thomson is a scholar-activist currently working towards a Ph.D. in sociology at the University of Florida. His areas of research specialization include global and rural issues with an emphasis on social geography and community engagement. He is a member of the UF Graduate Student Union and an active participant within the International Student Movement (ISM), Social Forum Peoples Movement Assemblies.

Diana Vallera is a fine artist with work shown in national and international galleries and is a part-time faculty member in the photography department at Columbia College Chicago. As the president of the Columbia College Part-time Faculty Union (P-fac) Diana served as chief negotiator during collective bargaining and was instrumental in helping achieve what has been described as one of the best contracts in the country. She has been recognized for her leadership by NEA and by AAUP for her leadership and commitment to academic freedom. Vallera's current fine art project is on gender roles, women and work.

Carey Vicenti is Associate Professor of Sociology at Fort Lewis College in Durango, Colorado. He is a member of the Jicarilla Apache Nation.

Gregory White is a Ph.D. candidate in the Department of Social Policy and Social Work at the University of York, UK. His research addresses the relationship between social movements and social policy. In particular, he is interested in post-crisis social movements and their influence on discourses surrounding the redistribution of resources, regulation of financial institutions, and social justice.

Richard J. White is a Reader in Human Geography at Sheffield Hallam University. Richard's long-standing research both (i) explores the pervasive anarchist geographies of community self-help in contemporary Western society, and (ii) promotes an anarchist (i.e., nonviolent) intersectional awareness of social justice and total liberation. He can be contacted at Richard.White@shu.ac.uk.

Index

RADICAL ANIMAL STUDIES AND TOTAL LIBERATION

Anthony J. Nocella II, S E R I E S   E D I T O R

The **Radical Animal Studies and Total Liberation** book series branches out of Critical Animal Studies (a field co-founded by Anthony J. Nocella II) with the argument that criticism is not enough. Action must follow theory. This series demands that scholars are engaged with their subjects both theoretically and actively via radical, revolutionary, intersectional action for total liberation. Founded in anarchism, the series provides space for scholar-activists who challenge authoritarianism and oppression in their many daily forms. **Radical Animal Studies and Total Liberation** promotes accessible and inclusive scholarship that is based on personal narrative as well as traditional research, and is especially interested in the advancement of interwoven voices and perspectives from multiple radical, revolutionary social justice groups and movements such as Black Lives Matter, Idle No More, Earth First!, the Zapatistas, ADAPT, prison abolition, LGBTTQQIA rights, disability liberation, Earth Liberation Front, Animal Liberation Front, political prisoners, radical transnational feminism, environmental justice, food justice, youth justice, and Hip Hop activism.

To order other books in this series please contact our Customer Service Department:

(800) 770-LANG (within the US)
(212) 647-7706 (outside the US)
(212) 647-7707 FAX

To find out more about the series or browse a full list of titles, please visit our website:

WWW.PETERLANG.COM